MW00775001

HOTEL CONSTELLATION

DAVID L. HAASE

2/8/2018

M.F.S.,

Everyone
needs an editor.
I was blessed w/an
honest, talented one. You
are my treasured friend.

Help!

YKD

Hotel Constellation
David L. Haase

C. Lawrence Publishing

© 2018 by David L. Haase.
All rights reserved.

This book is in copyright.

Subject to statutory exception
and to the provisions of relevant collective licensing agreements,
no part of this book may be reproduced in any written, elec-
tronic, recorded, or photocopied form without written permission of author and C. Lawrence Publishing.

Although every precaution has been taken to verify the accuracy of the
information contained herein, the author and publisher assume no
responsibility for any errors or omissions. No liability is assumed for
damages that may result from the use of information contained within.

Books may be purchased by contacting the publisher and author at:

www.DavidLHaase.com/Contact/

ISBN: 978-0-9994847-0-8

Library of Congress Control Number 2017915667

1. Memoirs 2. Viet Nam war 3. Laos

Cover design: Damon Freeman, Damonza.com
Maps: Karen Chin, KarenChinArt.com
Interior Design: Benjamin Carrancho, Chrissy Hobbs, Damonza.com
Editor: Sylvia A. Smith
Copy Editor: Donna Verdier

Dedication

Elizabeth Turner Haase
Liz, you know why.

C. Larry and Mary Jane Haase
For the worry I put you through.

Ronk, Carl, Buckle, and Doolittle
For your patience with a green kid.

Richard Mathias Turner (1949–1969)
For a life unfinished, killed in Viet Nam.

Richard, Xannie, Eva, and Nate
For you, so you will know.

Contents

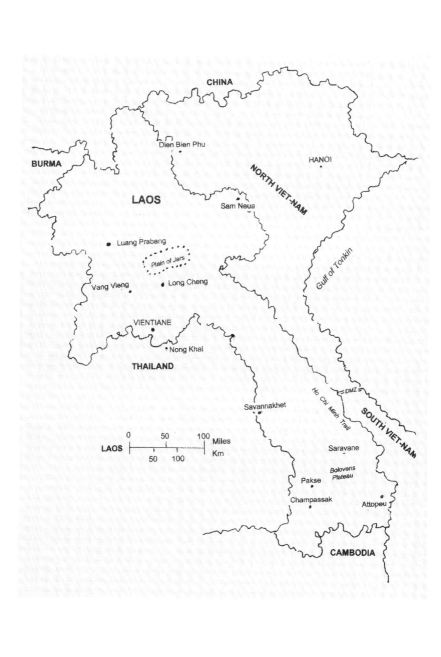

CHINA

Dien Bien Phu

BURMA

HANOI

NORTH VIET-NAM

LAOS

Sam Neua

Luang Prabang

Plain of Jars

Gulf of Tonkin

Vang Vieng

Long Cheng

VIENTIANE

Nong Khai

THAILAND

Savannakhet

Ho Chi Minh Trail

DMZ

SOUTH VIET-NAM

0   50   100 Miles

LAOS

50   100 Km

Saravane

Bolovens
Plateau

Pakse

Champassak

Attopeu

CAMBODIA

Prologue
In the Beginning
1945—1970

If we lose Laos, we will probably lose Thailand and the rest of Southeast Asia. We will have demonstrated to the world that we cannot or will not stand when challenged.

Chief of Naval Operations Admiral Arleigh Burke
December 31, 1960

B ETWEEN 1954 AND 1975, the United States waged war in lands on the western edge of the Pacific Ocean. The nations where Americans fought and died—Viet Nam, Laos, and Cambodia— never attacked or threatened our homeland. Americans died by the tens of thousands on foreign soil.

Rather, America's leaders from President Dwight D. Eisenhower through Richard Nixon treated the war as a crusade against an un-American ideology: International communism. The leading proponent of communism, the Soviet Union, had been an uneasy ally of the United States during World War II.

After the battles against Nazi Germany and militaristic Japan were fought and won, the United States and its democratic, capitalist allies—Britain and Western Europe—slid into a new type of cold war against the Soviet Union, its satellite countries in Eastern Europe, and China, which fell to the communists in 1949. This cold war was fought by proxy in developing countries all over the world. The Soviet Union—a communist empire built around today's Russia—and China supported and supplied the communist factions while the United States and allies backed any political party, movement, or strongman opposed to communism. Both sides wanted to avoid a "hot" war because the major adversaries had in their arsenals nuclear weapons capable of destroying Earth and everyone on it.

The cold war blazed into a shooting war in 1950 on the Korean Peninsula when the communist government of North Korea invaded the South. Noncommunist forces under the aegis of the United Nations, but dominated by the U.S., jumped in to prevent the takeover of the South. After two years of carnage, Korea reverted to the pre-1950 status quo, formally divided along the 38th parallel; the frightening and costly contest between communism and capitalism chilled again and shifted focus to the south, along the coast of China to the former French colonies of Indochina.

The French had colonized Indochina in the mid-1800s and created three artificial countries whose boundaries were drawn around the three predominant ethnic groups of the region: the Vietnamese, the Khmer of Cambodia, and the lowland Laotians. After World War II, when colonies throughout Asia and Africa were claiming their independence, Vietnamese nationalists led by Ho Chi Minh's communists defeated France and forced it to give up its colonies in Indochina.

Among the three newly named nations, Viet Nam was by far the largest and the most developed and aggressive. In fact, the French intervened to halt Vietnamese expansion into both Laos and Cambodia in the 1800s. The French recognized Vietnamese ethnic assertiveness and used Vietnamese to fill the ranks of the colonial bureaucracy in all three countries.

After the Korea experience, however, successive U.S. government administrations saw more than assertive Vietnamese; they saw aggressive Vietnamese communists seeking new territories to conquer. In particular, policymakers feared for Thailand, just across the Mekong River from Laos and Cambodia.

A hallmark of the Cold War was the wink-wink, nod-nod complicity of all parties in keeping their Cold War activities secret from their own people as well as the rest of the world. The Soviets, Chinese, and Americans knew what the others were doing, but they kept it quiet—except when they could score a propaganda victory—because they were doing similar things.

In this atmosphere, the United States tiptoed into Laos and South Viet Nam in 1954, using small teams of military advisers, CIA operatives, and a secretive airline—Air America—to contain the Vietnamese communists.

A decade into the fight, most Americans had still never heard of Viet Nam, Cambodia, or Laos. During the mid-1960s, however, television started to bring the growing war in Viet Nam into living rooms across America. The impact of those images far surpassed anything that newspapers and magazines could produce. As American involvement grew, so did casualties, from 416 dead in the nine years between 1956 and 1964 to 1,928 in 1965 alone.

As the casualties mounted, and more and more Americans knew someone whose family had lost a son, America started to tear itself apart over the war, split along generational lines, political lines, even geographic lines, riven by opinions about why we were fighting so far from home and whether we should use military conscription ("the draft") to fill the ranks of the armed services.

America had instituted a draft of fighting-age (18–26) men as the danger of World War II lurked on the horizon. After the Allied victory in 1945, the military downsized but the draft remained in place. As the United States shifted from advising the South Vietnamese to fighting battles for them, the administration of President Lyndon Johnson relied on the draft to fill the military's needs. Overnight, military service went from a relatively safe career option to a potential death sentence.

In 1966, American casualties in Viet Nam tripled from the previous year to more than 6,000 dead; they almost doubled again in 1967 to more than 11,000. In 1968, the number of dead rose to almost 17,000 young men—325 a week, almost 50 per day. The three TV networks—their half-hour evening newscasts a dominant source of news in a pre-cable TV, pre-Internet information environment—broadcast the deaths in living color to Americans as they ate their evening meals.

Suddenly, every American male faced an enormous, life-changing decision as his 18th birthday approached: What to do about the draft?

It was no simple decision, this question of the draft. The Selective Service System, as the draft was formally known, was full of loopholes and ruled by an alphabet soup of more than 30 categories of risk. A noisy few chose defiance, refusing to register for the draft and risking jail for doing so; others quietly slipped into Canada or fled to Sweden, beyond the reach of American law but also far from their families and friends.

Most tried to game the system. College students could be deferred from the draft from year to year as long as they remained enrolled or until they turned 24; college classrooms swelled with young men rated as 2-S deferred students. Married men and ministers were exempt altogether, and the ranks of young marrieds and divinity schools swelled. The unlucky majority—overpopulated by poor and working class kids who could not afford college—were classified 1-A, an open invitation to join the military.

I grew up during those years of the anti-communist crusade, but I didn't understand how they had shaped me and my country.

And so my story begins.

Chapter 1
A Pistol on the Desk
SEPTEMBER 1970

I'm leavin' on a jet plane;
Don't know when I'll be back again.

"Leaving on a Jet Plane," lyrics by John Denver

I NEVER PLANNED ON Laos. I certainly never intended to get caught up in a secret shooting war. I was a naïve kid—a would-be academic—trying to understand the big war of my generation and my complicated emotions about it. My peers[1] were fighting and dying in Viet Nam; I wanted to show I had the guts to go there but without engaging in the killing. Ending up in Laos was just one more thing that went wrong.

As we dropped out of the clouds just before twilight on September 24, 1970, I glimpsed my destination far below—Tan Son Nhut Airport, Saigon, Republic of Viet Nam.[2]

Out the left side of the plane windows, the South China Sea stretched to a hazy white horizon; on the right, a carpet of dark

---

1 My future wife's brother died in Viet Nam at the age of 19. I had met him once or twice and spoken with him by phone. He was a good guy. We named our first-born after him, and this book is dedicated to his memory.
2 Viet Nam is spelled many ways today, typically as one word, Vietnam. I use the spelling the Vietnamese used when I was in Viet Nam.

green rolled off to the west as far as I could see. A pencil-thin strip of white sand separated land and sea.

As we banked hard, I bit my nails—I was still doing that then. The closer I got to Saigon, the more I wondered about the wisdom of my plan to study for a year at a Buddhist university in a country deep into its second decade of internationally sponsored civil war. When my favorite professor at Antioch College talked about it at Ye Olde Trail Tavern in Yellow Springs, Ohio, it had seemed like a fantastic idea. As my plane dropped its wheels and lined up to land, I feared that the beer might have affected our judgment.

I was arriving in a foreign country with $500 in cashier's checks and only a vague plan for getting through the next 10 months.

My Vietnamese language skills acquired over ten weeks of intense six-hour days at Cornell University would allow me to hire a taxi or order pho, the cheap ubiquitous noodle soup I expected to live on. But there was no way I would be able to follow lectures about philosophy or Vietnamese history and economics, all topics I naively expected to take up.

I couldn't be sure of my safety. The war was not going well for the South Vietnamese and their American patrons. I discovered much later that my father had taken out a $5,000 life insurance policy on me. As one of his friends told me years later, Dad was afraid he couldn't afford to ship my remains back to our hometown in Iowa along the Mississippi River and give me a decent Catholic burial. And with good reason. We didn't come from money. With a wife and four other children to support, Dad earned his family's income as the owner and head carpenter for a small home building and remodeling company. Every dollar was spoken for before it came in the door. In fact, my college education was consuming one dollar of every ten brought in, despite my grants, scholarships, and loans. My savings, such as they were, were tapped out by the end of my sophomore year. At the start of my third year in college, I was carrying two bank loans and an I.O.U from a generous and trusting friend who had given me $700 to make the trip.

I carried all my belongings in a dark green hardside Samsonite suitcase that had taken a beating traveling from Antioch to off-campus co-op jobs in Madison, Wisconsin; Dayton, Ohio; and Boston. Antioch required students to alternate between periods of on-campus study and real-life learning. We took to the road as cheaply as possible every three months. It was hell on luggage.

As I stepped out of the frigid aircraft, a blanket of hot, wet air wrapped around me, and I started to sweat just standing at the top of the portable stairway. I could not recall a summer day on the Mississippi River as oppressive as this autumn day in Southeast Asia. I trudged down the steps, searched for my suitcase on the broiling tarmac and lugged it into the open-air terminal. Every Westerner I saw was sweating; the Asians, mostly Chinese and Vietnamese, were not. I wanted to learn how they did that—one more thing to put on my list of educational goals.

In those days, there were no X-ray machines to pass through, no customs officials rummaged through your packed underwear. What you saw when you arrived in a country were rows of immigration windows with separate lines for returning citizens and incoming foreigners. I had already been through the routine of "disembarkation," as it was called then, in Tokyo, Taipei (Taiwan), and Hong Kong. I expected the same dreary drill in Saigon.

I stood around taking in the sights. For every commercial airplane I saw there were five military planes as well as helicopters, old DC-3 prop aircraft, and huge four-engine supply planes looking out of place in their brown-and-green camouflage paint.

A skinny Vietnamese official in a brown uniform motioned me to move from the foreigners' immigration line to a table off to one side. My fellow passengers worked hard not to stare as I unlocked the Samsonite, opened its halves like a giant clam and stood back as the immigration officer lifted a flap securing my clothes and discovered a red plastic plate lying upside down on top of my pants and shirts.

This?

He pointed to the plate.

Frisbee, I said.

Free-bie?

No, Frisbee.

I wracked my memory. I had no recollection of a Vietnamese word for Frisbee.

You know, like this. I reached for the disk.

The official grabbed my wrist.

Whoa. What the hell? Most uncool, man, I thought. This guy was seriously uptight about a plastic Frisbee.

How had we failed him? Americans had introduced the Vietnamese to the latest weapons; rock and roll music, and blue jeans and bell bottoms, not to mention menthol cigarettes. Had we not introduced them to Frisbees?

He released my wrist, and I again reached for the disk—oh, so slowly—picked it up and mimicked tossing it.

He didn't get it, and I had no Vietnamese words to explain it. We stared at each other. Finally, he directed me to a chair against a dingy lime green wall and walked to an office nearby, watching me over his shoulder. Did he think I would run away? Where? The immigration line? Back onto the plane? He ducked his head into the office, spoke softly and turned back to me. An older, severe-looking official in a brown uniform—must be regulation issue—appeared in the door, stared at me, and walked slowly to where I sat.

He extended his hand. I'd been traveling through Asia for almost two weeks, and I knew this was not a handshake. The motion was in the universally understood argot of the bureaucracy: Passport. No please, no sir—just passport.

I stood and pulled my passport out of my back pocket. Not even two months old, the cover was curved to match the shape of my right buttock. I handed the damp document to him. He opened it, studying the hairy version of me in the passport photo against the "Be clean for Gene"[3] version standing before him. He flipped pages and found my yellow-and-green visa stamp allowing me to enter Viet Nam and stay for one month. (Our plan was to worry about the other nine months of my year abroad when the time came.)

Without looking at me again, he motioned me to follow him. I thoroughly understood even without resorting to my Vietnamese language skills.

He sat. I sat. Someone deposited my suitcase on the floor beside the desk. I didn't notice who, because my eyes were glued elsewhere: I saw only the pistol on his desk, which was pointed my way. It looked just like the one my father kept hidden at the bottom of a locked cedar chest at the foot of his bed. When I was a kid, I had held it once. My father told me it was a Colt .45, a souvenir of his Army service during World War II. It was big and ugly. I remembered needing two hands to hold it level. Now its twin lay feet away, pointed in my direction.

"Why are you here?" The Interrogator interrupted my flashback. He spoke better than passable English.

My eyes flicking between his face and his gun, I blathered, explaining my determination to learn all about Viet Nam and its development challenges by studying with the monks and Vietnamese students at the country's premier Buddhist university right there in Saigon. I assumed that he really cared, and I shared my story gladly. I had finally achieved my goal. I was in Viet Nam. Let the education begin.

"What are you doing here?"

I thought I had covered that pretty thoroughly, but I was enthusiastic and more than happy to go over it again. Which I did.

---

3 In 1968, hairy college students working on the presidential campaign of Senator Eugene McCarthy were encouraged to cut their beards, mustaches, and hair; bathe regularly; wear 'square' clothes and generally "be clean for Gene."

I never play poker because my face telegraphs everything. This guy, however, could well have survived the fall of Saigon five years later and escaped to make a living in Las Vegas. Not a muscle on his face had moved since he demanded my passport.

He sent me to a bench, nowhere near the immigration line, where I met a shaggy Frenchman about my age. He introduced himself as Christian Landeau. I felt like I had been consigned to the Group W bench in *Alice's Restaurant*.

"Any idea what's going on?" I asked.

"It's something to do with students."

"You mean like us?"

"Apparently, yes."

"When did you get here?"

"About ten hours ago."

Ten hours! my brain screamed.

As we traded stories, my spirits fell. Christian had been held almost half a day without being allowed to contact anyone, although he expected to be put on a plane heading for parts unknown at any moment.

A depression that would dog me for the next several months set in. My mentor at Antioch, Dan Grady, and my study-abroad adviser, Paula Spier, had discussed all kinds of contingencies with me. Missed flights. Lost passports. Stolen wallets. Even sickness and injury. One thing we had not discussed, however, was airport detention.

I was both beleaguered and outraged. How could they do this to me? True, it was their country, but I had done nothing wrong. I had done nothing, in fact, except disembark from the plane and show them my Frisbee. Were Frisbees illegal? I doubted it. Guns and grenades, bombs and bullets were allowed into the country— who cared about a lousy Frisbee? I knew it wasn't about the Frisbee. Problem was, I was a student. And somehow that mattered to the Vietnamese. Why? I wasn't here to protest or demonstrate. I was here to study. I had tortured myself all summer studying Viet Nam's tonal language. I was wearing a pants with a crease, a shirt with a collar, and even shined shoes. I used deodorant and had cut my hair.

Now I was stuck on a bench with a French hippie, actually a really nice guy, and wondering whether the Interrogator ever used his gun. Would they throw me on a plane, like Christian? He didn't even know where he was being sent. They hadn't spoken to him in hours. How long were we to languish on the bench? What about food and water? Would we sleep here? Would they let us sleep? And where was the bathroom? I couldn't ask Christian if they let him go to the bathroom. I was too afraid of the answer.

I thought a lot about the menacing gun. I didn't know if there was a round in the chamber, ready to bore a hole through the back of the chair I had sat in—and any part of me that might have been in the way. The Interrogator was hardly subtle. He counted on that pistol to scare me, and it worked. But I thought the prop was over-kill. Oh, god, I thought, why would I use a word like overkill with a gun pointed at me?

Judging by the light coming through the terminal doors, I could tell that the sun was setting, although the tarmac was lit up like high noon. I needed to pee, but The Interrogator waved me back into the office.

"You have someone in Saigon who knows you? Someone you can call?"

"Yeah, sure."

"Call them. Tell them to come here. Then we will see."

Of course I knew people to call. I had spent the better part of year planning this trip, writing letters, making contacts, asking advice, cadging favors. I had assumed I would meet them at an outdoor restaurant, a Ba Muoi Ba [33] beer in hand, not at the detention bench at Tan Son Nhut Airport with a possibly loaded gun haunting me.

I managed to reach the evening duty officer at the American

Embassy and asked him to contact Bill Herod, a volunteer with Viet Nam Christian Service, or VCS.

I had never met Bill or spoken to him, but I had corresponded with him during my nine hectic months of planning for the trip. VCS was one of a dozen nongovernment relief groups operating throughout Southeast Asia. Their volunteers dug wells, built schools, taught kids to read, and did other good deeds. One of my Antioch co-op jobs in the States had been with the American Friends Service Committee, a Quaker relief group, and the Quakers were generous in sharing contacts and referring people who might one day be helpful. Bill was one of them.

He eventually arrived, tall, skinny, and wearing sandals. Bill spoke at length with The Interrogator in impressive Vietnamese. Then he turned to Christian and me and said he had good news and bad news.

The Interrogator had canceled our visas, Bill said. We had 72 hours, no more, to straighten things out. This was a Thursday night—there was only one workday left in the week. We got the message: Stay or leave, we had only one day to work a miracle. The good news—for Christian, if not for me—was that Bill had also vouched for Christian, so he could finally leave the airport. Truly good people are not selective in their goodness; they're good to everyone.

As we left his office with our 72-hour papers in hand, The Interrogator spoke again: We could pick up our passports, he said, on our way out of the country.

Chapter 2
Chasing Butterflies without a Net
SEPTEMBER 1970

I take things for granted so quickly that I cease to see anything
unusual in my surroundings.

W. Somerset Maugham,
The Gentleman in the Parlour

USUALLY I CAN sleep anywhere, any time, under any circumstances, but that first night in Viet Nam sorely tested my talent.

Bill Herod deposited Christian and me at IVS House, the Saigon headquarters for the International Voluntary Service, an ecumenical aid group that worked and lived closely with the Vietnamese. IVS House had no air conditioning. The Vietnamese seemed not to mind. Americans, on the other hand, lived by their window air conditioners. I lay on the narrow cot in my underwear, with my skin sticking to the sheet. A ceiling fan made circles above me, but the mosquito net draped over my bed kept not only bugs but also moving air from reaching me.

Worries about my situation could have contributed to my insomnia. I was not under arrest, per se, but I was certainly not free to roam around—not without a passport. And I had picked up a second scruffy student along the way. His name was Larry

Lifschultz, which should have predisposed me to like him. My father is a Larry, and my grandfather is the original Lawrence; I had a cousin Larry; and legally, my name was Larry, too, although given all the other Larrys in the family, I went by my second name, David.

In this case, the name similarity just pissed me off. These two interlopers, Christian and Larry, were screwing up my gig. They looked like a couple of lost hippies in their ratty jeans and sandals. They didn't know anything about Vietnamese history and culture, its philosophy and development challenges. They didn't know a word of Vietnamese, and, worst of all, they didn't care. They didn't know anyone they could reach out to for help, and I couldn't figure out why they were even here. They showed up the same day I did, so I got lumped into the same basket of undesirables.

I had studied and prepared for this trip. I could pick up a grain of rice with chopsticks. I knew that the Vietnamese made *nuoc mam* (fish sauce) by burying fish heads in the ground and letting them rot. What's more, I liked nuoc mam.

I had studied how not to stand out any more than I had to, being a six-foot, skinny white American in a country of short, well-tanned natives. I knew to wear creased slacks and polished shoes, just like the Jesuits required at my high school. I had cut my hair back to where my ears stuck out like Dumbo's. I had connections— I actually knew *of* people whom I could call. In comparison, they knew nothing, and, besides, Larry had a big mouth and an obnoxious personality.

I finally gave up trying to sleep. I was miserable, hot, and cranky. My cold shower felt great, but I started sweating before I finished drying off. Going in search of other residents of IVS House, my mood improved. This would be my first day in the "real" Southeast Asia, where I would meet the locals and experience their way of life. I was ready for rice bowls and chopsticks. Instead, the IVS folks served me an egg fried over easy and half of a delicious baguette of crusty-on-the-outside, soft-on-the-inside French bread. Yeah, welcome to the real Viet Nam, where French influence on the culture still maintained a strong hold more than 15 years after they lost their Viet Nam war.

My first stop on the road to staying in Viet Nam took me to Van Hanh University. I worried the Buddhists would not want to have anything to do with me, given my trouble with the authorities. I was aware of the irony of my concern about staying in Viet Nam while every guy my age in the military would kill to get kicked out.

At the university, I discovered that my contacts were out of the country. I used my Vietnamese language training to speak with an administrator named Om Tong (Mr. Tong) and realized I should have spent even more time in the language lab at Cornel. Om Tong listened to my story and confirmed that I could be a special, non-degree student.

I didn't know if traveling around Saigon was violating the terms of my 72-hour visa, but I couldn't conduct business by phone. In fact, I wasn't sure how to conduct it, but I had to get out and meet people face to face, so I took the chance. All they could do is boot me out a couple days early.

By this time, I was hot and tired, and I didn't have a map of Saigon. I splurged on a taxi (100 piasters, or 85 cents) to the U.S. Embassy. There I spent an hour with a Mr. Lawrence E. Pope, a deputy consul, whom I took to calling Frank Fucking Pope in all subsequent journal entries and letters. He reeked of disdain and unhelpfulness. He made me write an affidavit, promising not to cause any trouble and to abide by the spirit of the Vietnamese Constitution. I was never sure what the hell that meant, but I pledged it just the same. Pope gave me a letter of introduction to the deputy minister of Interior, Le Cong Chat, and told me to show up at Chat's office at 2:30 sharp. (In Viet Nam and other countries, the Interior Ministry typically handles police and intelligence activities; it has nothing to do with trees or national parks as in the

United States.) Being told to show up anywhere in Southeast Asia at an hour "sharp" was ludicrous; no one was ever on time in Asia, but I needed a long-term visa so I would be on time.

Thus I began chasing butterflies without a net, a game I played with diminishing enthusiasm for more than two months across three countries.

Despite my promptness, Mr. Chat was not available. A clerk told me his higher-ups wanted me to see someone at the Ministry of Foreign Affairs named Diep Quang Hong. This sounded promising. I was apparently no longer a police issue, but a foreign policy matter.

I made my way over to Mr. Hong's office. He was in and expecting me. Again, promising. Maybe things would work out as I hoped. He shook my hand and sent me down the hall to Huynh Huu-Luan, the director of the Eurasian Affairs Bureau. Mr. Huu-Luan heard me out and expressed his greatest sympathy with my plight. He shocked me when he volunteered that this was not really his area of expertise; he had only been in Saigon three months and still didn't know the street layout. My fate was in the hands of someone who had only been in Saigon 89 days longer than I. With the hours left in the work week racing by, and the odds that anyone official would be at work on Saturday or Sunday approaching zero, my spirits sank.

Mr. Huu-Luan sent me back to the U.S. Embassy to meet with a Mr. Lewis, whom he knew. He promised to call Lewis later that afternoon (a Friday) to get a reference for me. Lewis was not available, so I was stuck a second time with Frank Fucking Pope. He passed me on to another vice consul, Mr. O'Boyle, who recommended that I be allowed to stay. (Why his recommendation mattered escaped me at the time; I haven't figured it out since.)

Trying to conserve money, I walked to all these appointments, each one a miserable expedition of 30 minutes or more. My creased pants chafed my inner thighs, starting a nasty case of crotch rot that lasted until I hit London on my way home two years later.

That evening, I ate dinner at the American Friends Service Committee headquarters with Don Luce, a legendary figure in both Viet Nam and the antiwar movement in the States. Luce had been head of IVS until he and three of his top lieutenants quit in a public protest over American policy in Viet Nam. Over dinner I learned that the *New York Times* was looking for a copy boy; two other dinner guests gave me a ride to the *Times*'s Saigon office, where I was offered the job pending approval of my visa.

It was not the last time that just showing up—and being able to speak, read, and write English—would help me.

* * *

Day Two in Viet Nam, not counting the partial day I spent at Tan Son Nhut Airport, began hot, miserable, and hopeless, despite the job offer of the previous evening.

Bill Herod joined Christian, Larry, and me at the IVS House to discuss strategy. We concluded we didn't have one.

I don't know how Christian and Larry spent the previous day. I hadn't run into them in my bureaucratic travels the day before, and neither Pope nor O'Boyle had mentioned them.

Bill hoped to use his contacts at the U.S. Embassy. He took me to a security officer he knew, who said he wished he could help out, but the only authority he had was to deport me. I already had people working on that, I said, but thanked him for meeting with me just the same.

Despite it being the first day of the weekend, we drove over to the Ministry of Foreign Affairs to speak to the secretary-general, an acquaintance of Bill's. Bill couldn't get in to see the guy, but I managed to speak with my new friend, Huynh Huu-Luan, who had definitive news. Not good news, but definitive. I had been denied a visa. The decision had been made above the ministerial level. What was above the ministerial level? I could only wonder. I supposed it could mean the prime minister, the president, or the American ambassador. Maybe even God. One of those four.

Mr. Huu-Luan didn't know how I could retrieve my passport. To help the nasty-tasting medicine go down, he presented me with a copy of "Viet Nam Realities, 1969," a glossy propaganda photo album that would probably add two pounds to my already over-weight luggage.

I rendezvoused with Christian and Larry at the Immigration Department, and we were taken into the office of Captain Sang of the National Police. Turns out Christian and Larry had met Sang the day before, and Sang had gotten heavy with them while I traipsed through Saigon yesterday. At least, I thought, he didn't use his pistol as a paper weight.

Bottom line: Having had our original entry visas canceled and having been denied new visas, we now needed to apply for exit visas (filled out in duplicate, without the use of carbon paper). It occurred to me only later that I might have been able to stay in Viet Nam simply by not requesting an exit visa.

Captain Sang told us we would receive our passports after we presented valid airline tickets for flights out of Viet Nam. He made it very clear we needed to do that by the evening of the next day, no longer than 72 hours after our arrival.

By this time, news of our hard-luck story had gotten out, especially among the nonofficial Americans, i.e., those not in the military or the U.S. diplomatic and aid bureaucracy. We told our story over terrible hamburgers to two freelance reporters, one of whom was John Steinbeck III, son of novelist John Steinbeck. Steinbeck III was in Viet Nam on his own Hemingwayesque wartime adventure.

Back at IVS House, we met with Bill Herod again. He tried to reach someone at the immigration office to let them know we had our tickets and were ready to pick up our passports. He couldn't reach anyone. So he called the press, and Christian, Larry, and I told our stories to Kim Willenson of UPI. Shortly thereafter, the U.S. Consul called me and asked what was up. If I had been paying better attention, I would have understood by this time that my experience was simply a metaphor for U.S. involvement in Viet Nam: No one knew anything about anything. Chasing butterflies without a net.

A short while later, the consul telephoned to say that Frank Fucking Pope had learned that the Vietnamese premier, Tran Thien Khiem, had personally made the decision to revoke my visa. Apparently it was nothing personal, however. All other American students were to be kept out, too. I later found this to be ironic, given that Khiem had had to leave Viet Nam himself a few years before I arrived after participating in one too many coup attempts; getting thrown out of his own country apparently did not generate sympathy for others in similar straits.

His decision was a culmination of a number of events and would have made a certain amount of sense, had I not been snared me in the net. Viet Nam was having trouble with students, foreigners as well as its own. Eleven Vietnamese student leaders being held in a Saigon jail were on a hunger strike, and two were said to be very close to death. In recent weeks, two American students had visited North Viet Nam, then came to Saigon and held a press conference during which they praised the North. Finally, a rumor was floating around that the U.S. National Student Association was sending four student representatives to Saigon to show solidarity with the fasting Vietnamese.

* * *

With my fate determined, I had to call the *New York Times* and let them know I couldn't accept their wonderful offer of employment. The reporter who took the call, Gloria Emerson, asked me a few questions—my third media interview of the day—and promised to call back. She never did, despite her reputation for empathizing with innocents in trouble.

Christian, Larry and I huddled again, this time over whether to issue a statement to the press about how the South Vietnamese government was treating us. Larry pushed hard for it; Christian and I were less enthusiastic. I didn't see what it would get me, and I hoped this same government that I was about to criticize publicly would let me return after things cooled down. Saving face is extremely important to Asians. I'd learned that in my studies dating back to high school. I figured it would be poor form to slam them and then ask for the privilege of returning to their country.

We decided to consult with Don Luce, who'd had his own experience making statements to the press several years earlier. I guess we came up with something to say because Larry and I exchanged words in the cab on the way back to IVS House. In my journal I wrote:

> *I called the joint statement off and went to bed angry. Larry came in later and said Christian was going to Bangkok (Thailand) without publicity. We apologized to each other, but the issue remained to be settled.*

I spent another muggy, miserable night under a mosquito net, churning my sheets into damp rags. I had planned and studied and worked hard for a year to create this opportunity. Dan and Paula, my Antioch mentors, had called in chits and incurred professional debts on my behalf. My sponsors at Van Hanh University, Dr. Ton That Thien and Thich Minh Chau, had endorsed me with their government. I had gone into considerable hock—taking out loans and tapping my parents for one more year of help with college tuition—to create this once-in-a-lifetime opportunity. Now it was all a bust. I didn't know what to do or where to do it.

I was running low on cash after underestimating my costs for visiting Japan, Taiwan, and Hong Kong before landing in Saigon. My hotel bill in Hong Kong for three days was $167 Hong Kong—almost $29 in U.S. currency. That sounds like nothing now, but I had about $500, and I needed that to last for—well, that was the problem. I didn't know how long it had to last because I didn't know what would come next. Neither Antioch nor my parents even knew I was being tossed out of my study program country. All I knew is that come noon the next day, I was stepping onto an airplane bound for Thailand—a country I had never studied, in which I had no interest and about which I knew nothing. From there, who knew where I would go? Back to the United States? That would be one expensive "Around the World in 80 Days" experience.

The sun rose as I started to doze off. I showered, packed, and slurped pho for breakfast. Among the many things I did not know was when I would eat next.

Our guide and sponsor in this adventure so far, Bill Herod, arrived after breakfast. We confronted him with our debate over making a statement. He counseled against it, which was good enough for me. Christian and I wrapped up our preparations to depart. Larry went to the Vietnamese immigration office to demand that he be allowed to fly to Pakse, Laos. I had no more idea of where Laos was than Thailand; at least I had heard of Bangkok. UPI promised to keep an eye on him; he would plague me again and again, although we never met a second time.

Leaving Viet Nam—ending my Antioch year abroad after 68 hours—was anticlimactic. I trudged through the lines in the unair-conditioned civilian terminal at Tan Son Nhut, climbed the steps to the plane, and settled into my seat, wondering whether I would ever return and what the hell I would do next.

Chapter 3
On Becoming a Man
1964–1970

Give Campion a boy. Get back a man.

Campion Jesuit High School slogan, 1960s

I CHOSE ANTIOCH COLLEGE because it had coed dorms. As a senior at an all-boys Jesuit prep school in sparsely populated western Wisconsin, I dreamt of beautiful girls with naked breasts rooming next to me, bouncing down the halls to the unisex bathrooms, asking me to wash their bare backs (eyes closed, honest).

During my years at Campion Jesuit High School in Prairie du Chien, I can remember seeing only three women regularly; they had a combined weight of about 600 pounds, give or take. I still managed to drool over them now and again.

When I heard about Antioch, a small liberal arts college with a radical bent, nestled in a town about the size of Prairie du Chien in the southwest corner of Ohio, I envisioned a paradise far beyond anything I had read about in the Old Testament. Jack Spicer, the older brother of one of my closest friends, made the jump from Campion to Antioch and told hardly believable stories about the freedom from Jesuitical rules, the lack of supervision by teachers and administrators, and the anything-goes atmosphere of coed dorms. I and two others from my graduating class—Tom Spicer and Tom Schlenker—followed Jack to our image of Nirvana.

Gaining admission to Antioch, whose standards rivaled those of Harvard back then, was hardly a one-and-done thing. The Jebbies, which is what we called our Jesuit minders, started us on the road to college in our junior year and expected every student to devote the first months of senior year to filling out applications to a minimum of five or six colleges, including one "clutch" college, a place even a public high school grad could enter. Campion's Jesuits had high expectations but were ultimately practical: Any college acceptance is better than none.

I left Campion with a degree in discipline as well as college prep academics. It was impossible not to. The Jesuits regimented our lives from the moment clanging bells awoke us early for daily Mass to the selection of our classes and the amount of time we studied to the flashing lights five minutes before they turned the lights out.

Our sophomore year rule book ran to 24 pages with sections on the bell system, room care, chapel behavior, dining hall manners, dress regulations (class days, Sunday, and free time), and theater rules (for Sunday night movies featuring Doris Day, Walt Disney, and other wholesome fare featuring fully clothed women). To keep our lusty teen-aged male minds off sex, we were also required to participate in sports—football, soccer, basketball, swimming, and softball, in seasonal order—and to memorize the separate Intramural Sports League rulebook.

The Jesuits censored our mail, incoming and outgoing. Our *Newsweek* and *Time* magazines arrived weekly with offensive material, usually pictures of women in bathing suits, cut out. Pity the poor Jesuit scholastic armed with a scissors and charged with excising the same suggestive photos from hundreds of copies each week. Once or twice a night, the Jebbies silently opened our doors to make sure we were in bed and asleep. It didn't matter if you were studying for a test under a stifling, light-blocking wool blanket. We were expected to do what we were expected to do at all times, or face the consequences.

Jesuits punished infractions—talking too loudly, walking too fast, moving too slowly, missing a bed check—with "jugs." Each jug mandated one hour of additional silent study—writing or doing homework, no novels, and certainly no magazines or comic books—to be served Monday through Sunday during our "free" time. If the jugs piled up, or if the infraction was severe enough—talking back to a teacher, say—you were called to your dorm rector's office after lights-out for a session with the paddle, usually five to ten whacks on the bare bottom. Really serious stuff—like possessing a copy of *Esquire* magazine—merited expulsion. Immediately. Without appeal. A handful of guys a year simply disappeared.

To further our education in discipline, in sophomore year all but a handful of Campion students joined ROTC, Reserve Officer Training Corps, taking the same classes as college students preparing to become officers in the Army. (Dad was a proud WW II veteran who would have liked to have had a career in the Army. I assumed his career ambitions for quite a while.) I rose through the ranks, becoming a captain and commander of the honor company my senior year.

Senior year, 1967–1968: Was there ever a more tumultuous period in our lives, especially those first six months of 1968? Not since World War II, perhaps. At the end of January, Viet Cong guerrillas and North Vietnamese regulars launched attacks throughout South Viet Nam in what became known as the Tet[4] offensive. Some attackers even penetrated the U.S. Embassy in Saigon during the month-long battle. Opposition to the war mounted, and CBS News anchorman Walter Cronkite, a white-haired almost godlike figure in the news business, returned from a trip to Viet Nam and pronounced the war unwinnable.

In March, Democratic President Lyndon Johnson, who had inherited the White House from John Fitzgerald Kennedy when he

---

4 Tet is the Vietnamese lunar New Year and usually falls in February.

was assassinated in 1963, dropped out of the race for the presidency after barely beating an unknown Minnesota senator named Gene McCarthy in the first Democratic presidential primary of the 1968 election season. McCarthy ran on an antiwar platform, and young people all over the country thronged to his campaign, cutting off their beards and long hair to "Be Clean for Gene."

Civil rights leader Martin Luther King Jr. was assassinated by a white racist in April, and black Americans rioted in all of the major cities, burning down swaths of their own neighborhoods in outrage and frustration.

John Kennedy's younger brother, Bobby, jumped into the race for the Democratic presidential nomination and was assassinated in a hotel kitchen in Los Angeles just weeks after Campion graduated the 120 survivors of the Class of 1968, myself included.

I was overjoyed by graduation but stricken with anxiety about the draft, the war in Viet Nam, and a heartrending conversation I needed to have with my father before my 18th birthday on June 27.

* * *

My college selections had been eclectic to say the least.

Antioch led the list with its coed dorms, but I had also been accepted at the University of California at Berkeley, a hotbed of long-haired radicalism, free sex, and cheap drugs, and Georgetown University, a Jesuit-run institution in our national capital.

I chose the University of Wisconsin, Platteville, a short drive up the road from my hometown in Iowa, as my "clutch" college. Two of my mother's brothers, Uncles Kenny and Leonard, had graduated from the engineering program there, and we all thought that was recommendation enough. I was accepted in about a week—such a short period of time that I felt embarrassed by my choice. Other classmates had chosen UW at Madison, which at least was the mothership of public college education in that state. The cost was the same.

My other college choices surprised many of my classmates, and quite frankly they confused me as well: The U.S. Military Academy at West Point and the U.S. Air Force Academy at Colorado Springs. My father never once asked me to apply, but I am told he was pleased when I did. His lack of interference in my life choices was un-Jesuitical and raised the pressure on me to perform.

Dad was so proud that he took time off work, which he could not afford, to pick me up in Prairie du Chien and drive me to my academy entrance physical at an air base outside Champaign-Urbana, Illinois, in the southern part of the state. We even stayed overnight in a hotel room together, a closeness we never shared before. The all-day physical was far more comprehensive than the one draftees got on their way to Viet Nam.

Trouble was, I didn't know whether I wanted to pass or fail. My father had told me of men in his generation who had failed the physical for WW II because of flat feet; I was so afraid of failing for that reason that one night I dumped a bucket of water on the concrete floor of the garage and walked through it and then onto the dry concrete. The imprint showed marvelous arches; no flat feet for me.

At the same time, I was leading a double life at Campion, devouring radical alternative weekly newspapers like the *East Village Other* and the *Berkeley Barb*, full of antiwar, free love, dope, and long hair. If the Jebbies had tried to censor the papers, I would have received nothing but confetti. For some reason, they didn't. I recall my parents had been asked to visit with the Jesuits a month or two into my senior year and spent an hour or more with the vice principal, Father Dutkiewicz, our head disciplinarian. I don't know what they talked about. It might have been the underground newspaper I was putting out with two friends or the newspapers I was reading or the state of my immortal soul. Dad never said, and the Jesuits gave me freer rein than I expected.

During this turbulent academic year, I also joined an intense class run by some of the younger Jesuit scholastics with a hand-picked crop of students. We read existential philosophers like Jean

Paul Sartre and the rebel, mystical Jesuit theologian Pierre Teilhard de Chardin. We probed the history and philosophy of our Catholic religion and challenged one another to be open and honest about our feelings. I typed a 17-page, single-spaced, anguished, and conflicted review of my religious and philosophical life; I concluded that I could not believe the New Testament stories and Catholic catechism. A virgin birth, assumption into heaven, turning water and wine into flesh and blood. It was all too crazy. I got an A-minus, no mean feat. (The Jesuits never ceased to amaze.)

Meanwhile, we seniors debated Viet Nam. We were all facing the draft, although we assumed that we would be in college and eligible for a student deferment. My closest friend at the time, a Campion dropout who introduced me to my wife, wrote long letters to me from his home in Ohio. Erich vehemently opposed the war; rather than register for the draft, he moved to Canada and has lived a life outside the United States since. How, he asked over and over, could I read what I was reading and still want to go to West Point? My answer was that I believed every American had the right to oppose government policy, and I was willing to fight to preserve that right. Erich didn't buy it; apparently neither did I.

Word eventually came to me at Campion that my congressman had nominated me to attend West Point. Admission to West Point required an appointment—you couldn't just send in an application. You needed a political sponsor and glowing character references from community leaders as well as appropriate academic and extracurricular records and high test results.

Then the results of my physical came back. My poor eyesight disqualified me for an appointment to the U.S. Air Force Academy. I chickened out and informed my parents that this disqualified me from West Point as well. No more military career for me. Antioch, here I come.

The final hurdle before reaching Antioch was that decision about the draft and the conversation with my father. I was appalled by what I was learning about Viet Nam. I decided that I could not fight this war or any war like it. I registered with the draft as a conscientious objector.

Dad was lying in bed when I asked my mother for a few minutes alone with him. I was on the verge of tears. I was about to hand him a huge disappointment for the second time in six months. I believed in what I was doing, but I hated breaking the news.

Like every kid in a farm family during the Depression, my father grew up dirt poor, the last of nine children and the only boy; as a skinny child, he was expected to do a man's job, and his education ended in sixth grade after failing fourth grade twice for sleeping through class.

When World War II started, he welcomed the call to military duty and escaped from poverty forever. He once told me the Army provided him with his first new suit of clothes and three square meals a day. Despite his lack of formal education, he was curious and learned fast. He rose from private to sergeant during the American invasions of North Africa, Sicily, and Italy. At the killing ground in Italy known as Anzio, he won medals for bravery and a rare battlefield promotion to second lieutenant. He liked the Army, its order and routine, the clear rules and discipline. If he had possessed more formal education, he would have happily made a career of the military.

This was the man I had to face. I could only assume—and did assume—that he would think me a coward, something I had suspicions about myself.

Once again, my father shocked me, revealing how little I knew or understood him. He told me he had served with conscientious objectors and admired their courage in tending the wounded without bearing arms. Nonetheless, I never lost the sense that I had disappointed him.

A time would come soon when I would try to, if not make amends, at least face my fears. I knew I would have to go to Viet Nam.

Chapter 4
Deported... Please Advise
SEPTEMBER 1970

Deported from V-N due to student crisis. Believed blacklisted and unable to return.

Telegram to Dan Grady, September 27, 1970

NOTHING GOOD EVER happened to me in Bangkok.

I hated it before I got there, a glaring reminder of my failure in Saigon and constant disappointment in my effort to fulfill a dream.

Christian and I landed shortly after lunch on a sleepy Sunday afternoon. If anything, Bangkok was hotter and more humid than Saigon.

I spent an hour on the phone with Christian hanging over me before I was able to reach one of the names I had collected in Saigon: Lance Woodruff, an editor at the English-language newspaper *Bangkok World*. The *World* was the smaller of the two English-language papers run by British and American expatriates. The *Post* was larger and considered closer to the Thai power brokers.

For the second time in three days, I was asking for help from a man I had never met.

We took a taxi to Lance's home. He heard our stories, and then

Christian and I split up. Christian took a room in the Pepsi Hotel near the railroad station and dropped out of my journal.

I got a room at the Niagara Hotel, a short walk from Lance's place on Silom Road in the Soi Susaan neighborhood. I would learn later that the Niagara had a reputation as a hot-sheet hotel or, as I wrote to Paula Spier at Antioch, a "bring-your-own brothel." I found it to be quiet, clean by anyone's standards, close to Lance (my only connection in Thailand), and full of friendly, helpful people, none of whom appeared to be in the "trade," if you know what I mean.

And it was cheap. Only $4 U.S. a night for a single room with a private bath. (Asian hotels, at least the kind I could afford, offered rooms with just a toilet and a shared shower down the hall; some just offered a bed with both the toilet and shower shared with the entire floor. With my own honest-to-God bathroom right in my room, I felt like I was staying in the lap of luxury.)

Lance escorted me to the Central Post Office so I could wire Dan Grady and let him know that my Antioch Education Abroad experience appeared to be heading back to the United States prematurely. Counting words as if they mattered—and they did, because telegrams were expensive, especially ones going halfway around the world—I summarized my plight:

Deported from V-N due to student crisis. Believed blacklisted and unable to return. Please advise further instructions. Care of Bangkok World.

Including Dan's address, the telegram contained 35 words and cost 122.5 Thai baht — $6.13 in U.S. currency, a night and a half at the Niagara.

Thailand is twelve hours ahead of the U.S., and a telegram, even using the Telex machines of the 1970s, could take half a day to travel from Bangkok to Hong Kong, then on to Tokyo, San

Francisco, and Chicago; and finally to Dayton, Ohio, and Antioch College in Yellow Springs, Ohio. Lance said I could not expect a response before Tuesday, local time. This was only Sunday.

I turned to filling time, something that would occupy the months remaining in 1970.

At first, I had some administrative and domestic tasks to work on. I wrote Grady a minute-by-minute recitation of my experience, eight single-spaced pages written slowly to make my left-handed chicken scratch as legible as possible. Then I did laundry, pouring a handful of local detergent into the bathroom sink and scrubbing the old-fashioned way: Dunking the stinky laundry in soapy cold water and rubbing one edge of cloth against another edge, squishing and kneading as I thoroughly soaked myself. Repeat to rinse, until the water created no soap bubbles. Wring by hand, shake out, spray more water over myself and the bathroom walls. Carefully hang the dripping material over a thin clothesline stretched taut between the showerhead and the bathroom door knob. A pair of black socks or boxer shorts took a few minutes; a shirt, five minutes or more; a pair of pants could take longer than 20 minutes.

"What a hassle to do a pair of pants!" I wrote in my journal.

* * *

The telephone woke me Monday morning around 9:00, the latest I had slept, I observed in my journal, since leaving Cornell. It was Lance; he wanted to know what I wanted to do. He had offered to write a story about what a good person I was and how I had been caught up in a bureaucratic nightmare and was determined to fulfill my dream of studying in Viet Nam. (A story like that ought to make the G.I.s enjoying R&R with young Thai hookers on Patpong Road shit their pants, assuming they ever read the local paper, which was not what they were in Thailand to do and therefore not very likely.) I told him I wanted to do the story and that I planned to visit the embassies.

Thus began another six weeks of chasing butterflies without a net.

At the Vietnamese Embassy way out on Sam Sen Road, the lady I spoke with sympathized with my plight, told me the visa requirements (in triplicate, no carbon paper), and explained that she should have an answer in one to three months. By the way, she warned, don't overstay the 15-day visitor's visa in Thailand; the Thais take that very seriously. Good to know. Three months divided by 15 days: I would only need six more visas for Thailand to find out if I got one for Viet Nam.

From there, I taxied to the U.S. Embassy.

Compared with Saigon, which has a compact city core, Bangkok is spread out over miles and miles of clogged roads and smelly klongs, the canals that parallel every major road. In Saigon, I could (and did) walk most places except when I was in a hurry. Walking was less of an option in Bangkok, given the sprawl.

It appeared I had only three transportation options. Buses were big, smelly, and perpetually overloaded—I never saw a bus that did not have three or four riders hanging out the doors. They were unmuffled monsters spewing black smoke. Despite their low cost—50 stang (two and a half U.S. cents)—they were exceedingly slow, making stops to transfer hangers-on every block or so. In fact, they moved so slowly in traffic that a passenger could safely board or step off just about any time.

Taxis, on the other hand, were hot, unairconditioned, asthmatic noise boxes that cost a lot, never less than 20 baht ($1 U.S.), subject to negotiation since they didn't carry fare boxes. And they didn't travel very fast, following all those buses.

The alternative was the tuk-tuk, a three-wheeled motorcycle with a top that covers the driver in front and passenger(s) wedged into a bench over the rear axle. Their small motors roar like they're doing 80, and they ride like they have square wheels. The drivers are clueless, typically stopping as soon as the passenger boards to query other tuk-tuk drivers about how to reach the address they swore they knew how to reach. And they break down. A lot. When that happens, the passenger walks away without paying. But they cost about half what a taxi does, and even at their normal speed of 10-15 miles an hour, they move a little faster in traffic because they can maneuver around trucks, taxis, and all those buses.

I rode a tuk-tuk to the U.S. Embassy and managed to speak with Vice Consul Donald R. Tremblay. His title sounds more important that it was, and after hearing me out, he explained that he was powerless to help. He warned me not to overstay my 15-day visa because the Thais take that kind of thing very seriously.

Back at the hotel, I read the *Bangkok Post* and the *World* and wrote a half-dozen letters. These activities would become mainstays of those days when I awoke with no specific plans and nothing to do, which is to say everyday going forward.

On Tuesday, the day I expected to hear from Dan Grady, I figured I should probably get out and about and see some sights. (I only had so much laundry to do.) I grabbed my new 35 mm camera, purchased in Tokyo at the bargain price of $80—marked down from $200 to $91 and bargained down from there—and went in search of adventure, dramatic Asian sights, red and gold Buddhist temples. What I found was a con man who offered to show me the out-of-the-way sights of everyday Thai life. We piled into a narrow, wobbly flat-bottomed boat near a temple and motored toward the nearest crowded klong. There he told me I would have to pay double or he would throw me in the river. He was fat and greasy, and there was no way he could do that; the guy driving the boat, however, was lean and muscular. And I am terrified of water, having at that point almost drowned twice in my young life. (Kids who grow up along the Mississippi River do not necessarily learn to swim.) I promised to pay the bastard after he put me back on firm land; as I was paying him, he grabbed all my money—$9.50 in baht—shoved me onto the landing steps, and escaped in the boat with his confederate.

If I had viewed myself reflected in a shop window, I would have seen a red-faced kid with a pouty lip on the verge of tears. I was humiliated. I was furious. But I was also too embarrassed to call for help or go to the police. I still had my camera, and unknown to the son of a bitch, I had a little more money hidden in my shoe for just such an emergency.

In Japan, I had met an American couple on a tour bus to see Mount Fuji on a foggy day. We didn't see the mountain, or even much of the road for that matter, but we shared lunch, and they told me horror stories about "thieving, slant-eyed" Asians. Their obvious disdain for Asians was both confusing and off-putting— Why are you touring Asia if you hate Asians so much? I thought— but they knew tricks about pickpockets, beggars, and con men.

Never carry a wallet, they advised. Pickpockets in Asia use razor blades to slice your pants open; you lose your money and ruin a pair of pants. Always wrap the strap of your camera around your wrist. Hit and run artists, mostly kids, steal cameras hanging around your neck or shoulder. Always hide enough money in your shoe to get back to your hotel. Use only legitimate tour guides, not strangers wanting to "practice their English" by squiring you around. I should have heeded *all* of their advice.

I had 20 baht, a dollar, in small bills in my shoe, enough for a taxi to my hotel. Bangkok was showing me a little hate, and I was hating it right back.

Chapter 5
Professor Daniel M. Grady
1968–1970

I think you should go to Viet Nam.

Dan Grady, 1969

DAN GRADY'S RESPONSE to my telegram arrived late Tuesday: He would call me at the *Bangkok World* sometime the next day.

I rose at 5:45 a.m. so I could go into the newspaper office with Lance. It rained on us all the way in, waves of monsoon rain, creating lakes in the streets and submerging my feet up to my ankles, brown leather shoes, black socks, creased pant legs and all.

Dan hadn't said when he would call, so I hunkered down at a vacant desk and read the *New York Times* and *Bangkok World* cover to cover. I was becoming the best-informed person in Thailand, with nothing to do with my newfound knowledge.

Finally, an hour after lunch, the call came through. Given the 12-hour time difference, that meant he was calling in the middle of the night, Ohio time. Two tin cans and a wet string would have been as good as the international telephone connection between Yellow Springs and Bangkok. We could barely hear one another. He yelled; I yelled. We both yelled, "What did you say?" a lot.

I was elated to hear his gruff voice and chronic cigarette cough, and his message pushed me to the heights of happiness. Even my sour stomach, now becoming a real menace, felt comforted.

Antioch would back me all the way, he said. I should sit tight in Bangkok while the college raised holy hell in the United States. Dan had the contacts and the Irish brashness to make me wish I could be there to watch the show. He promised to call my parents and reassure them that everything was cool. After 15 minutes of back and forth, a few other instructions emerged, and he promised to stay in touch via the *Bangkok World*; we hung up and gave our voices a rest.

I thanked Lance and headed back to the Niagara. With no place to go in a hurry and the rain on hold for a while, I ventured onto a bus and missed my stop by only three blocks.

I was probably daydreaming about Antioch.

God, Antioch was fantastic, especially after four years of confinement in an all-boys Jesuit boarding school.

If it had a rule book, I never saw it. You chose your own course schedule or, like me, made up your own independent study plan. No one kept attendance in class, and lots of students never went—ever.

Jack Spicer, the older brother of a close high school friend, landed at Antioch a year before his brother and me and reported back that girls lived in the dorms with guys and didn't wear bras, or much of anything except in winter. I was deeply disappointed, however, to discover that rather than being overpowered by lust, most Antioch men came to look on the girls in their dorms as sisters. If you wanted to mess around—and who didn't?—you looked to other dorms. And you looked askance at any males visiting the girls in your dorm. You knew what they had on *their* minds.

Despite the freedom and the coed dorms, the financial burden of paying for Antioch wore on me. Already a sophomore at this point, I didn't know what I wanted to study or what I wanted to be when I grew up. I didn't realize that that was the norm for college students, even many graduates. I had a deep interest in Southeast Asia fed, no doubt fueled by the war in Viet Nam, but deeper than that. Buddhism, as a philosophy and way of life—its absence of ritual, lack of a hierarchical clergy, and focus on individual salvation—intrigued and attracted me. I was beginning to wonder about its role in politics and in the development of impoverished countries. These interests, however, would not put bread on the table, and unlike most Antioch students, I did not come from upper-middle class parents.

All this Antioch fun was costly. I was a needs-based scholarship student at Antioch, just as I had been at Campion. I worked as a short-order cook in the student union to help pay tuition and raise a little spending money. As I started my second year, I had two bank loans and was hitting up my parents for 10 percent of their net income. This seemed unfair in a family with five kids. I started toying with the idea of dropping out of school and going back to Iowa to work in the door and window mill where I had worked the summer after graduating from high school. That, of course, assumed the draft did not snatch me first.

About this time, the Antioch "You can do anything you want" spirit kicked in, aided by supportive faculty and administrative staff.

I had latched onto Dan Grady, a professor of political science, my first quarter. He taught a class on the politics of Southeast Asia, informed in part by his own work in Viet Nam for the RAND Corporation, a think tank that was negatively identified at Antioch with the "repressive regimes" of Presidents Lyndon Johnson and Richard Nixon.

Grady was something of an outcast among Antioch's radical upper-middle-class students. He came from a working-class neighborhood in Worcester, Massachusetts. While hardly conservative or a Republican, he was not popular with the radical kids who ran the school.

Dan was the perfect example of the adage that the only thing worse than being wrong is being right, especially when it comes to delivering unwelcome dire warnings and predictions of doom that come to fruition.

A pragmatic Democrat, Grady worked to nominate and elect Vice President Hubert H. Humphrey as president after Johnson dropped out of the 1968 race because of growing opposition to U.S. involvement in Viet Nam. People who supported Gene McCarthy, a liberal senator from Minnesota, and then Bobby Kennedy, also a senator and a brother of the assassinated President John F. Kennedy, were not being practical, Dan said. He predicted neither could win against former Vice President Richard Nixon. Neither could Humphrey, as it turned out.

The majority of students felt he was not liberal enough for Antioch, not like the other truly socialist members of the faculty. Grady attracted a few loyal adherents willing to discuss something other than socialist heterodoxy; one of his fans went on to become a member of Congress. (It was not I—my claim to Antioch fame was getting kicked out of Viet Nam.)

When I started talking about dropping out because the education I chose was not matching the financial sacrifices my family and I were making, Dan came up with a truly radical idea: I should go to Viet Nam to study for a year under the Antioch Education Abroad (AEA) program.

I don't remember exactly when he presented it as an option. Well, you could do another co-op term, or you could go to Viet Nam, he probably said. Hey, there's an idea, Dan. I think I'll go to Viet Nam. I hear it's quite the spot.

We might have been sitting in a booth at the Olde Trail Tavern, a dive on the main drag through Yellow Springs. Dan and I downed a few pitchers of beer there, he holding court for me, the avid acolyte.

AEA sent a lot of kids to foreign countries, mostly in Europe, a few to South America, and even fewer to places like Kenya, Nigeria, and India. Going to Viet Nam was an intriguing idea, straight out of the "put up or shut up" school of decision making. We noodled over what it would take and how it would work. Paula Spier, a middle-aged, motherly member of the AEA staff, bought into it.

Dan, who had worked out of the RAND Corporation compound in Saigon on a massive study of Viet Cong defectors, started calling his contacts to see what could be done. Paula did the tedious work of finding funding, making travel arrangements (including shots for smallpox, cholera, typhoid-paratyphoid, and plague), and keeping me calm. I wrote applications and essays and filled out documents by hand until my fingers went numb.

Working through the former ambassador of the Republic of (South) Viet Nam to the United States, Tran Van Dinh, Dan got me admitted to the Van Hanh University School of Social Studies in Saigon for the academic year starting in September 1970. Two of the university's leading monks, Thich Minh Chau and Thich Nhat Hahn, sponsored me. Perhaps we should have considered this more carefully since they ranked high on the list of critics of the government of South Viet Nam, whose approval I would need to enter the country.

In June, I moved to Ithaca, New York, and started ten weeks of intensive Vietnamese language study at Cornell University as a National Defense Foreign Language fellow. I agonized over accepting the fellowship, which paid for absolutely everything and gave me spending money to boot, because I feared the "national defense" aspect might conflict with my conscientious objector application on file with my draft board in Iowa. Dan convinced me that the terms only required me to defend the Constitution, and I felt I could do that in good conscience if called on to do so. I figured there was more than one way to defend the Constitution without taking it out on the Vietnamese.

At Cornell, housed in a graduate dorm, I spent six hours a day in the classroom followed by hours in the language lab and doing written homework at night. My roommate, a former GI fluent in listening to Vietnamese, and I broke for beer around 11:00 p.m. and closed down the student bars, frequently crawling up the steep Ithaca hills to our dorm so we could do it all over again the next day.

At the end of the course, I flew off to visit a girl I knew in Youngstown, Ohio, and then on to Dubuque, Iowa, to see my family before leaving for Saigon.

Chapter 6
Night Train to Nong Khai
OCTOBER 1970

P.S. So I'm going to Laos for a while.

Letter to My Sister, Bonnie, October 10, 1970

MY DAN GRADY high faded quickly.

Hearing his familiar voice from halfway around the world reminded me of how few people I knew and how much I was on my own. In fact, I knew only Lance Woodruff and his Thai wife, Liz. I had written a few dozen letters to everyone I knew but had not received any mail in return. How could I? No more than a handful of people knew where I was.!

Making my loneliness and homesickness worse, my gut was causing all kinds of problems. Two days after our call, I observed in my journal:

> *"It appears to me that I have broken my ass. It just stopped working. Beware the creepy crud."*

I was eating "on the economy", which is to say wherever the locals ate—in restaurants, at noodle kitchens, off street carts. I loved the taste of Asian food, but my gut was struggling to acclimate, and nothing stayed with me very long. As my father used to say, rather prosaically, my waste could pass through a screen door and not touch a wire.

As a result, I was spending as much time on the toilet as off. I took to reading on the commode, and before this diarrhea or dysentery passed, I had read every word Ernest Hemingway had written that was available in Southeast Asia.

This stomach upset, combined with my lack of interest in Thai culture and my unfortunate mugging by the con man, resulted in my staying homebound and avoiding sight-seeing or adventuring, which a curious student might have been expected to do.

It also meant that I ventured out only when absolutely necessary, as when I needed to chase butterflies without a net. Two days after speaking with Grady, I had to get my paperwork, in triplicate without benefit of carbon paper, back to the Vietnamese Embassy. Before I could do that, I had to get my photo taken because I had used up the few spare passport photos I carried.

Walking out to find a camera shop that did passport photos, I mused about Bangkok and its brand of Buddhism, which I thought compared poorly with what I had seen ever so briefly in Saigon.

I don't like the superficial elaboration [who knows what I meant?] *of Bangkok, especially the Buddhist temples. It's ridiculous to see beggars worshipping these monstrous gold figures.*

My interest in Buddhism contributed to my desire to see Viet Nam. Buddhism, particularly the meditative "What is the sound of one hand clapping?" Zen variety, was quite popular among the smart cool kids, and we all read Herman Hesse's *Siddhartha*, the story of one man's search for spiritual self-discovery. By the time I left the States, I had studied enough about Buddhism to know it would not totally guide the rest of my life, but I was very curious about how a pacifist philosophy could confront dictatorships of the left and the right and how it might affect modernization in the underdeveloped nations of Southeast Asia.

My problem with Buddhism, at least in Thailand, was that like most theologies, it had split. I had focused on Mahayana Buddhism, the "Big Wheel" version found in China, Japan, and Viet Nam. Thailand, Laos, and Cambodia followed the teachings of the elders, or Theravada/Hinayana Buddhism. Theravada temples were gaudier than Mahayana temples, and I had a problem with that. In fairness, however, the garish red-and-gold temples of Bangkok might have reflected Bangkok more than Buddhism because the rundown and faded temples of Laos did not offend me at all.

It was just one more reason to get out of Bangkok.

Anticipating the need to leave Bangkok so I could get my visa renewed (so that I could return there to again wait for news from Saigon), I located the Royal Lao Embassy—within walking distance!—and filled out the paperwork to get a visa to enter the administrative capital, Vientiane, twelve hours northeast of Bangkok by overnight train.

On October 7, a little over a week since talking with Grady, he wired that Saigon had agreed to give me a visa. The U.S. Embassy in Bangkok confirmed the good news. The Vietnamese in Thailand knew nothing about it and suggested I come back in another week.

Two days later, fed up with the Vietnamese as well as Bangkok, I decided to accompany Lance to Laos. He had to renew his residency visa every six months, and his deadline was getting close. We chose the 6:30 p.m. express train from Wah Lampo Station to Nong Khai, the end of the rail line just opposite Vientiane, Laos.

I paid my bill at the Niagara Hotel—960 baht, or $48 in U.S. currency. I was appalled. Money was dribbling through my fingers like water; my supply was limited, and despite Dan's telegram, I was no closer to getting back into Viet Nam than I was the day I got booted out.

At Wah Lampo, I shelled out another 221 baht, more than

$11, for a roundtrip second-class seat. Lance and I found our seats and settled in for the overnight ride. Our departure time came and went, but the train sat in the station. I played the naïf. I marveled at the soldiers on board carrying M-16 rifles; I assumed they were loaded or could quickly be loaded. That concerned me just a bit as the soldiers downed a bottle of Mekong, a kind of rice whisky with a light brown tincture cast that cost less than a baht for a flat pint bottle.

Around 8 p.m., word spread through the train that we might never leave. No one knew why, but people began gathering their belongings. Then a conductor came through announcing a terrible crash on the tracks north of us, near Ayutthaya, a key railway junction about 50 miles from Bangkok. Our train was canceled. Try again tomorrow.

Lance and I cashed in our tickets, and Lanced decided to show me the town, at the least the parts with booze and women, including the Venus Turkish Bath and Massage, the Roaring 20s Speakeasy Bar, Duke's, and one other place whose name I could not recall the next day when I wrote my journal entry. We returned to his home after 1:00 a.m. and rose four hours later to catch the 6:10 express train to Nong Khai. We splashed water on our faces, tossed on the previous day's grubby clothes, and raced out the door; we purchased one-way tickets and made it onto the train just as it fired up the engine to pull out of the station.

The train was packed with its regular supply of riders as well as the overflow from last night's canceled train. We couldn't find a seat anywhere, much less in our designated car. Anticipating the all-day trip, we kept squeezing our way from one car to the next until we found one seat. I collapsed, and the rest of the trip we took turns sitting and standing.

We reached Ayutthaya before 8:00 a.m., and the train stopped, apparently so we could gawk at the wreckage. Five or six passenger cars lay on their sides in the water on either side of the tracks. Lance guessed that it had been a head-on collision. "*I was amazed that only two people had died,*" I wrote in my journal, "*and I wondered if they had drowned.*"

As we sat and wondered, we stifled in 95-degree heat. The train windows were open and five overhead fans never stopped spinning; my crotch rot itched but I could not scratch it; it was just too crowded, and I didn't want to offend Thai sensibilities.

Three miserable, boring hours passed before we moved again. After seeing the wreckage, I stopped feeling sorry for myself, and the moving train generated a baked, but welcome, breeze.

I saw my first water buffalo, a rotund cow with hide the color of mud; in fact, it probably *was* mud since the hulking animal stood up to its knees in a paddy beside the rails. Then I saw hundreds of buffalo, usually in ones or twos, looking doleful, knee-deep in mud.

Patches of paddy fields with an isolated tree or two made up the landscape. Houses with thatched roofs perched on stilts above the floodwaters. People traveled on long, narrow wooden boats. No one seemed unduly concerned about the high water everywhere, but I wondered how it would affect the rice crop. Thais grow rice in flooded fields, but this looked more like flooding than fields.

Every time I rode a train I remembered my first train ride, from East Dubuque, Illinois, across the Mississippi from my hometown, to Youngstown, Ohio, via Chicago. I wondered about the lives of the people who occupied the houses we passed. Did they wonder about the lives of the people passing on the train? This trip was no different, and I suspected the wonder passed both ways.

At every stop—and we stopped at every road crossing—men and women hefting round flat woven baskets of food crowded around the train, selling bananas, mangoes, small packages of cooked rice wrapped in green leaves, and what I came to think of as barbecued chicken pancakes. I grew up watching my mother cut up whole chickens, and I had even participated in chicken roundups, chasing headless chickens that would soon become dinner. I was no stranger to chicken parts. But I had never seen an entire chicken, minus feathers but with the head and feet attached, split in half, flayed and cooked over an open fire. I bought one and recorded my impressions:

> It was not hot, but it was tasty, like barbecued chicken in the States. I hope it didn't have something.

Fourteen and a half hours after leaving Bangkok, the express pulled into Nong Khai station. The border with Laos was closed. Lance hired a pedicab, an oversized tricycle with a seat between the rear wheels. An ageless Thai cyclist with calves the size of an Iowa ham pedaled Lance and me over to the Pongvichit Hotel. We got a room with a double bed for 20 baht, a dollar, each.

> It's not air conditioned but it has a fan. Is fairly clean by Asian standards.... Cold water shower. Toilet with an over-enthusiastic flusher. Lance says it's not bad for the sticks, and Nong Khai is the sticks.

After a quick dinner, I took a cold shower and shampooed my hair three times. It still felt dirty. The train had been completely open, and we had picked up a 14-hour accumulation of grit.

There's a knack to taking a cold shower even in a hot climate. During the day with the sun shining on the hotel walls, the water in the pipes warms and produces a comfortable stream. Of course, the warm water quickly runs out, and icy needles shock naked skin. The secret is not to get caught standing under the water. You take a deep breath, jump under the water, flailing your arms to get as much water over you in the shortest possible time. Then you step out of the stream, lather up, take another deep breath and rinse. There was no such thing as a long, hot shower in the hotels I patronized.

After the long train ride and the Pongvichit cold shower, I

considered that perhaps Bangkok was not totally without merit after all. Tomorrow, I would try life in another country.

Just before midnight, Lance and I climbed into bed, both of us wearing just shorts. We tried to act as though two robust young heterosexual men sharing the same bed was not at all awkward. Lance was a great guy and had shown me nothing but kindness; I still hugged my side of the bed all night long.

But more than Lance's loins getting too close to mine, I worried about something more, something bigger, something potentially deadly. The Mekong River was in flood; we were on one side, and Laos was on the opposite. There was no bridge between them. I would need to get into a small boat and ride across the swollen, swift-flowing Mekong, and I couldn't swim.

Between thoughts of my current bed partner and the coming river crossing, I did not sleep well.

Chapter 7
Nice Town, Nice Guys
October 1970

The place was always one where people could bury themselves anyway, and somehow justify it by saying they were press.

Letter from Don Ronk, May 1974

W E ROSE AROUND 6:00 a.m. and gobbled fried Chinese dough and hot tea at a food stand by the river. Lance was in a hurry to get to Vientiane; he had work to do and a family to get back to. All I thought about was whether I would upchuck my greasy Chinese doughnut into his lap on the trip over the Mekong.

To carry us across the river, Lance and I found a ferry with a roof to keep the sun off us and wide enough so we could sit across from one another. The boat had room for fifteen, but we were its only passengers. I assumed we were being charged for the other thirteen. Dealing with taxi drivers in Bangkok had made me just a little cynical.

I could say the driver rocked the boat dangerously as he pushed the boat away from the bank and clambered aboard. I could say the boat raced downriver sideways in the flood as the driver yanked on the motor cord over and over trying to start the engine. I could say I took a photo of Lance, looking peaceful and happy, to mark the occasion of my first river crossing. But I would be ignoring the central fact of that trip.

I was terrified.

I am afraid of a lot of things—snakes, rats, the dark, meeting strangers, meeting strangers, rats or snakes in the dark—but nothing approaches my fear of drowning. On the fear scale of 1 to 10, my anxiety about water reached about 13-1/2.

With just Lance, the boatman, and me aboard, the boat's wooden sides rose mere inches above the river. Its flat bottom looked rotted from exposure to rain and river water. A small puddle sloshed under the floorboards. The propeller worked on a shank at least six feet long that stuck out the rear of the boat—contributing to its name as a dragon boat. The driver ran the engine full out all the long way across that muddy brown expanse of water.

Several times he slowed as he recognized a friend piloting a similar boat in the opposite direction. The engine continued its roar with the prop raised out of the water. We wallowed and raced sideways down a river clogged with who knew what kinds of debris as the drivers laughed and chatted above the noise of their lawnmower engines, the propellers spinning wildly and throwing spray just above the river.

I had adopted in my travels a kind of frozen nonchalance to hide my fears, namely dealing with new people in lands strange to me. I sat with my legs crossed, leaning against the low back of the seats that lined both sides of the boat, feigning interest in the horizon over Lance's shoulder. He smiled, as if to say, "Neat, huh?" I smiled back, never once loosening my white-knuckled grip on the back of the bench.

When we arrived at the opposite shore, I let Lance take the lead so he wouldn't see my relief. I wanted to kiss the muddy earth. I could not imagine crossing that river again.

* * *

It would have been impossible to tell when we entered the city of Vientiane, save for the small road sign in Lao and French that announced, "Bienvenue au Vientiane." The reason was simple: There was no city, just small collections of houses separated by palm forest and rice fields.

We had landed at the immigration outpost at Thadeua, Laos, more or less directly across from Nong Khai. The officials there happily collected our entrance fee—no receipt, thank you—and ignored our passports. The difference from Saigon was glaring.

Lance negotiated the taxi fare into the city, and we traversed mile after mile of dusty dirt road, passing rice paddies, palm trees, bamboo houses on stilts, men in shorts and shirts driving carts with rubber tires pulled by plodding oxen. It was Thailand all over again, which should not have surprised me since the Thai of northeast Thailand are as much Lao as Thai. Borders didn't matter, and in fact, I don't ever recall seeing ordinary Thai and Lao going through immigration on either side of the river.

As the road turned from rutted orange dirt to rutted dusty black asphalt, I suspected we were approaching the heart of Vientiane, or at least leaving the country suburbs. Then the road forked, with our lane easing off to the right while the oncoming traffic disappeared to the left. Instantly the character of the buildings changed; gone were the bamboo and thatched huts, replaced by stolid, squat two-story faded orange stucco buildings. We sped through several blocks of shops, past the Ministère de la Défense and stopped in front of the Anou Hotel.

We had arrived. Vientiane. Another stamp in my passport, joining Japan, Taiwan, Hong Kong, and Viet Nam.

It reminded me of midsummer in Hazel Green, the tiny farm town in southwest Wisconsin where my father grew up on a 40-acre farm, but with an Asian accent. The "business district" was measured in blocks, not miles. Any exposed wood turned gray, then black, and cracked in the weather. Water buffalo, in lieu of cattle, grazed in open patches of green beside dusty streets. The sidewalks ended with step-up curbs, but there were neither gutters nor storm drains. Water accumulated in low pools until it evaporated in the 90-plus-degree heat. Small piles of trash and sewage waste lay where they were thrown or blown or washed. The wind and an occasional passing car whipped fine orange dust into our eyes and ears. And always the terrible twins, heat and humidity, smothered, soaking shirts with sweat and seeping into red rashes where clothes meet moving body parts.

Vientiane felt familiar, knowable. I felt at home, a small-town boy in a small town.

Bangkok's smelly klongs and smellier traffic were gone. The garish Buddhist temples were replaced by faded, worn, almost working-class temples. There wasn't a skyscraper to be seen. In fact, hotels of three and four stories seemed to be the major buildings. This had the look and feel of a manageable town that I could get used to, if only for the three or four days I planned to stay while arranging for a new entry visa for Bangkok.

The next day, a Sunday, this sleepy town drowsed as Lance and I set out on foot with our cameras to record the early morning sights. A few blocks away, we found in a row Wat Ing Peng, Wat Ong Teu, and Wat Mixai—the first of many Buddhist temples we would explore as we roamed from the river down the main boulevard and out toward That Luang, a stupa (place of meditation) that dates to the third century A.D.

On the way back, we spotted a beggar lying unconscious in the sun on a sidewalk outside the Lido Hotel, a mere block or two from the king's palace and the Lane Xang Hotel, which is what passes for posh in Laos. Later I would recognize him as a homeless heroin addict, one of dozens with descriptive names like the Horse Face Girl and the Mad Street Feeler.

After photographing the man, one arm outspread, a leg bent at the knee, Lance and I stepped into the air-conditioned chill of the Lido Bar and ordered a Lao beer, which is different from lao-lao, a rice whisky made from the waters of the muddy Mekong. I marveled at the slot machines—such decadence!—at the bar girl whose affections were obviously negotiable, and at the way the heat crept back upon us despite the air conditioners and slow-moving ceiling fans. I did what any red-blooded American boy would do in the absence of anyone to act as his conscience: I ordered a beer, chugged it down, and ordered another. Compared with Saigon and Bangkok, Vientiane was cheap and showed promise. A guy could learn all kinds of things here, even on my budget.

Lance won at the slot machines, but we got into a serious hassle over our bill with the old Vietnamese woman running the place. I kept learning that cheating customers was a way of life, and the best approach is a swift departure.

Near our hotel, we found a small French café and ate a real dinner of steak and pommes frites. Lance raced off to catch the overnight train back to Bangkok. I planned to stay longer to do a little butterfly chasing at the Vietnamese and Thai embassies and walked back to the hotel alone.

The Anou Hotel was that odd mixture of Vietnamese, Lao, and French commerce. It was named for the last king of the Lao Kingdom of Vientiane, not to be confused with other Lao kingdoms, Luang Prabang, Champassak, and Xieng Khouang. The Anou cost more than the Nong Khai dive we stayed at the night before ($3.60 vs. $1) and had fewer amenities: The cold water shower was down the hall, and despite the ceiling fan running at takeoff speed, my room was hot, stuffy, and noisy.

Around 7:00 p.m., Carl Strock, the local Associated Press stringer, rode up to the Anou on his 100 cc Honda motorcycle, the vehicle of choice for the less than wealthy but much better off than most in Southeast Asia. Carl was lean, neither tall nor short, mustachioed. He couldn't have been more than eight or ten years older than me, but he possessed decades more experience and wisdom.

I pegged him as a hero. He spoke fluent Vietnamese with a South Viet Nam accent. (I had heard enough accents at Cornell to identify northerners from southerners.)

He moved and spoke slowly, but he made me feel comfortable as I recited my oft-told story of eager anticipation, expulsion, and endless waiting for butterflies to light.

Carl couldn't stay long: He had a wife and child and was working on some unexplained big project, but we both wanted to talk more. We agreed to meet for lunch in three days. In the meantime, he suggested I check out the Hotel Constellation, where the expatriate Americans, Brits, and Aussies gathered.

It seemed strange at the time that one of the first persons I should meet in Laos would be an American war correspondent. I realized later it would have been impossible to miss me. Vientiane is a very small place. The number of Americans—or white foreigners, whom the locals called farangs—is even smaller. Any new face is an immediate attraction for the old timers, and it takes only weeks to become an old timer.

Following Carl's advice, the next day I walked the three blocks to the Constellation and changed $20 into kip, the Lao currency. Kip made me feel wealthy: the exchange rate was 500 kip to the dollar. The most common denomination of the colored script was the 100 kip note; it was twice the size of an American dollar bill, and locals carried them folded in half and then in half again, creating a wad with very few kip. After the transaction, my right pants pocket bulged with 10,000 kip, far too many of them 100 kip notes. I learned to insist on 500 and 1,000 kip notes in the future and resisted accepting one hundreds in change.

The expats had not yet convened, so I took a taxi to the Thai Embassy, filled out the same visa application four times—doing things in triplicate now seemed a luxury—and paid the required fee of 1,700 kip ($3.40). I walked back toward the Constellation, shooting photos of anything that did not move, had lunch, and then walked out to IVS House near the airport—a couple of miles at least—to meet Al Best, a name the IVSers in Saigon had given me. We arranged to meet the next day, and I ventured forth again on foot, noting the experience in my journal that night:

> *I walked back to the Anou and took a shower. I am get-ting a very nice case of crotch rot. Balls of fire—literally! The hemorrhoids are doing well. Yesterday they hurt, but today I walked slowly and they are not bothering me. I cannot take the medicine because it melts in the heat—too soft to insert.*

Around five o'clock, I set off again for the Constellation. I found two of the expats sitting in front of the hotel bar's huge front window in low red leather seats separated by a coffee table. Neither was speaking. I introduced myself, and they invited me to join them. They seemed to be expecting me, probably having been alerted by Carl Strock.

Jerry Doolittle, the tall, lanky, sardonic one with thinning hair combed back on his head, had been the press attaché at the American Embassy. When his tour of duty ended, he had resigned from the Foreign Service and stayed on in Laos, apparently giving what I called the "Official Americans" heartburn over thoughts of what he might do, say, or write about what he knew.

The other guy, similar in stature to Carl but reserved to the point of being gruff, was Don Ronk. He had worked in Viet Nam for IVS—those people were everywhere and seemed never to go home from Southeast Asia.

Both seemed to be in their early 30s, perhaps a few years older than Carl. Doolittle was sipping a Heineken; Ronk had a coffee that he toyed with. I ordered a Pepsi, the only soft drink available. Apparently the owner of the Constellation held the concession on Pepsi for all of Laos and pushed it hard.

I noticed that so far every American I had met—Saigon, Bangkok, Vientiane—carried few extra pounds. I was pretty skinny myself and would get a lot skinnier on a native noodle and rice diet, but I wondered if all the overweight Americans had stayed back in the States.

As I told my story yet again, Carl stopped to check for mail and joined us briefly. A row of open-fronted wooden mailboxes at the back of the bar may, in fact, have been the reason this Algonquin Round Table convened at the Constellation. Carl, Doolittle and Ronk each had an unmarked mailbox. One day, I would have one, too, but that's down the road.

Carl soon left, and Doolittle followed, heading home to his wife and five sons. Ronk, a bachelor, asked if I wanted to join him for dinner at a noodle kitchen nearby. His brusque manner put me off, but I was as hungry for company as I was for food, so I agreed to meet him at 9:00 p.m. Later I wrote my impressions:

Don is an impressive person—cynical, tough, [illegible]—by his own standards, which tend to glorify him, although not unjustifiably. Spent 4 years in V-N. Knew Don Luce well since he was in IVS from '65 til the time Don [Luce] quit and Ronk followed w/ 3 others. He says that he started the boys' homes in V-N, not Dick Hughes, and that Dick has fucked them all up. Don R. is a "damned good photographer." Right now he doesn't appear to be working regularly. His cynicism and overconfidence bother me, but I may just be chickenshit.

I did not sleep well that night, "disturbed by Don Ronk."

Chapter 8
Hemorrhoids and Hemingway
OCTOBER–NOVEMBER 1970

You've had a classic "learning experience."

Letter from Dan Grady, October 14, 1970

Too soon I found myself back in my least favorite place on earth, suppressing memories of crossing the Mekong twice in four days and chasing butterflies again.

I'd spent a long evening on Tuesday with Ronk at his favorite Chinese noodle kitchen—from 9:30 p.m. to 2:00 a.m. The soup kitchen stays open as long as it has customers. He talked about stories he was writing. One in particular grabbed my attention: The Meo army, the only real Royal Lao Army combat force in the northeast part of the country, is composed of boy soldiers, 8–14 years old, he said. Six out of ten soldiers are now 16 or younger. I did not know whether to believe such an outrageous tale. I was still focused on Viet Nam; Laos was a sideshow, nothing more.

The next day Carl and I had our long-delayed lunch at an outstanding, and cheap, French restaurant. The conversation did not match the caliber of the cuisine, as I noted in my journal.

Carl and I had a rather dismal and discouraging talk. I was very depressed about not getting into V-N; confused over

*what to do next; and almost despondent in my impotence
to effect change or even forge a future for myself. Carl
was not much help in coming up with ideas or in giving me
moral support.*

I knew Carl didn't owe me anything, nor did anyone else. People I met as strangers—Bill Herod and others in Saigon, Lance in Bangkok, and now Carl and Ronk in Vientiane—had gone out of their way to be helpful. I was young enough to expect others to solve my problems, and I just couldn't get over my disappointment.

I arrived back in Bangkok Thursday morning after sitting up all night on the train because there were no sleepers available. The disappointments just kept piling up.

The crotch rot was getting worse: *"I itch most of the time and scratch the rest of the time. My balls are burning up and are about ready to fall off."*

I found no mail or telegrams waiting for me at the *Bangkok World.*

At the Vietnamese Embassy, I learned they still had not heard about the alleged approval of my visa; the consul told me it usually takes six weeks for these things, and only three weeks had elapsed since I made my application. If I left a forwarding address in the United States, he said, he would be happy to let me know how it turned out. I explained that I was not going back to the States.

Perhaps to placate me, since I refused to leave, he told me that my application was being reviewed by the Minister of Foreign Affairs personally. Then the consul threw me a curve and asked me about Larry Lifschultz. I hadn't given that loud-mouthed pain in the ass a thought since leaving Saigon, and here he was intruding in my life again. Larry had made a big stink about being expelled; the Vietnamese wanted to talk to him but couldn't find him. The American Embassy suggested they ask me, as though we were traveling companions. I couldn't shed him any more than I could my crotch rot.

On the way back to the Niagara Hotel, I stopped at the Bangkok Christian Hospital to schedule hemorrhoid surgery, fallout from my habit of eating on the local economy. The cheapest available bed cost 300 baht ($15). I had stopped at Chase Manhattan Bank to get more baht, and I learned I couldn't afford that bed. I had only $345 in my account. The doctor and I agreed we would do it the next week when a cheaper bed might be open.

To finish my day, I continued reading Hemingway's *For Whom the Bell Tolls,* his tragedy of the Spanish Civil War and easily his most depressing book.

Over the next three days, I did little but sleep. I worked through the dirty laundry by washing my clothes in the sink; I caught up on the news each day and read Hemingway on the toilet, but mostly I slept.

At the start of the new week, I popped out of bed, trying to jumpstart a new attitude. At the Christian Hospital, I bowed and spread my cheeks and got the first pleasant surprise since arriving in Southeast Asia: I didn't need surgery.

More good news arrived from Lance: I had mail. Two letters from Dan Grady instructed me to sit tight, stick it out and go to the American Embassy. There I got the same old, same old, with a dose of inquisitiveness about my antiwar activities in the States. I explained that I'd worked for the Quakers at the American Friends Service Committee and spoken to small groups about the war.

While waiting around the embassy for my turn to be questioned, I visited the mail section and found a heavy 9 x 12 manila envelope from Grady, full of thirteen pages of back and forth between the U.S. Embassy in Saigon, Vietnamese officials, and Dan. In it, many questions were answered. It was Lifschultz again.

Three days after we were expelled, Lifschultz wrote a single-spaced, four-page "formal statement of objection" to the Vietnamese

foreign minister. He lumped Christian and me into his protest—
this after our arguments about not wanting to make a stink. The
only good thing he did was to point out how in 1969 President
Nguyen Van Thieu had invited the students of the world to come
and see for themselves the "truth of Viet Nam." It was a cheap shot
from a guy I did not like and one that I knew would be counterpro-
ductive, but it still felt good reading it.

The next document was from the U.S. Consul in Saigon to
Huynh Huu Luan, the new man in the Ministry of Foreign Affairs
who had still been learning the street layout when I spoke with
him. The consul noted that our expulsions "had some unfortunate consequences."

A week later, Luan wrote to Lifschultz at his upstate New York
home. He noted that he hadn't met him or Christian but "had two
most interesting interviews" with me. Responding to the Thieu
invitation, Luan got to the heart of the matter:

> You arrived in Vietnam a few days after two American
> antiwar students had left the country. As you are
> aware, those students while in Saigon had resorted to
> all kinds of subversive activities, unworthy of a citi-
> zen from an allied country. Our Government was very
> unhappy about the incident, with the result that spe-
> cial instructions had been given to Airport authorities
> to carefully screen all visitors to Vietnam and you were
> victim of those stringent measures for security.

There it was: America's Southeast Asian ally in the battle against
godless Communism had accepted America's military support but
not its values. Pesky students speaking their minds would not be
tolerated. I was a student, therefore I must be pesky. I would not
be tolerated. (The correspondence may have been addressed to
Lifschultz, but it applied to Christian and me. Woody Allen always

said that 90 percent of life is just showing up; I'm sure he has a corollary about bad timing.)

On October 10, when Lance and I were chugging our way to Laos, the U.S. consul explained to Lifschultz (again at his home in New York State) that he would be granted a three-day transit visa, but that if he wished to stay longer, the Ministry of Interior would have to review his application first.

> This is not a special procedure in your case, but rather the new regulations applying to all foreigners. There is also a regulation that you cannot enter unless you are well groomed and here the concern is with the length of one's hair.

It's a failing on my part, I'm sure, but I have never understood the obsession with the length of my hair. My mother wanted me to keep every strand of curls as long as possible, leaving me with shoulder-length Shirley Temple curls at the age of 5 when every other boy in America had a butch cut. The Jesuits insisted on military-style haircuts every two weeks whether we needed/wanted/liked them or not. Here were the South Vietnamese locked in a losing civil war with their northern brothers, and still they had time to worry about foreign visitors' hairstyles. After Lifschultz went clean, cutting off his long hair and shaving his beard, Lance would chastise me for allowing my hair to grow over the tips of my ears. (Lance had my interests at heart and didn't really give a hoot about my hair, so this is not a criticism of him.) So I got a damned haircut. Did it get me into Viet Nam? No, it did not.

During this back and forth, Grady had chimed in with a wonderful, precisely worded one-page letter to the U.S. consul, drawing his attention to my case and calling me "that rarest of birds, a Viet Nam specialist." (Trained by no less a specialist than Professor

Daniel M. Grady, Acting Chairman of the Political Science Department of Antioch College. God, I loved that man.)

Here was the zinger:

For the time being, I intend to treat this matter as a simple misunderstanding and shall even operate on the dubious assumption that the Saigon authorities will right the situation once they see that an error has been made. I... shall refrain from raising hell in hopes that it can all be straightened out quietly.

I would be most appreciative of any assistance which you can give and hope that we can reach, if you will pardon the expression, a negotiated settlement.

Here was the evidence I needed that someone was on my side. I never doubted that Dan and Paula Spier were with me; I just didn't have the proof. On the contrary, Dan zinged me more than once about my behavior. "You should be aware that extraordinary efforts were made for you by individuals who did not really have to do anything," he wrote at one point along here. Ouch. Then added the spoonful of sugar that makes the medicine go down: "Whatever, you've had a classic 'learning experience' so far. Doesn't that make your day?"

Things looked so different on the other side of the world.

The consul responded with the usual bureaucratic rigmarole, couching unreasonable ideas in reasonable language.

My favorite was this:

Various Vietnamese officials have suggested that it might be better if Mr. Haase did not name a specific university in Viet Nam. These officials have particular concern with Van Hanh University, where there has been some considerable student activity.

That might be a reasonable if I had not already filled out several affidavits and visa applications that pointed very specifically to my association with Van Hanh. I'm sure Grady saw it as I did, a lame attempt to push the burden of my expulsion onto me.

Finally, this packet of depressing material did contain one positive note. The consul pointed out: "The Vietnamese authorities have decided not to admit persons with long hair and lack of grooming. This should not be a problem in David's case."

As I already noted, it did not do a damned bit of good.

*   *   *

Back in Bangkok, I fell into the bad habit of staying up late reading and not rising until well past noon. In truth, I didn't have anything to do. One day droned into the next. Trips to buy bread, my staple for two meals a day. Long periods reading the English language Thai papers, the *Bangkok World* where Lance worked and the *Bangkok Post*. Walks to American University Association library to borrow books. Laundry in the sink. Time on the toilet. Visits to Lance and his wife, Liz, who were experiencing some marital discord owing to his long hours and, I suspect, some cultural differences. I liked them both and hoped for the best. Lance was very, very good to me.

At the end of October, I paid my hotel bill for the month: 1,360 baht ($68) for 17 days, and no end in sight.

At one point, Lance told me that a clean-shaven, short-haired Lifschultz was skulking around Bangkok but didn't want me to know about it; he didn't want to be associated with me. The rat bastard was the source of my trouble in Viet Nam, and he was avoiding me. That was rich. Things like this contributed to my frequent dark moods and disgust. I was learning lessons from classes I had not enrolled in.

I continued to experience severe diarrhea and cramps, and

I isolated myself in the bathroom, with only Ernest Hemingway for company.

During the second week of November the *Bangkok World* carried a piece by Ton That Thien suggesting that Vietnamese Premier Nguyen Van Thieu should step down in favor of General Duong Van "Big" Minh, who was considered a neutralist at the time. *"This will not bode well for my visa,"* I wrote. *"Thien is a sponsor."*

With my 30-day Thai visa about to expire, I prepared to make another trip to Laos. It took me three trips to the Royal Lao Embassy to get a visa that could have been handled while I waited. This experience just added to my frustration.

At the American Embassy, my regular contact whined at me to "call off the dogs" since he couldn't do anything. I assumed he meant Grady, and I silently cheered Dan on.

In fact, however, my affair with Viet Nam had ended in the Niagara Hotel: *"My enthusiasm for Viet Nam has waned to the degree that I don't give a damn about getting there."*

Chapter 9
Vee-en-chun
NOVEMBER 1970

Everything in Vientiane is legal. Nothing is forbidden here.

Maurice Cavalerie, *Far East Economic
Review* May 22, 1972

I SURPRISED RONK AND Carl when I walked into the Hotel
Constellation bar from my room upstairs. They figured, as I had,
that we had met and gone our separate ways never to meet again.

They asked me what I planned to do, and I told them honestly
that I was getting tired of waiting on Saigon, always chasing butterflies. Beyond that, I had no plans. Ronk gave me tips on housing—
his apartment building had a one-room vacancy; jobs—the Lao-
American Association always needed English teachers; and mail—I
could use his mailbox at the Constellation.

In one conversation with these two semi-strangers, a future
started opening for me. I wasted no time.

I tracked down Ronk's landlord at his day job at the Lane Xang
Hotel and arranged to rent apartment No. 6 in the four-story stucco
building at 20 Rue Manthatourath for 20,000 kip ($40) a month. I
checked out of the Constellation and hauled my suitcase the three
blocks to my new home.

Apartment is not an appropriate name for this dwelling [I wrote in my journal] *since it consists of only one large room and shower-in room with a toilet and sink thrown in incidentally. It is located on the first floor (French method of floor counting) of a large building one block from the Mekong River. It is equidistant from the Anou and the Constellation Hotels.*

As you enter the room, everything is situated to your left. Straight ahead is a table and two chairs. On the immediate left is a stand-up dresser-vanity, which is the only storage space in the place. The double bed is beyond it. In the far corner of the room are two easy chairs and a small smoking table with magazine space below. A small nightstand and lamp near the bed complete the furnishings.

The "shower closet" is just that. A toilet and sink with mirror seemed to be added as an afterthought.... I like the little place.

P.S. It has a large set of three windows. No view. It is spacious but not huge. Totally unpretentious. Clean by Asian standards. Very livable, even by U.S. standards.

This single bit of permanence in my life, the simplest symbol of stability, boosted my mood as I settled in, with the Hotel Constellation as the center of my new universe.

Like most cities and towns along the Mekong River, Vientiane sits on a flat plain, occupying an often flooded crescent of land where the river makes a sharp right turn from a west-to-east flow to a north-to-south flow. In the dry season—November to March—the river shrinks to a stream flowing along the Thai embankment to the south, leaving Vientiane with a mile-wide beach where previously just a small island sat.

Ronk often sat on a wooden bench perched at the top of the riverbank a block from our apartment building. It was a quiet, private place where he could be alone with his thoughts. When he wasn't using it, I too sat for hours looking across at Thailand or watching magnificent sunsets upriver.

Altogether, my universe stretched a half-dozen blocks east to west and four blocks, at most, from the river to the north. On the east, Rue Lane Xang, a six-lane boulevard and the city's widest thoroughfare, ran from the Vientiane Palace on the Mekong at a northeast angle to the Victory Monument, fashioned after the Arc de Triomphe in Paris. Most Americans called the squat monstrosity the Vertical Runway since it was built with concrete the U.S. government had provided to extend the runway at Wattay Airport. Beyond the Vertical Runway, Lane Xang doglegged to the right, the northeast, out to KM 6, a walled, gated compound of American suburban ranch houses where a large number of Official Americans lived. Rue Khoun Boulom, an asphalt ribbon, arced from Lane Xang west behind the soccer stadium and then south to the Mekong, marking the northern and western boundary of the neighborhood. The river made up the southern border. This was essentially downtown Vientiane. Beyond it lay ordinary Laos.

Two one-way streets bisected the downtown east to west. Rue Samsenthai ran from east to west; Rue Setthathirath moved traffic from west to east. On the west, the two streets joined to create Rue Luang Prabang, which continued to the airport; on the east, they joined to create Rue Thadeua, which followed the river south to the ferry crossing over to Nong Khai, Thailand.

The real heart of the neighborhood, where I spent more time than any other place outside my apartment, was the Hotel Constellation. It was the hotel for out-of-town journalists, and the bar, restaurant, and meeting place for in-town journalists and those wanting to meet the press. I thought of it as my living room. I arranged to meet people here. I poked my head in the door at least several times a day just to see what was happening. It was my post office once owner Maurice Cavalerie realized I just would not go away. It was also the phone booth for most journalists, with Maurice's daughter, Danielle, acting as international operator-interpreter.

From November 1970 until the day I left Southeast Asia, I spent at least an hour or two every day in the Constellation bar, which also served as the hotel lobby and entrance to the restaurant. (I know there was a restaurant in back, but I never saw anyone eat there.) We expats ate in the bar, perched on the edge of calf-high red leather seats, our elbows resting on our knees. Maurice's cheese sandwiches with spicy mustard on fresh French baguettes contributed to the European flair of the Constellation, and we expats resembled complaisant groupers just out of the water, big-eyed with curiosity over anyone who passed through the swinging glass doors into Maurice's air-conditioned heaven.

The Constellation was convenient to every place that was any place.

The American Embassy was a block away, just past That Dam, an ancient moss-covered stone stupa blackened by antiquity. The embassy was protected by eight-foot-high concrete walls with razor-sharp concertina wire curled across the top. A garden of antennas sprouted from the green roof of the embassy, sending and receiving who knows what secrets.

The embassy sat on the corner of that little no-name half-block street and Lane Xang Boulevard. Across the boulevard was the Morning Market, one square block of open-air booths selling everything that could be bought in Vientiane, from live animals to butchered meat, fresh fruits and vegetables to imported canned goods like Carnation evaporated milk, a key ingredient of the delicious tea sipped all day long. It offered sleeveless white blouses and colorful sarong-like, ankle-length skirts known as pha-sins, the everyday wardrobe for Lao women. Everything anyone would need to live a normal life sat piled in heaps. The market also gathered the longest line of taxis and pedicabs in the city; from here you could go anywhere wheels would take you.

At the southern edge of the market—the part closest to the river—not a long stone's throw from the American Embassy stood a two-story French colonial home covered in faded orange paint and fresh orange dust. Inside lived Soth Petrasy, the Communist Pathet Lao representative to the Royal Lao Government. One or two PL soldiers stood guard, staring into space in the most unthreatening way. What these avowed communists thought about the largest showcase of free market capitalism in Laos is anyone's guess, but day after day, month in and month out, they stood and stared. I never saw them leave for a short stroll downtown; I rarely saw anyone visit.

I could fill most of my needs in the single block of Rue Samsenthai where the Constellation stood. Next door to the hotel was a camera shop that developed black-and-white film. Ronk swore by it, and he knew his cameras. I bought my Kodak Tri-X black-and-white film there and returned it to have contact sheets printed.

A few doors farther down was the entrance to Tammy Arbuckle's apartment. Arbuckle was a Scottish expat, reporting for the now-defunct *Washington Star*. He was the envy of the other freelance reporters in Vientiane: He actually got a salary. I shared several holiday meals at his place, which was a real apartment with a kitchen and bedrooms and a living room and such. It took up an entire floor. I suspect he didn't pay much more than I did for my one room, he being married to a Thai woman (Somboun, whom he called "Soupy") who took shit from no fellow Asian, least of all a mere landlord.

Directly across Samsenthai from the Constellation stood two Indian shops, Haja Store and Habeeb Store. They sold exactly the same things at the same price and appeared as competitive as two capitalists could be. Clerks stood outside each and were happy to escort potential customers past the competition. I suspected the shops were secretly owned by the same family who lived all together in the back of the premises. The clerks were nice young guys watched over by a single authority figure, friendly, smiling and always willing to help; I tried to split my commerce between them, but Habeeb probably got more of my money.

Bunches of other shops filled both sides of Samsenthai, but I never stepped inside. I had no need for dressmakers or jewelers. Buying gold was a big deal in Laos. American pilots with Air America loved wearing gaudy gold bracelets. One of them explained over a game of dice that the gold was ready cash, useful for a ransom or to pay for help in the event of a mishap up-country where planes were shot at daily and shot down regularly. Gold was cheaper than in Saigon or Bangkok, probably because the overhead costs were so ridiculously low, and Official Americans came from both places just to buy it. I never understood where the gold came from or why it would be cheaper in Vientiane than elsewhere. It reminded me a lot of things that "fall off the back of the truck" in the United States.

My route home from the Constellation rarely varied: West (right) down Samsenthai to the first intersection, left on Pang Kham, a short block to the fountain which contained water only during the monsoon season—and was to be avoided then because the mosquitoes bred in the stagnant water—right onto a no-name street for another short block, left onto Rue Manthatourath, past the first shop on the left, and left down a short open hallway to the stairs. My room was up one flight and to the left. Later I would move from the back of the building to the front and up one more flight. On one or two occasions I made the trip up the concrete steps on my hands and knees, too drunk to walk upright.

On the western edge of my small universe, where the map would be labeled "Here be dragons," was the Anou Hotel, the movie district—it had two theaters—and catty-corner from the Anou, the Cuong Ky noodle kitchen. The first time Ronk invited me to meet him for dinner, he told me to meet him at a Chinese restaurant on a no-name side street parallel to Samsenthai about six blocks from the Constellation. I was shocked to discover I had already seen the place, having taken a photo of it from the balcony of my room at the Anou Hotel. I should have realized how small the world can be.

We never called it Cuong Ky. It was always "the Noodle." (In my journal, I noted it as CN, short for Chinese Noodle.) If I wanted to arrange a rendezvous with Ronk, I would ask, "See you at the Noodle later?" Later always meant around 9:30 or 10:00 p.m. I felt I had worn Lance out with my presence in Bangkok, so I tried not to do that with the guys in Vientiane.

* * *

I arrived in Laos on November 10, a Wednesday, and having set myself up at the center of the universe—the Constellation—soon I ran into a former G.I. named Fred who was studying tropical diseases in Bangkok and was presumably in Laos doing the visa routine. He quickly demonstrated that he knew less about Asia than he thought, but I was still starved for company and put up with him. I learned something useful about Ronk from Fred. Don joined us at a table in the Constellation bar, listened to Fred carry on for a while, then just got up and moved to a different table. Subtle as a hammer, that Ronk. But that one move put a value for me on his friendship. If he hadn't liked me, I would have known it.

The next day, Ronk surprised me with a message from an official at the American Embassy. This guy—his name was Ed Kelly—came looking for me at the Constellation. He said he was a graduate of Antioch College. Hah! I thought. Fat chance an Antioch grad was in the Foreign Service.

At the Noodle, I met a Brit name John Cornell. John was 26, spoke with a slow drawl, possibly owing to his opium experiments. Opium—indeed, all drugs and narcotics—were perfectly legal in Laos at that time. John occasionally visited one of the many opium dens behind the soccer stadium and often stopped at Ronk's table to chain smoke hand-rolled cigarettes and eat fried Chinese doughnuts dunked in sa nam hon, a creamy brown confection, half tea, half Carnation evaporated milk.

John was the first, but hardly the last, Westerner I met who played around with opium. John was assistant director of the Lao-American Association, an American Embassy project that provided inexpensive English language lessons to hundreds of young Lao, Thai, Vietnamese, and Chinese students. He suggested I apply for a job; there were no immediate openings, he said, but they always needed more teachers, most of whom were the wives or girlfriends of Official Americans. In fact, the LAA building, a beautiful white edifice with arches three stories high, sat right behind my apartment building. If I got a job, it would be a short walk to work.

The next day, Ed Kelly stopped by the Constellation again. This was such odd behavior for an American official that I actually believed he might be an Antioch grad. When he started asking about South Hall, the Little Theater, and the Olde Trail Tavern, I knew he was legit. He told me he had read a telegram saying I had been readmitted to Viet Nam. Great news, if it was true. I had heard that before; unfortunately the Vietnamese here had not.

On John Cornell's recommendation, I stopped at the LAA and spoke with Penny Khounta, the director. Penny was an oddity among Official Americans. She was a woman, and official women were in short supply. (I never met another.) She was married to a Lao. (I never met another American, male or female, married to a Lao. Vietnamese, yes. Thai, yes. Lao, no.) She was bossy. That made her official.

Mrs. Khounta, as she wanted to be called, said she had no openings, and all teachers had to have a residency visa, but she hired me on the spot as a substitute teacher.

Less than a week after I set up housekeeping in Vientiane, one of the journalistic powerhouses of Southeast Asia breezed into town and settled into the Constellation. Arthur Dommen—he might have been in his 40s, but who knows how old old people are?—was the Saigon bureau chief of the Los Angeles Times. He played tennis with the U.S. Ambassador to Laos, G. McMurtrie "God" Godley, and drank after hours with the guys at the Constellation. I listened in and learned that he was publishing a book about Laos that would come out soon. I made a mental note to borrow it from someone who could afford to buy it.

After his short visit, a familiar lassitude set in. I noticed in my journal entries a preoccupation with bedtimes and sleep. When you have nothing to do, I guess sleeping counts as a daily achievement.

The time, which appears to pass so slowly, is melting the days and running them together. This afternoon I could not remember the day. It was indeed Thursday, but what had happened to Wednesday? Or Tuesday or Monday, for that matter? I have been here nine days, but I can't remember the first week having gone by.

The highlight of my second week in Vientiane was the sudden appearance in my apartment of a desk. I hadn't asked for one; I hadn't thought to—I didn't know it was an option. I guess my Lao landlord saw the mess I was making on the tables and figured I needed a desk.

That suggested I needed to get serious about my studies, not that I planned to stay on in Laos. But I was a student, and students study.

Chapter 10
In Search of Laos
November 1970

If you think you know what's happening in Laos, you just don't know the facts.

Anonymous Foreign Diplomat, 1960

I HAD NO IDEA how long I would be in Laos—a couple weeks, maybe a month—waiting for the elusive visa, but I knew from my weeks in Bangkok that I needed something to do or I would go crazy.

The Stephen Stills 1970 hit song, "If you can't be with the one you love, love the one you're with," came to mind. I applied it to my situation and set out to learn something about Laos.

Wanting to put my time to good use was a noble idea. I had two problems, however: I didn't know enough about Laos to know what to study, and from what I had seen so far, I didn't think Laos had a library, much less a university.

I turned to my trio of advisors at the School of Life, Hotel Constellation campus: Carl, Ronk, and Doolittle. Laos has a technical school, they thought, but it was more like Grade 13 in high school and not so much a university. Doolittle had a bunch of books and monographs from his days working at the American Embassy and invited me to stop by his lending library at the Lido

Hotel. Trouble was, he was hard to catch. He had a wife and five sons; his days were full.

Just three days after arriving back in Vientiane, I wandered down Lane Xang Boulevard slowly so as not to aggravate my permanent crotch rot. Near the Vertical Runway, I discovered the U.S. Information Service Library. Surely, I thought, they would have what I needed, just like the AUA Library in Bangkok. I learned three things here. First, I discovered that what seemed to be logical assumptions did not apply in Laos. Second, the role of USIS is to provide materials not about the host country but about how great the United States is. And third, Official Americans were far more interested in learning about me and what I was doing than they were in giving out information. The library had not a single book, magazine, brochure, or pamphlet on Laos, and the Official Americans made no offers to provide from their personal collections.

I thought to visit my new Indian friends, Haja and Habeeb, whose emporia across from the Constellation sold everything and advertised on their nameplates that books were among their stock. Always trying to differentiate themselves from the other, Haja called his store a purveyor of "General Merchandise and Book Sellers"; Habeeb advertised himself as a "General Merchandise and Books Seller."

When I put in my request for books on Laos, the young clerks looked at me in puzzlement. I might have been asking for a rhino hide (which they probably could have provided if I could wait a day or two). They looked through their stock and came up with a Mickey Spillane mystery. Not what I wanted, but I bought it anyway because I like to reward enthusiasm.

Once put on notice that I would buy anything about Laos, the boys unearthed a copy of Father Matt Menger's *Valley of the Mekong*. Menger was a Catholic priest, and his book was an anticommunist screed. Then the guys found a copy of *Remous du Mekong* (Mekong Whirlpool) by Frenchman Pierre Gentil.

It was starting to dawn on me that Laos was seriously different from Viet Nam and Thailand, and not just in the absence of libraries and universities. Here was a country at war, yet I saw almost no soldiers. Police in their khaki uniforms and military hats roamed the downtown streets now and then, but in a crunch I wouldn't know where to find a cop. The only troops I saw with regularity were the two guards fighting sleep in their sentry boxes outside the Ministry of Defense. There were no sandbags, either. In Saigon you ran into soldiers and sandbags everywhere. Interesting, I thought, inspired to find some source that might explain this peculiarity.

I scored my first book the day after my excursion to USIS. After dinner with Ronk at the Chinese Noodle, John Cornell, the assistant director at LAA, joined me in dunking deep-fried doughnuts into creamy hot tea. (Ronk didn't eat doughnuts very often and when he did, he didn't dunk, but he was willing to watch John and me. I was still in the skinny "nothing makes me fat" days of my just-turned-20s; he had already entered his 30s and knew better.) I placed my dilemma before the educator. Like a magician, he pulled the solution out of his ornately sewn Lao shoulder bag: A British Information Service booklet aptly titled "Laos." I was off and running.

BIS told me the general story: An 800-year-old kingdom often overrun by its larger neighbors, especially Viet Nam and Thailand. The timely arrival of the French in the 1800s kept the neighbors at bay. An urban elite considered itself more French than Lao. A multiplicity of ethnic groups—Lao, Phutai, Tai Nyo, Tai Deng, Tai Dam, Tai Hao, Tai Hat, Thai Then, Wa, Lawa, Katu, Ho, Lahu, Lolo, Lusi, Yi, Yao, Meo, and more. Ethnic groups ranked in order of social importance by how far up the mountains they lived, the higher the dwelling, the lower the status. The country had no major natural resources or commerce; no bridge across the Mekong; no railroad.

It was a start, but I craved more. I wanted to *understand* Laos.

When I tracked down Doolittle at his writing lair several days later, he recommended that I start with Hugh Toye's *Laos: Buffer State or Battleground?* Toye had been the military attaché at the British Embassy in Vientiane just a few years earlier; he knew the political and military landscape firsthand. Material I would find later filled in details, but Toye provided the big picture, documenting Laos' unhappy location between Viet Nam and Thailand.

Arthur Dommen's *Conflict in Laos: The Politics of Neutralization* was the other basic book for newbies. Dommen had been kicking around Asia for quite a few years. He made one of his periodic visits to Vientiane in early December, and I was able to question him for a few hours over Lao iced tea at the Constellation. Dommen clearly held the Official American view, whereas Toye was more skeptical.

Oddly enough, *Conflict in Laos: The Politics of Neutralization* never sold in Vientiane that I am aware of. The copy I read made its way into the country from a bookstore in Bangkok.

Ed Kelly, my Antioch connection in the U.S. Embassy, offered two monographs by the embassy's resident Laos expert, Edwin T. "Win" McKiethen. The titles sounded academic—*Life under the P.L [Pathet Lao] in the Xieng Khouangville Area* and *The Role of North Vietnamese Cadres in the Pathet Lao Administration of Xieng Khouang Province*—but I was warned that they were propaganda.

On a repeat visit to the USIS library at the end of November, I unearthed two histories of Southeast Asia, one by British historian D. G. E. Hall and the other by John Cady, the foremost American historian on French Indochina. When I eventually returned to the States, I studied at Ohio University with Cady, then in semiretirement, and discovered that he was more interested in picking my brain than in sharing his. Still, he was a nice guy, even though he only gave me a C and told me my work was not up to graduate-level standards. (I left grad school greatly disillusioned shortly thereafter and never looked back.)

As I scoured the city for material, I discovered a French

bookstore not far from the Constellation. Nothing was far from the Constellation. Another nearby store, Casa Lao, also sold books. Unfortunately, both catered to a French-speaking clientele, and my two years of high school French barely carried me through book titles. Nonetheless, I bought a French-English dictionary and pushed on, tackling *Place Historique du Laos en Asie,* by Khamchan Pradith, the private secretary to Prime Minister Souvanna Phouma. Oh, the stories he could tell, but didn't.

I hadn't given up on finding a library, and after much searching—it amazed me how little everyone knew about Laos—I located the Lao national library, the Bibliothèque Nationale, behind the Morning Market. Having been founded by the French, its materials were in French and Lao, but that language barrier was small compared with its policy of not lending books and the surprise of its staff that anyone would want to read one of their volumes, much less borrow it.

Having heard that the Soviets had a library in their Soviet Cultural Center, I dropped in. They were more surprised than the people at the Bibliothèque Nationale. So surprised, in fact, they called for a political officer from the Soviet Embassy. He questioned me about what I was looking for and why I was looking *there.* I was naïve, but I quickly sussed out that I was in the wrong place and exited pronto. Walking back to the Constellation, I imagined that going forward I would be followed by Soviet intelligence agents as well as the CIA and maybe even Lao intelligence, assuming the Royal Lao Government had an intelligence branch. (Paranoia ran high in Vientiane, and everyone assumed that everyone else was nosing into their business.)

Next, I tried the Asia Foundation, despite being leery of its connection with the CIA. It had been widely reported that the CIA provided most of the funds for the foundation's operations, and the serious Southeast Asia scholars at Cornell University considered it both suspect and worthless. I learned it didn't have any books on Laos.

I heard that the Indian ambassador to Laos was very knowledgeable and might have a private collection of material from which I might borrow. (India was one of three countries selected to oversee the 1962 Geneva Accords that ended one Lao civil war and sparked the proxy war between communism and capitalism in Laos; Poland and Britain were the others.) I showed up at the Indian embassy, unannounced and without an appointment, and actually got in to see the ambassador. (The Indians at that time had little power anywhere in the world, and I think he was lonely.) I told him my story of planning to study in Saigon, and he sympathized. He suggested instead that I could make a very good study right there in Laos and encouraged me to continue my research. Unfortunately, he had no books to lend, but he invited me to return any time. I did—many times.

As I read deeply—I was knocking off a book every two days or so, taking extensive notes by hand—I fulfilled my need for history, but I craved information about what was going on in Laos *now*.

Conversation at the Constellation swirled about CIA spies in northern Laos running a "clandestine army" made up of Meo hill tribesmen and lead by General Vang Pao. VP's army—everybody called him VP—was all that stood between the North Vietnamese and Vientiane.

Air America, the CIA's secret airline, flew unmarked planes out of the second-busiest airport in the world (second to O'Hare in Chicago), located in a mysterious fog-shrouded valley less than 100 miles northeast of Vientiane. The place was called Long Cheng; VP made his headquarters there, although he was constantly on the move, hopping by air from one outpost to another.

Another American agency, USAID—which everyone called "you-sayd"—provided food, clothing, equipment, shelter, and other logistical support to both VP's independent army and the

Royal Lao Army from a huge base less than a 10-mile hike north-northwest of Long Cheng at Sam Thong. Air America pilots called Sam Thong "Lima Site (LS) 20;" Long Cheng was "20 Alternate." Such was the symbiotic relationship between the two.

The Constellation regulars talked about the American bombing, directed from an inaccessible mountaintop in far northeastern Laos just a few miles from the North Viet Nam border. I heard stories of tens of thousands of hill tribe refugees, the result of American bombing, according to some, or of North Vietnamese attacks, according to others. The biggest refugee camp, Sam Thong, was almost as large as the city of Vientiane. In addition, the Meo were taking enormous casualties, so many that only boys were left to recruit, and the CIA had lured Thai mercenaries to replace the casualties.

Part of my effort to fill the countless hours of every day was reading *Lao Presse*, the government's daily propaganda sheet. It was mimeographed on coarse legal paper—six to eight sheets of paper per edition folded in half, and the ink bled through to the opposite side, making it extremely hard to read. Also making it hard to read is that it was printed in Lao and French. It stretched my limited French to the limits, but I had a French-English dictionary and nothing better to do.

I began visiting the paper's office on the fountain circle[5] behind my apartment and searching through its archives. At first, the staff was shocked, although pleased, that someone wanted to read *Lao Presse*. They made me comfortable in a reading room with four library tables. To be accurate, they tried to make me comfortable, but the reading room had neither air conditioning nor fans; I had to exercise extreme caution not to sweat on the editions, as this tended to blur the ink further. In fact, I could only tolerate working there an hour or two at a time before I either fell asleep or

---

5 Nam Phou Circle, also Fountain Circle or, literally, Water Mountain Circle.

came dangerously close to passing out. But I persevered and made the trip to *Lao Presse* every day until I finally got a full-time job as a reporter not long before I left Laos. Starting with the June 2, 1952, edition, I worked through the dusty archives, filling 276 pages of red-and-white Habeeb-special composition notebooks with my translations of official pronouncements, declarations and laws, and lists of officials' names, positions, and titles. The latter helped me identify key figures over time, lending a rough structure to my study of Lao elites and family politics, the only politics that mattered in Laos. I didn't read every issue back to 1947. I don't think that would have been possible without causing brain damage. Rather, I focused on periods of important change: Mid-1952 when the French, then losing a war to keep their Indochina colonies, granted Viet Nam, Laos, and Cambodia "associated state" status within the French empire; 1954–1956, when an international conference in Geneva recognized the complete independence of the three nations and partitioned Viet Nam into two states, following the Korean model and launching the civil war there; 1960, when an obscure Lao captain staged a coup, overthrowing a right-wing government in favor of neutrality and deepening U.S. military involvement; and 1962, when a second Geneva conference established the neutrality of Laos, a fiction that neither communists nor noncommunists ever intended to abide by and which led to the current war, albeit one kept secret by all parties so as not to undo the '62 accord.

The more I studied, the more I discovered about Laos that strained the mind. Many journalists came to this "tiny landlocked jungle kingdom"—that's how they invariably described it—and after a day or two declared it not a nation but a "state of mind." Clichés for sure, but clichés often contain more than a grain of truth.

When I arrived, Laos had been independent from France for less than 20 years; power was dispersed regionally, ethnically, and along family lines. Political parties and governing institutions existed in name only, and the ordinary people—the majority unable to read in any language, much less French, the language of power—were irrelevant to governance and decision making.

Two half-brothers, Souvanna Phouma and Souphanouvong, illustrated perfectly the interplay of family, regional power, and politics.

Souvanna and Souphanouvong shared the same father, Bounkhong, a cousin of the old king and the viceroy of the Kingdom of Luang Prabang in French colonial days. Bounkhong had seven wives who produced at least 20 children.

Souvanna came from the second wife and was the fifth child overall. Souphanouvong was the youngest child of Bounkhong's fifth wife. Like the king (Samdach Brhat Chao Mavattaha Sri Vitha Lan Xang Hom Khao Phra Rajanachakra Lao Parama Sidha Khattiya Suriya Varman Brhat Maha Sri Savangsa Vadhana, or Savang Vatthana for short), they could trace their ancestry back to the first king of Luang Prabang in the seventh century.

Both were educated in France and returned to their native land to work in the French colonial government. Cut to 1970: Souvanna was the prime minister of the Royal Lao Government, a neutralist in name but dependent on the United States for his survival despite having been deposed by the American government in the 1950s. Meanwhile, Souphanouvong married a Vietnamese—significant for conspiracy theorists—and became the titular head of the Pathet Lao, the Communist Party of Laos.

For a time after the 1962 Geneva agreement, the brothers shared power in a coalition government along with a right-wing leader, but those days were long past. The civil war that raged was orchestrated by foreign powers: Neighbors like Viet Nam and Thailand, with their own territorial concerns, and a trio of Cold War ideological foes, the United States, the Soviet Union, and China.

Family dynamics affected the hill tribes as well. Touby Lyfoung, the self-proclaimed "king of the Meo," told me how a bridal kidnapping gone wrong had split his clan generations earlier, resulting in a Hatfield-and-McCoy depth of animosity that led part of the Ly clan to side with the French and later the Americans, while another side of the bridal dispute sided with the Vietnamese, first against the French and later against the Americans.

Nothing was simple in Laos. Nothing was as it appeared. Laos was more a state of mind than a real nation.

Chapter 11
Peaceniks and Paranoia
DECEMBER 1970

Now come on mothers throughout the land,
pack your boys off to Viet Nam;
Come on fathers don't hesitate,
send your sons off before it's too late;
Be the first one on your block
to have your boy come home in a box.

Country Joe and the Fish, "Viet Nam
Song," Woodstock 1969

No MATTER HOW far I ran or how hard I tried, I could not
escape the American student peaceniks who frightened the
Vietnamese authorities and got me booted out of the country.

Three members of the National Student Association delegation
that I had heard about in Saigon landed in Laos on December 9.

I tried hard to dislike them, to disagree with them, to resent
them, but I just couldn't. They were simply nice guys my age doing
something they believed in, and I almost immediately became
embroiled in a Lao version of the "pistol on the desk" game.

They were hardly the first peaceniks I ran into in Laos.

The day I moved from Bangkok to Vientiane to wait for my
visa in a cheaper country, I heard of a "mystery woman from

Saigon." Her name was Cynthia Fredericks; she was a representative of the Committee of Concerned Asian Scholars, a group trying to balance the anti-communist Cold War scholarship that dominated American universities. I had run into some CCAS people at Cornell, and they seemed pretty solid in their scholarship. They weren't pro-communist; they just didn't buy the "my country right or wrong" kind of patriotism espoused by some American academics.

I had read a lot about Viet Nam, and I had a pretty good feel for Uncle Ho (Chi Minh), the leader of North Viet Nam. Like most revolutionaries, he was ruthless with his opponents. I had no illusions. I just didn't see that the United States had a stake in this civil war, but the communism argument colored everything.

I don't recall who mentioned Cynthia to me. She was just a mystery girl who had been kicked out of Viet Nam like me. It took me a couple days to track her down, even though we were both staying at the Constellation. She had been a liaison between the Vietnamese students and the world before she got kicked out.

I wrote a brief note about our encounter in my journal:

> *Cynthia didn't have much to say. She had intended to go to Hanoi but a mistake was made and there was no visa. She then traveled to VN, Saigon. Talked with Mike Morrow and Don Luce and a lot of students. Now she is returning to States to organize in favor of students.... Apparently 200 students are living in the Saigon Student Center for fear of being arrested at home.*

> *Cynthia is very active/emotional leftist. Not much on thought. Reads a little Vietnamese but doesn't speak it. Was there 3 years ago, 1967, for 1 year as a student of some sort.*

I knew who Don Luce was, having met him and received his wise counsel in Saigon, but the name Mike Morrow was new to me.

I turned to my encyclopedia of all-things-Viet Nam, Ronk, who of course knew Morrow and his wife, Christine. Morrow and a few other folks had founded something called Dispatch News Service (DNS) in 1968 with the goal of providing in-depth reporting of the war in Viet Nam; it was, in effect, an alternative to the traditional wire services like AP, UPI (United Press International), Reuters, and Agence France-Presse.

Ronk contributed to DNS, although I don't know that he made any money on it; so did Don Luce. I knew or had at least met other contributors, not realizing their connections to DNS: Gary Porter I knew from Cornell, where he was a grad student while I took Vietnamese language. We had partied together with his wife, Pat, and their circle of friends. John Steinbeck IV had interviewed me (and Christian and Larry) over that awful hamburger lunch in Saigon weeks earlier. John Everingham I met later; he went native, wearing the black Meo pajama-style clothing, and traveled extensively throughout northern Laos while I sat in the Constellation. He knew the backcountry intimately because of his travels, but I never saw any of his reporting.

DNS had credibility by the time I encountered it because of Seymour Hersh's report on the "mass killing of between 347 and 504 unarmed" old men, women, and children in the village of My Lai on March 16, 1968. Hersh and DNS won the Pulitzer Prize, journalism's highest honor, for international reporting in 1969.

Despite the honor, or perhaps because of it, Official Americans shunned and suspected DNS reporters of harboring anti-American feelings. To be antiwar was to be anti-American or—worse—procommunist. It was an accusation that would taint anyone who questioned U.S. policy, strategy, or tactics in Viet Nam, Laos, or anywhere in the world. I was quickly falling in with the unofficial American side of things.

One thing Cynthia said, the part about the students being afraid to go home, gave me pause. If I succeeded in returning to

Viet Nam, what would I be getting into? I had to assume that some Van Hanh students were among the fearful ones. How would they view an American who just happened to show up to study there?

In truth, I was getting a little paranoid.

I was still smarting big time over my expulsion from Viet Nam. Getting mugged in Bangkok didn't help. The curiosity of Official Americans about what I was really doing contributed, despite the friendly visits from Ed Kelly, the former Antiochian. Throw in the really stupid attempt to find books in the Soviet reading room, and I had a bad case of paranoia going. I saw evidence of the conspiracy against me everywhere. Take the mail, for instance. It disappeared. People I wrote to didn't get some of my letters explaining in detail what was going on in Southeast Asia; I received letters referring to previous letters that never arrived. Was that a coincidence? Or incompetence? That's the problem with paranoia: You just don't know.

I was also nervous about a letter I had hidden in the lining of my suitcase. My friend from Ohio, Liz Turner, asked me to mail it when the time and place seemed right. So far, that had not occurred. The letter was from a woman Liz knew to her POW/MIA flier husband. How could I refuse the favor? The problem was that I did not think that the South Vietnamese would take kindly to a letter addressed to North Viet Nam, even if was addressed to a POW in a prison camp. When I arrived in Laos, I still had the letter, the heaviest piece of paper I had ever held, and I didn't know whether the Lao government would feel any better about it. I had heard the North Vietnamese Embassy refused to accept such letters.

Dan Grady didn't help with the mail paranoia. In one letter he wrote of helping someone travel to "points north." That meant Hanoi. So here he was helping some academic get to North Viet Nam, and he was being a touch careful, too. It was as if he thought someone was reading his (or my) mail.

It was already widely known—not just suspected—that J.

Edgar Hoover's FBI was creating files on all kinds of antiwar activists. (I discovered later they had a huge file on Antioch College.) The Constitution's First Amendment protections did not prevent the U.S. government from spying on people who opposed its foreign policy, and Democratic administrations did as much as Republicans.

I had not joined hundreds of thousands of Americans, mainly students, at huge antiwar marches in Washington. Instead, I had put on a sport coat, tried to comb my tangled shoulder-length curls into something civilized looking, and spoke to small groups of high school students about how the United States got involved in Southeast Asia. That was probably more subversive than marching anonymously in a crowd.

I naively assumed I had that right until one of the Official Americans at the embassy in Bangkok asked me about my antiwar activities in the States. That made me paranoid. How did he know? Did he simply assume it, or had he seen some FBI file with my name on it?

It seemed to me that I was constantly being dragged into things that I wanted no part of.

For instance, a week before the guys from the National Student Association (NSA) arrived at the Constellation, I walked into the bar and up popped someone I knew: Gary Porter, my grad student friend from Cornell. Gary was a legit scholar, but he was also an antiwar activist of the worst kind: He was trying to prove the Official Americans wrong. As often as not, he succeeded. (I have learned over the years that the only thing worse than being wrong is being right, especially in a prescient way.) Gary and his wife, Pat, were heading to Saigon to spend the year leading up to the Vietnamese presidential elections in late 1971.

Over the course of the next week, Gary roamed around the city interviewing people and acting like the academic he was. I shared many a meal with him, and he allowed me to copy his notes. Here was a book in the making, and I was getting a first look.

Gary did one thing that I envied and regretted at the same time: He sneaked up to the refugee camp at Ban Son and spent a day talking with the residents about American bombing in northern Laos. I wished I'd had the balls to do that. It was illegal for Westerners to leave the city without government approval. Gary was not the kind of person to let that stop him, but I was different. Having been kicked out of one country, I didn't want to get booted from another. I hated being associated with that kind of behavior but I valued the information he gathered. I felt I should be doing Gary's kind of reporting, but the thought of the potential consequences reinforced my paranoia.

Then along came the National Student Association guys, self-appointed representatives of antiwar students all across America. What attracted them to Vientiane were the two weekly flights to Hanoi, one flown by the Soviet Union's Aeroflot airline and the other a regular charter for the International Control Commission—a misnomer if there ever was one, given how little control it had over anything—the three-nation group allegedly monitoring the implementation of the 1962 Geneva Accords that had ended a previous civil war in Laos.

I ran into the guys at the Constellation. Where else? It always amazed me that people seemed to congregate at the Constellation, but so few stayed there—it made me wonder how Maurice could stay afloat. The guys were staying at the Settha Palace, a French colonial dump around the corner and across from the soccer stadium.

One stood out, for me at least: Jim Doherty, a 21-year-old philosophy major and president of the student government at Wheeling College in Wheeling, West Virginia. He knew a classmate of mine from Campion. That's one for the "small world" file.

My adventure with the NSA started when I ran into Jim on the street and walked with him to the Constellation to change some money. While there, a Lao police colonel walked in and asked to see our passports. I had been in a half-dozen countries since September, and I had never been asked for my passport except at immigration checkpoints. Official America, in fact, recommended keeping your passport locked up somewhere safe.

Neither of us had our passports. I explained what I was doing and showed him my Iowa driver's license. He advised me to carry my passport but apologized for the inconvenience. He was looking for Doug Hostetter, a member of the NSA delegation. As soon as he satisfied himself that we were not Doug, he left; Ronk, who had witnessed the encounter, told us to go clear out Doug's room.

We followed the cop out the door to the right and down to the corner, then passed him. He didn't know where Doug was but suspected we did; he followed us. We stopped in midblock, and I took Jim's picture; the cop passed us and ambled into the 555 cigarette factory across the street. We continued to the Settha Palace with the colonel watching us from a distance.

This was getting downright Cold War-ish. During my 68-hour stay in Saigon, I felt that eyes were on me, but nothing quite like this. You could be paranoid, I thought, and someone could still be following you. Like our colonel.

At the Settha Palace, Jim quickly moved Doug's stuff into his room. Shortly after the switch was made, the colonel arrived with backups and asked to see the passports for the three members of the NSA. Jim explained again that Lao Immigration had their documents. The colonel said he would wait, although how he expected the passports to get from Immigration to the Settha Palace was beyond us.

When Doug eventually arrived at Jim's room, we briefed him. The colonel asked to see Doug in his room, and Jim went along as a witness. (Paranoia can apparently be contagious.)

I returned to the Constellation and told Ronk what was going on. He rounded up Carl, and the power of the international press corps went down to the Settha Palace.

I lost track of the NSA guys for a while and ended up eating lo mein at the Chinese Noodle with Dennis Ross. Dennis was Australian, and I could never figure out what he was doing in Laos. After dinner, I strolled over to the Settha Palace and found the guys in their room making plans. Doug decided he wanted to see Ronk again, and I offered to guide him. We caught up with Ronk at La Paix, a cheap French restaurant across from the Chinese Noodle. Ronk had probably watched Dennis and me eat dinner. He was a guy who needed his privacy after attracting every street kid and beggar wherever he lived. The French did not tolerate beggars the way others did.

Doug told Ronk his story, and I entered it into my daily journal:

Colonel and at least one plainclothes man searched through everything in his luggage. They were always very polite and kind. Even funny. Told Doug. 'Watch how we do this—just like the Americans.'

They asked Doug if he had any more and he said, 'Yes,' and went to retrieve the other bag from the other [Jim's] room. They were looking for 'illegal items.'

Asked him to go to police station, but insisted if he didn't want to go, then he did not have to. At the office, they looked through his papers, then locked them up and went out to dinner. Halfway down the stairs Doug thought of taking the papers with him, but the colonel assured him that they were safe, he had the key, etc.

When they returned, Doug noticed the air conditioner was on and later that 2 pictures in his book were upside down. They obviously had copied the whole file. The colonel asked to copy 3 innocuous documents and that was it.

I suppose only in Laos would the Interior Ministry police invite a suspect to dinner. Laos: Not a country, just a state of mind.

Doug, Jim, and the two others had been invited to North Viet Nam as representatives of the National Student Association by the Union of North Vietnamese Students. They were to join ten other members of the NSA delegation who arrived in Hanoi one week earlier. How such a large group could escape the notice of the Vientiane press corps was beyond me, but I suspect they must have flown through Moscow rather than through Laos.

Our group of NSA guys had intended to visit South Viet Nam, but all except Doug were denied visas. Doug was no stranger to Viet Nam and its ways. He had worked for the Mennonite Central Committee in Tam Ky, Quang Tin Province, from 1966 to 1969, setting up schools for refugee children. He got back into Saigon because he identified himself as a sociologist on the visa application rather than as a "student."

While I liked the guys, I thought they were on a fool's errand. They told me they intended to sign a people's peace treaty to end the long, costly conflict "even if the governments can't agree." They did, but there was never any evidence that it hastened the end of the killing by even a day.

It did, however, make me think again about my plans for Viet Nam.

Chapter 12
Fish or Cut Bait
JANUARY 1971

The trip has not turned out as I had planned it.

Journal entry, Thanksgiving Day, November 26, 1970

B Y THE TIME the entire National Student Association delegation passed through Wattay Airport on December 19, I had been trying to get into Viet Nam for three months.

My patience was wearing thin, and Saigon and its Official American allies may have been counting on that. Maybe I would get tired and go home if they stalled long enough.

I *was* getting tired, but I had no intention of going home. The truth was, I was getting used to life in Vientiane, and it appealed to me. In fact, I was starting to take control of my life.

I recalled Shakespeare's Falstaff from my days at Campion. In *Henry IV, Part I*, Henry said, "If every day were holiday, then holiday would be work" or words to that effect. My everyday life had been a holiday after being expelled from Viet Nam. My only goal was to do whatever Dan and Paula needed me to do to push forward on the visa. Having nothing specific to do most days, I fell into the habit of staying up until the wee hours of the morning and sleeping past noon and even 1:00 p.m. In Vientiane, I started to whittle away at my rising hour, trimming it from noon to 10:00

a.m., then to 9:00 and eventually 8:00 by mid-December, and this despite continuing to consume glass after glass of sa nom yin and sa nom hon, strong tea laced with Carnation evaporated milk. The milk made it smooth and easy going down, but did nothing to diminish the impact of the caffeine.

Besides, those late night conversations at the Chinese Noodle amounted to grad school seminars, with Ronk and Carl, Dennis Ross, and John Cornell presiding.

My new routine improved my diet considerably, which cut down on the diarrhea and cramps. The crotch rot remained, but I was learning the art of locomoting in the tropics: Never run when you can walk; never walk when you can stand; never stand when you can sit; never sit when you can lie; and go out of your way to walk in the shade rather than in the sun. I powdered myself liberally with Desitin foot powder, raising white clouds about my waist every morning and night, whether I had showered or not.

My favorite breakfast place was Boua Kham, a noodle kitchen just like Cuong Ky, Ronk's Chinese Noodle, which served an outstanding cheese sandwich that become my favorite breakfast food.

These sandwiches are made from a small loaf of bread, 9" long and about 2-1/2" in diameter in the center. 3 or 4, sometimes as many as 5 slices of cheese are placed end to end in the middle and thus your CS. No mustard. Bread is always fresh and the CS is made at that time – not pre-prepared. A small, very tasty salad of greens, onions and 4 thin slices of tomato are also served with it. Cost: 100 kip—U.S. $0.20.

When I ate lunch, I liked the pho at Biboun, a hole in the wall like every other restaurant, around the same corner from the Constellation as the Settha Palace. Dinner was the important meal, and although I often ate with someone, I also enjoyed solitary meals that did not require me to be sociable. The Chinese Noodle got most of my business, and many days I took dinner at 7:00, ordering beef lo mein more often than not, and returned around 9:30 or 10:00 for fried Chinese bread and tea with Ronk and whoever else might be there.

On special occasions, I splurged for spaghetti at the Pizzeria or bifteck et pommes frites avec salade at La Paix, meals that cost as much as 750 kip ($1.50).

For work, I wrote detailed notes from the nightly Chinese Noodle sessions as well as journal entries and long handwritten letters back to the States. I had my book-hunting and reading with extensive note-taking. Having discovered mysteries, I started devouring them, reading one every couple days.

The older guys were generous in sharing their fiction with me. Someone got hold of *The Hobbit* and *The Lord of the Rings* trilogy, and I polished the entire set off in a day and a half, despite proclaiming it not all that good.

We expatriates reconnected with the world every Wednesday in late afternoon. That's when the truck arrived from Bangkok carrying not just the daily *Bangkok Post* and *Bangkok World* but *Time*, *Newsweek*, and the Monday edition of the *International Herald Tribune*, which included the "Week in Review" section from the Sunday *New York Times*.

It was funny to watch us troop out of the Constellation, then skitter among the cars as we crossed Samsenthai to Haja and Habeeb, where each of us bought a copy of everything that had arrived. Back at the Constellation, we gathered like a group of Quakers in silent meditation. No one spoke. No one suggested a game of dice. We all slouched into the low red-leather chairs and began reading the news weeklies, starting at page one and going through the entire issue. After several hours, hunger, a sore back, or something that we read would drive one of us out the door. The bar would empty, and we would take our precious readings off to dinner, to the wooden bench on the Mekong or back to our apartments, our heads filled with thoughts of what was going on in the real world.

Wednesday was a day like no other, and the failure of the Bangkok truck to arrive made us all a bit testy.

Any other late afternoon, however—including weekends—would find the bar filled with the rattle of 10 dice in a much-used red-leather cup followed by a thump and the sound of ivory tumbling across wood. The game, which I thought of as poker dice, was called Cameroons or, in our slang, 'Roons. It was a combination of poker, dice, and Yahtzee, and it was played for serious stakes.

Maurice played for $100 bills with the occasional Air America pilot wearing gold on his wrists and armed with more money than sense. Maurice's games were grim business, although he always paid his losses with a smile and the promise of a better day. I wondered if he threw games to keep the big spenders coming back.

Our group didn't have any money—even the older guys—so we played for bragging rights, or the right to humiliate the loser. Once I learned, I was a frequent victim, humiliated for being a kid, for not knowing anything, for not trying to become a writer, for wanting to go to Viet Nam, and for not making up my mind about Viet Nam. Never for losing, however. That seemed to be a given.

In truth, I was having a hard time deciding about moving on to Viet Nam.

Grady telegraphed me in Bangkok on October 7, a few days before my first trip to Laos, with what appeared to be good news:

State department says you are readmitted.
See Vietnamese Embassy for new visa.
Congratulations.

But when I showed up at the Vietnamese Embassy, of course they had not gotten the news. Come back in a month, they said.

Chasing butterflies without a net: It was my own Catch-22 mantra.

Later in October, I vented my frustrations in a long letter to Mom and Dad:

Here I am writing from Bangkok—again and still! I am beginning to wonder whether I will get to Viet Nam. And I am beginning to wonder whether I <u>want</u> (emphasis in original) to get there. I spoke to the Vietnamese consul here on Thursday. He said my visa was being considered by the Minister of Foreign Affairs personally. But it may still take 3 weeks or so. That would be the 2nd week of November before I got in. I am getting angry and disgusted.

At the end of the first week of November, I summarized the situation in a letter to my older sister, Bonnie:

...My Thai visa expires the 12th so I am leaving Thailand and going to Vientiane, Laos, on Tuesday, the 10th. I do not plan to return to Bangkok. I also do not think that I will be given a Vietnamese visa. I am not unhappy about this thought though. I can work in Laos as well. I may begin writing for the Bangkok World *up there...."*

On moving to Vientiane, my first stop was at the Vietnamese Embassy. Same story as in Bangkok, only worse. They could not issue a visa, because they had not been told to, and anyway, the Bangkok embassy was going to do that.

See the pretty butterfly.

In mid-November, I wrote Grady recommending that I stay in Laos until January 12 so I could pursue my studies here. A week later, the Vietnamese Embassy suggested I check back in a month, just before Christmas.

Thanksgiving came, and I treated myself to a solo dinner at the

Pizzeria, then went back to my apartment to write up an assessment of the trip so far:

I am satisfied, to an extent.... The trip has not turned out as I had planned it, but it has more than enough merit on its own. The future is uncertain; I have enough money to carry me through May if nothing exceptional happens. What I do with my time will be a heavy factor in a further evaluation. I have been lonely and confused. Mail has been very scarce. I have been a little paranoid.

A week later, during one of my continuing visits to their embassy, I discovered the Vietnamese had a visa for me—and had had it for a while. In fact, they had received a telegram two days after I brought in my application. The bureaucrat I spoke with, the same one who predicted it would take a month, said he could not inform me because he did not have an address for me—that despite it being on every page of the application. All I needed to do was to present a valid airline ticket to Saigon and pay the 750-kip tax, and the visa would be mine. I rejoiced in a letter to Grady, who had still not responded to my earlier piece, and informed him I expected to depart for Saigon on January 12.

Then bad news arrived. First, the National Student Association guys arrived with word of Saigon's hostile feelings toward students, their own as well as American.

In a letter to my friend, Liz, I spelled out the more serious developments:

Mike Morrow of Dispatch News Service, who was recently expelled from Viet Nam, and Jerry Doolittle, a freelance writer just back from Saigon, are both here in Vientiane pour[ing] forth all sorts of bad news about the situation there. I am a little anxious (that means scared shitless) about conditions there, but I am also getting impatient once again to get there and see for myself. I am trying to get accredited as a newsman so I don't have to rely completely on my student status. Being a student means nothing in Asia, and in the U.S., I suspect, also.

Mike and Doolittle brought words of anti-American violence by the South Vietnamese in Saigon. Our allies were turning against Official America, and all Americans were lumped together. This seemed a poor time to relocate.

In mid-December, the *Bangkok Post* carried an article saying that U.S. military commanders in Viet Nam had ordered the G.I. presence in Saigon reduced to the minimum because of fire bombings by students. Another story told of Vietnamese students attacking U.S. jeep patrols over the killing of a student by an American soldier.

During one Constellation bull session, Doolittle told of witnessing a gang of Vietnamese toughs beating up four G.I.s in front of the National Assembly building. He also reported hearing that students had pulled two M.P.s (military police) from their jeep, beaten the Americans, and burned their vehicle, just for driving through the University of Saigon campus.

"It [Saigon] just gave me an impression of total anarchy," Doolittle told me. I asked if he'd advise going to Viet Nam to study. A cynical smile curling the corners of his mouth telegraphed his answer. "No.... No, I don't think I would advise that."

The next day I observed in my journal: *"I feel like a fool to continue planning my excursion to V-N. But it is just something I must see myself."*

To back up my words, I turned down a full-time teaching position at the Lao-American Association, which would have paid me a comfortable wage, and invested $85 in a round-trip ticket to Saigon. Meanwhile, Grady remained silent; it was almost as if he had other things to do than hold my hand.

I was gathering a lot of omens; I just didn't know whether they pointed me toward going or staying.

I dropped my watch and broke it, which made me heartsick. My mother had given it to my father as an engagement gift before he left to fight in World War II. He had given it to me before I left for Antioch.

Then my camera stopped working. The shutter opened but would not close. I had shot more than 18 rolls of black-and-white film documenting life as I saw it. Now I would have to rely on word pictures, and that would not be pretty.

The day after Christmas—like Thanksgiving, another holiday spent solo—I made a decision:

> *Time is so short and I like what I am doing here. I would only go to Viet Nam because Dan and Paula have worked so damned hard trying to get me there. I shall write Dan tomorrow and present my feelings to him. Maybe something will come of it that way.... I really don't care to go to VN anymore.*

Chapter 13
Foreign Correspondence 101
January 1971

*The American people would not understand; if they saw what
we are doing here, they would not like it.*

U.S. diplomat quoted by CBS News, July 23, 1970

I STARTED THE NEW year in a brothel with Carl and Ronk watching
a naked young woman smoke 13 Virginia Slims—all at once and
in a way I had never in my innocent life thought possible.

The dens of iniquity in Vientiane, I heard, specialized. The
White Rose where I watched the smoker was next door to the
Pizzeria, where the young women focused on what we will call
acrobatics. The place had rooms—or curtained alcoves—but much
of what took place occurred gladiator style, as it were, with all the
world as eyewitnesses. Passing it in broad daylight before, I had
noticed the wooden wagon wheel towering over a row of sad flowers
in front, but I had never imagined what took place behind its front
door after dark. Now I knew.

Most of the entertainment places in Vientiane were like that:
Discreet.

Madame Lulu's looked like a ramshackle French colonial building, its sign out front—Rendezvous des Amis—offering no hint of
its specialty: Oral sex. A rather high-ranking American Embassy

official was fond of describing it as "a turkey farm—they're all gob-blers." Word had it that each girl studied under Madame herself; Madame spoke French fluently, and I did not, at least not to the extent of questioning her training methods.

The Purple Porpoise, on the other hand, was legendary for its clientele, not its offerings. It was the hangout of choice for Air America pilots and CIA operatives overnighting in Vientiane rather than in Thailand. Monty Banks, a boozy Brit, owned the place. To this day I can't believe that was his real name—it's just way too close to mountebank, the hoaxer or trickster, but I never met the man and so couldn't ask. Local reporters were not welcome at the Porpoise. Some outside newsmen stumbled into the bar looking for a beer and lived to tell the tale. Only Tammy Arbuckle, who quali-fied as a non-American and a big supporter of the war, probably had special privileges. Tammy was close-mouthed about his sources.

Just down the street from The Porpoise, the Lane Xang Hotel was the most expensive hotel in town. Sitting next door to the royal palace on the Mekong River, it had a bar, but it was just a bar. It catered to people who thought they were important, including a lot of middle-class Vietnamese kids and the local French. From time to time, Carl and I would spend hours there playing chess over a single Pepsi.

Our bar of choice, of course, was the Constellation. People with interesting stories congregated at Maurice's; I felt most comfortable there, but I can't recall ever ordering a beer or booze. I subsisted on creamy iced tea; only Doolittle and out-of-towners ordered the Heineken. (Maurice had the Heineken concession; it was the only beer he served.)

My New Year's introduction to Vientiane's more adventurous nightlife was timely. I was getting accepted by the regular press guys as a serious student of Laos and the war, and having actually read every book I borrowed I could, and did, provide documented facts, relevant citations, and historical perspective as my contribution to the conversation. As I was about to learn, however, journalists had needs for things other than what was covered in books and dusty old documents. While not an expert, I could at least give accurate directions.

Ronk, Carl, and Doolittle were my first mentors, sharing books, background notes, and plenty of criticism of my laid-back lifestyle. They thought, and on more than one occasion said, that I should be more like them. I took that to mean long-term impoverished; they meant enterprising freelance writers. But it amounted to the same thing. Without a steady market for your writing, you were nothing but a poor student waiting for a visa that was never likely to arrive.

Through attrition, the guys divided the writing market into stringerships. Stringers are freelance writers loosely associated with a news organization. This arrangement worked to the benefit of both freelancers and news organizations. The stringer received a small allowance in return for providing tips, story ideas, and occasionally full-blown stories to a particular newspaper, magazine, or wire service. The news organizations got a source of steady news bits without the expense of employing a full-time correspondent. This was true all over the world and had been for decades, perhaps even centuries. Evelyn Waugh wrote a hilarious account of stringers and war correspondence in his fictional narrative, *Scoop*. It may have been a novel, but I used it as a textbook when my turn at a stringership came.

Until then, Ronk had the *Washington Post* and *Newsweek* concessions. Carl had AP and *Time* magazine. They could manage two stringerships apiece because they worked for noncompeting outlets.

For instance, the *Post* did not compete directly with *Newsweek*, and vice versa, because of their publishing schedules. The *Post* was a daily and required immediate exclusive material, while *Newsweek* was a weekly and needed more perspective or thematic news. A smart stringer could package the same news to meet both needs. That was the trick: Multiply your opportunities to sell the same news to different outlets. It didn't always work out that way, and I was soon to witness a blowup between Carl and a *Time* correspondent over exclusivity.

Correspondents were the royalty of the foreign news beat, with full-time salaries and travel allowances, and TV correspondents ranked higher than the full-timers for the weekly news magazines and the daily newspapers. Wire service correspondents, who often filed several stories, or several updates of the same story, every day, ranked below the others, but still possessed a status, i.e., a salary, greater than that of any stringer. Still, being a stringer at the right time and in the right place could and did lead to bigger things for many. I was about to make connections, just hanging around the Constellation offering a fact here and a discrete correction there, that would pay off in the long term.

Doolittle was a bit different. He had been the press attaché at the U.S. Embassy in Vientiane but resigned from the Foreign Service when his term was up. He became a true freelance writer, selling stories wherever he could. His favorite market was the girlie magazines with names like *Penthouse* and *Oui*. I think Doolittle was also writing the initial draft of *The Bombing Officer*, his book about the war based on his inside knowledge, which was not published until 1982.

Doolittle was the only writer I ever met who could mix sex and politics successfully. He spun his most fabulous tale of sex in Southeast Asia for *Penthouse*, whose photographs specialized in showing more nude skin than *Playboy*. He theorized that the war in Viet Nam was about women: Middle-aged Official American men burdened with uncomely middle-aged wives back home could get beautiful young Asian women to live with them very cheaply. They had no incentive to end the war—quite the opposite. If the war ended, they lost their lovelies and had to return home to the suburbs. It made as much sense as any rationale the Official Americans offered.

Tammy Arbuckle, a.k.a. Buckle, first appeared in my journal a few months after the others. I assume that was because he had been traveling. He wrote for the *Washington Star,* a full-time gig with a full-time salary and a small expense allowance, which enabled him to get to Viet Nam from time to time. Buckle brought to the job a strong dislike for the North Vietnamese and a lovely family—his wife, Soupy, and a preteen daughter, Linda—that invited strangers into their home as long-lost friends. Buckle also squired me on my first deadly combat experience.

I met Irwin Block about this time as well. Irwin, a Canadian, owned the *Bangkok Post* franchise, an important job because the *Post* served as the English-language daily of record for Laos. What Irwin wrote one day appeared on the streets of Vientiane the next. It also informed the Thai leadership, which had a hidden hand in the war in Laos. Irwin's stories could not be ignored.

Perhaps the most informed member of the stringers was Pon Chantharaj, the editor of *Xat La*o (Lao Nation), the largest Lao-language paper in the country. Pon spoke English well and wrote for UPI, Carl's direct competition. This competition was never personal; Carl introduced me to Pon, and when I replaced Carl, Pon never failed to let me know in advance when he had a big story coming. I could not do anything about it, but at least I was not caught flat-footed.

I never figured out all of Pon's political connections, but they must have been deep, which probably caused him no end of complications. I assumed he knew stuff he could not report for fear of offending his patrons and their friends. And while the rest of us could always leave Laos and go home if we got into trouble, Pon was already home.

Max Coiffait was another full-timer, but we didn't see much of him and never saw his stories. He wrote for Agence France Presse, and because his material was published in French, it did not appear locally. He undoubtedly had a direct line to all of the French advisors in Laos; they may have known what the Lao were doing, but they may not have known much more than we did about what the Official Americans were doing.

Ton That Ky, a South Vietnamese expat who dressed in TV correspondent khakis, rounded out the local press corps. He strung for Reuters, the British wire service. Ky kept to himself, appearing only rarely at the press gang bangs in the American press secretary's office. It was whispered that he was an agent for the South Vietnamese Embassy. True? It didn't matter. Any South Vietnamese reporter would have been tagged as a spy for Saigon. Had I known that earlier, I would have tried to enlist his help in getting into Viet Nam.

The writers I came to know best were, not surprisingly, the English-speaking natives who hung out at the Constellation. They taught me the two most important things about journalism: First, anyone could be a writer; all it takes is the ability to read and write English. Second, you have to make money: no money... well, no survival.

Chapter 14
The Great Press Offensive of 1971
JANUARY–FEBRUARY 1971

We're breaking the Geneva Agreements, and we don't want to advertise it.

Anonymous American Official, quoted by Carl Strock

I DETECTED SOMETHING UNUSUAL going on a few days after New Year's. I stopped in at the Constellation and found Carl and Buckle talking about a press war with the American Embassy.

I had been in Laos long enough to understand that the embassy called the shots. It controlled the bombing in both the north and south. Doolittle had told me about the bombing officer who ostensibly reviewed hundreds of bombing sorties a day to ensure they did not cause civilian casualties. USAID—the U.S. Agency for International Development, ostensibly a nation-building agency of the government, but in Laos, it was the logistics arm of the CIA—fed, clothed, housed, and moved as necessary the tens of thousands of refugees caused by the bombing and fighting. The CIA, reporting to then American Ambassador G. McMurtrie Godley, controlled Vang Pao and his Meo army in the northeastern part of the country. The United States paid the monthly salaries of the Royal Lao Army and clothed and equipped the soldiers not under VP control.

The U.S. Embassy also decided what information would

be released to the press. It even controlled where the press could travel, limiting excursions to a few cities, including the royal capital at Luang Prabang, a few refugee centers, and its prized economic development project, the Nam Ngum Dam. Americans were fighting and dying in Laos, and the embassy was handing out to anyone willing to look at them photos of a small dam about 37 miles north of Vientiane, far from the fighting.

What galled Carl and Tammy, Ronk and Irwin, was that in Viet Nam, the U.S. military not only provided priority transportation to reporters, they also fed and housed them when they visited military bases outside Saigon. All the Vientiane reporters wanted was permission to leave the city.

Two weeks after I witnessed the discontent, the *Bangkok Post* ran an AP story under the headline: "Press seeks end to Laos war secrecy," explaining that members of the foreign press in Vientiane had sent a letter to Prime Minister Souvanna Phouma asking permission to travel outside the city. Carl, of course, was the AP stringer, so it was obvious where the story originated. It came to nothing, but Carl gave it another shot, sending a piece to the *Far East Economic Review*, an English-language weekly news and business magazine headquartered in Hong Kong and read from India to Japan. In it, he quoted a high-ranking American official as saying, "We're breaking the Geneva agreements, and we don't want to advertise it." I was about to witness the absurd limits of that secrecy.

I was sitting in the Constellation with Ronk when Doolittle walked in and pulled Ronk into a private discussion, a highly unusual occurrence. I could have asked Ronk and Doolittle what was up, but I learned more by just keeping quiet, biding my time, and hearing the details in good time. After all, I had only known these guys for three months, and they already shared their confidences. I didn't need to know everything, but I was sure curious. In my journal that night, I wrote, "*Something rather large is up.*"

A little later Max Coiffait told us that the Pathet Lao's chief negotiator, Souk Vongsak, planned to leave Vientiane on January 22, not having made any progress in the peace talks that started 10 months earlier. The day of Souk's departure, I rode behind Carl on his motorbike to Wattay Airport to see off the Pathet Lao negotiator. Without press credentials, I was barred from the departure lounge to interview him. Had I been more enterprising, or sneaky, I would have listened in at the open windows, but I assumed his departure was no big deal; Souvanna had talked peace off and on for years with various Pathet Lao representatives, including his half-brother, trying to get them to return to the government. The Pathet Lao always insisted that the Americans stop bombing and leave the country first. In 1971, the country was no closer to peace than it had been before the 1962 Geneva agreement mandated that all foreign forces, i.e., U.S. and North Vietnamese forces, leave the country.

A week and a day after Souk left, Carl dropped the bomb I had been expecting. It was bigger than anything the Official Americans had loosed: The South Vietnamese had invaded southern Laos. All of a sudden, Souk's departure took on a different light. Tammy and Irwin confirmed the story later in the day.

Smart observers in Southeast Asia had long assumed that the U.S. military, as well as its South Vietnamese and Lao allies, ran small raids into North Viet Nam to gather intelligence, plant listening devices, and capture prisoners. The North Vietnamese used southern Laos as a key route to funnel troops, supplies, and equipment into South Viet Nam and had done so since the partition of the country back in the mid-1950s. It was just tit for tat.

What Carl was reporting was on a vastly different scale, however. This invasion apparently involved tens of thousands of South Vietnamese troops. It was an invasion worthy of the name. The goal was to disrupt, if not actually stop, the flow of men and materiel along the Ho Chi Minh Trail into South Viet Nam.

The next day, a Sunday (January 31), the *Bangkok Post* carried an AP story out of Saigon. Whether Carl got his information from AP's Saigon Bureau or whether Carl gave Saigon enough information to run a story from there, thus protecting Carl and his source, I never knew.

"It is only speculation," I wrote of the invasion news, *"but it will undoubtedly prove to be the trigger of bigger things in Indochina."*

That evening Ronk and I were discussing the story over a game of Cameroons when Kevin Buckley walked into the Constellation with his wife, Pasqual. Buckley was the Saigon bureau chief for *Newsweek* and, in that role, Ronk's immediate boss. He had been on vacation in Bangkok when *Newsweek* headquarters ordered him to Vientiane. Something big was up in Laos, or at least the Saigon press corps thought so.

Buckley was the first correspondent to fly into Vientiane to cover the Laos invasion. The Great Press Offensive of 1971 had begun.

The fallout was immediate, and not at all what I expected.

Ronk, Buckle, and Kevin Buckley mulled the odds of Souvanna Phouma surviving as prime minister if either Long Cheng or the Bolovens Plateau fell to the North Vietnamese. Long Cheng was Vang Pao's headquarters, the center of CIA operations in northern Laos, and only 80 miles from Vientiane. I had no idea what it had to do with the ARVN—Army of the Republic of Viet Nam—campaign against the Ho Chi Minh Trail. Losing the Bolovens made more sense; it was a 3,000-foot plateau that dominated southern Laos between the Trail and the Mekong.

Later that evening Carl stirred the pot of intrigue. He joined Ronk and me at the Chinese Noodle immediately after meeting with Major General Etam Singvongsa, the chief of intelligence for the Royal Lao Army. Etam had dropped a few bombs of his own. He told Carl that Laos had a secret military alliance with South Viet Nam and Thailand. This blew up the fiction of Lao neutrality and demolished any moral high ground Laos had over the North

Vietnamese. Lao generals had been meeting with their counterparts in ARVN and the Royal Thai Army for some time in South Viet Nam, and Lao generals in the south had agreed to allow ARVN to invade the country whenever the South Vietnamese felt the need.

But Etam's news did not stop there.

He told Carl that right-wing Lao generals were planning a coup to oust Souvanna as prime minister and bring back General Phoumi Nosavan. The United States had backed Phoumi after an earlier coup dumped Souvanna in the late 1950s. After the 1962 Geneva agreements returned Souvanna to power, Phoumi exiled himself in Thailand where a distant cousin, General Sarit, ruled a military government backed by the United States. Ah, Laos, more a state of mind than a real country.

General Etam said the timing of the next coup would depend on military conditions in Laos. If Long Cheng or the Bolovens fell, Souvanna would go.

Even Burmese strongman U Nu and the Kuomintang Chinese—remnants of the anti-communist Chinese army still operating along the Chinese border in Burma, Thailand, and Laos—knew about the plot and the military alliance.

Everyone seemed to know except Souvanna.

The next day—February 1—Irwin's version of the plot story made the front page of the *Bangkok Post*. (Irwin's *Post* connection obviously trumped Carl's scoop, which may have run elsewhere.) Irwin added only a few details. The generals, he reported, had concluded their invasion agreement two years earlier in South Viet Nam but not in Saigon. For reasons I never understood, that detail was important. Given that the northern part of South Viet Nam abuts southern Laos, it seemed likely to me that the generals from those areas would be involved. The understanding, which Irwin described as "verbal," allowed incursions up to 50 kilometers— about 30 miles—inside Laos. Six Lao generals participated in the agreement, and Souvanna had not been aware of it until recently.

With a story this big, the guys were scrambling, and I was spending more time alone at the Constellation. I watched it unfold on the front pages of the newspapers delivered to Haja and Habeeb, where the young clerks were fascinated by my obsession. The news meant nothing to them.

The same day Irwin's story on the coup appeared and two days after Carl dropped his bombshell, the *International Herald Tribune* wrote: "Heavy B-52 raids may herald Laos drive by Saigon." That seemed oddly vague, given what Carl and Irwin had already reported.

Veteran *New York Times* correspondent Tillman "Till" Durdin arrived in Vientiane, joining Buckley and others. On February 2, his story appeared in the *Herald Tribune* with Souvanna's point of view: "Laos repeats opposition to any incursion." (This word, "incursion," means invasion. It gained popularity in the United States after President Richard Nixon ordered the invasion of Cambodia in the spring of 1970. Someone in Washington must have calculated that an incursion was somehow more legitimate than an invasion. Until then, I'm not sure anyone had ever seen the word outside of a crossword puzzle.)

Meanwhile, *Lao Presse*, the Royal Lao Government's official news organ, reported that the military situation in the country was relatively calm. In fact, that was correct, but *Lao Presse* had such a poor reputation for accuracy in my circle that we didn't believe it. Two days later, I recorded the opposite in my journal:

> *Don then told me that there was a general PL-NVN offensive going on in the north. Muong Soui had fallen or was falling. Long Cheng is surrounded.*

It's all relative, I guess.

Also on February 3, the *International Herald Tribune* reported "Washington is silent on Laos as reports of invasion grow; no

American combat troops operating there, [Secretary of Defense Melvin] Laird says." Closer to home, the *Bangkok Post* carried the headline, "N. Vietnamese incursion reported."

This was becoming absurd. The gathering horde of reporters in Vientiane was not allowed to venture south to confirm or refute reports of the ARVN invasion. It was like the old Bud Abbott and Lou Costello "Who's on first?" routine,

Irwin contributed to the confusion with a bylined piece head-lined "N-VN paratroops 'in south Laos.'" He took tons of guff for that, given that North Viet Nam had no air force to speak of and no paratroopers that anyone had seen or heard of. He agreed it was probably not true; he was just reporting what he had been told.

His obviously bogus story recalled to mind a conversation between Carl and Doolittle over journalistic ethics. Carl was strug-gling with whether to report something that Souvanna had said but that Carl felt certain was wrong. From my notebook:

> *Jerry said that he should file what SP said, even if untrue, but SP [Prime Minister Souvanna Phouma] saying it is the news. Jerry's 3 points—Moral Principles of Writing Copy as I prefer to call them—are (1) Do what you are paid to do; (2) add enough disclaimers to satisfy your own sense of integrity; and (3) let the rewriter back at your headquar-ters be responsible for getting rid of the disclaimers, etc.*

That put Irwin's situation into perspective. He and Carl had both reported the coup, but Irwin's story appeared in the *Bangkok Post* where everyone in Laos would see it. Anyone reading between the lines would conclude that Souvanna was either incredibly out of touch or duplicitous in allowing his generals to make a verbal agreement on his behalf while providing the tiniest of fig leaves to hide behind—Souvanna doesn't know about this even though his chief of intelligence is the source? The prime minister could not have been happy.

For Irwin, the best thing to do was to write a truly not believable story painting the North Vietnamese as the bad guys. I was finding this whole "news" business more complicated than reporting the "truth."

Meanwhile, foreign reporters poured into Vientiane. On February 5, U.S. Press Attaché Andy Guzowski told me that 25 media people had already arrived, and more were coming, including full-time correspondents for the major U.S. news wire services, AP and UPI. Others included ABC, CBS, the Canadian Broadcasting Corp., and Danish radio. None spoke Lao; few spoke French, the language of the Lao elite. Few had ever reported from Laos before. It was a gathering of the ignorant into the hands of the secretive.

As a result, when Souvanna held a press conference—actually, it was supposed to be a *Time* magazine exclusive interview, but other reporters just showed up at the prime minister's office—few in attendance could follow his remarks. Doolittle, who managed to participate, later briefed Tammy and me. I wrote it up in my journal that night:

> There is a general PL-NVN offensive throughout Laos," [Souvanna said]. "[The royal capital at] Luang Prabang is surrounded, with large troop movements north and northeast of LP. NVN within 12 km of LP—artillery range.
>
> There is a big buildup in Military Region III (immediately south of Vientiane Province). Muong Phalong, the RLG advance outpost on Rte 9 (which links North Viet Nam and Thailand) fell. Activity around Long Cheng-Sam Thong.
>
> No comment on RLG-Thai secret alliance. Didn't know anything about ARVN invasion. Said, however, that if there is an invasion, the US will (not would) tell him.

Those coup rumors are false. Probably due to the increase in security around Vientiane and Wattay Airport against PL attack.

Souvanna refused to address the question the reporters cared about—Is ARVN invading your country?—and there was no way to confirm anything else he said because reporters were not allowed to leave the capital.

Well, there was one thing we could test: His report of increased security around Vientiane. I had seen no truckloads of troops roaring through town; I saw no tanks at intersections or barriers around the Ministry of Defense, which was only a block from my apartment.

Ronk gave me an assignment: Take a taxi out to the airport and shoot photos of the extra security. Since my camera lay dead in my apartment, he fixed me up with an old camera body of his and a spare 100 mm lens of Carl's. My payment would be the indefinite loan of the camera, which allowed me to keep taking photos of my own.

My trip to the airport for Ronk had a second purpose. He also wanted me to find an airline passenger at the airport willing to carry a roll of film to Bangkok. This was the normal routine for getting photos out of the country in a hurry. Some Good Samaritan would put the roll of film in a pocket—there were no searches or X-ray machines at the time—and fly to Bangkok. There, he would call the AP bureau, which would send someone to pick it up. The bureau would develop the film and transmit one or two usable photos via telex around the world.

At Wattay Airport, I found no evidence of additional security—or even any security. No tanks or troops with machine guns. No checkpoints or barbed wire. Like the rest of Vientiane, it was calm. In fact, it was so calm that I went over to the Pathet Lao headquarters and took photographs of the solitary bored guard on duty. Laos, more a state of mind than a country.

In the midst of all this, I carried on my life as usual. I was told I needed a haircut and submitted, noting in my journal that I had been clipped twice. The haircut cost 400 kip, or 80 cents U.S., which I considered "pretty steep," given how little I spent on food.

On February 1, the same day Carl told us about his chat with General Etam about the potential coup, I started teaching 19 lovely Lao girls to speak enough English to be able to take jobs as bus drivers for USAID. I recorded what I considered to be the important details of my initial experience with them.

The majority are very pretty. One or two are stunning. None are really offensive to look at. LAA [Lao-American Association] predicts that up to 75% will fail. I believe it. There are only two or three that are doing well. During the 4:30 break, they all left. So I did too. Will have to straighten that out tomorrow. Class is supposed to last two hours, not one.

Meanwhile, on Friday, February 5, the *Bangkok Post* cited various wire services in Saigon for its story: "Huge VN drive under way." More than 40,000 U.S. and South Vietnamese troops had opened an assault along an 800-mile front on and across the Laos-Cambodia borders, at least according to the *Post*.

The *International Herald Tribune* headlined its story out of Washington: "U.S. and Saigon troops in major drive near Laos; White House hails secrecy of buildup."

It boggled the mind. Carl had the story of the invasion a week earlier. Souk Vongsak, the Pathet Lao negotiator, had flown off unexpectedly for Hanoi on January 22. Ronk and Doolittle had their private little chat on January 14. What kind of secrecy was the Nixon White House talking about?

On February 6, the *Bangkok Post* seemed to backtrack on everything that had been reported so far with the headline, "ARVN launches Lao probes," as if the South Vietnamese attacks were just raids.

Because of the U.S. Embassy's policy of secrecy, the foreign reporters who had flooded Vientiane after the initial invasion stories found themselves sitting around in bars with nothing to report. Not only would the United States not provide transport, the Official Americans would not even consider granting permission to leave the city. All the action was in Saigon.

Rather quickly, the press invasion of Vientiane ended, and the correspondents fled the country, leaving the resident stringers to play dice and complain about U.S. Embassy secrecy and travel restrictions.

For the record, Lam Son 719, the ARVN invasion of the Ho Chi Minh Trail in southern Laos, started on Monday, February 8. Reporters in Saigon were briefed on the attack much earlier, but the news was embargoed, which meant that anyone who attended the briefing was sworn not to report on it in advance. In fact, even the existence of the embargo was embargoed.

The Great Press Offensive of 1971 was simply an attempt by the Saigon press corps to find a way around the embargo. I had a lot to learn about journalism.

Chapter 15

Foreign Correspondence 202

MARCH 1971

Everyone wants to sell papers, so everyone has to cover the same shit. And shit it often is.

Jerry Doolittle, February 4, 1971

A LL THE DRAMA of Lam Son 719 caused concern back in the States, and even before the operation actually lifted off, I found myself having to soothe nerves around the world. Part of this involved explaining how the news gathering business actually worked—lessons I'd learned just a few days earlier.

On Saturday, February 6, I wrote a long letter to my parents, hoping to reassure them of my safety by providing glimpses of the mundane life I led in the face of doom-and-gloom news reports:

You may have read about Laos in the papers during the last week. About all I can say is that nothing has happened here. There are a lot of rumors here and speculation about what could happen if this or that occurred. But nothing has actually happened yet. There are a lot of newsmen coming into Vientiane but there is no news here. I am preparing an article now entitled "Laos: The Great Press Offensive of 1971." I want to mail it out by Wednesday at

*the latest. I should be able to do a pretty good article on
this. I just need time to work it over.*

*After [teaching my bus driver class], I usually retire to the
Constellation bar for a few hours to talk to the "regulars"
there. There are many people there who know about Laos.
It certainly beats sitting in a classroom.*

I tried to convey the same sense of ordinariness to my friend Liz:

*My water and electricity still go off about twice a week.
I still sit around the Constellation Bar drinking tea.... I'm
teaching 19 young Lao girls to speak English and that's
about it.*

When Liz chastised me for not writing more frequently, I
blew a gasket: "GODDAMNIT there is NOTHING FUCKING
NOTHING AT ALL GOING ON IN LAOS!"

What I meant, of course, was that there was no combat activity anywhere near me. My life was as mundane as could be. In fact,
since winning Antioch's agreement in early January that I should
remain in Laos, I had even fewer worries. I failed to make clear how
far away southern Laos and the ARVN invasion were. It was that
Laos, not a country but a state of mind, thing all over again. Unable
to explain that, I unloaded on the news-gathering process:

*Regarding these news programs: They are full of bullshit.
You will notice that they all lack depth and perception. But
just because CBS is told that there is fighting going on,
don't think that it's new. It happens every year, just like
the rains. CBS, of course, doesn't mention that.*

*...Let me explain how journalism over here works. The Laos
"crisis" started about three weeks ago when the NY Times
had a story about an NVNese invasion of Laos. Actually*

Till Durdin was passing through Laos when we heard the rumors of the ARVN invasion. Till arranged an interview with Prime Minister Souvanna Phouma, who said that he feared an NVNese invasion.

Well, with that story and the ARVN rumors, about 35 correspondents began flowing into Vientiane. So far nothing had really happened, but the NY Times headlines said it did, while Till's story said it might happen just like every year. Once the reporters got here, they had to put out. Their editors were paying a lot of money to have them here and they expected big news. (What does an editor in NY or DC or London who has never been to Asia know about Laos? Nothing.)

Now the correspondents know that nothing is happening, but they don't want to lose their jobs so they too write about what will happen and the papers headline it. The public, which doesn't know anything, *believes all this because they do know how to read. (Note definition of such words as "rumors," "reported," "speculation," "alleged," "believed," and so on. Check your newspaper.)*

As for television—phew! They can't get to see the fighting—no one can. The U.S. does not allow it. But they must have pictures, or create verbal pictures—"fierce hand-to-hand fighting," "red onslaught,"" etc. But as long as the Lao are involved, there is little blood—about as much blood as screwing an 80-year-old virgin.

This is how you get your news. And most of it is just not true or else distorted beyond recognition. The whole thing has destroyed my image of newspapers and so on....

Doolittle was more succinct when I spoke with him about it

during those crazy days leading up to the actual invasion. Writing in my journal, I noted:

> Jerry also described the process of a press invasion. First, something newsworthy occurs. News reporters, i.e., the media, respond and react after the fact by sending in a reporter. In doing so they expend a sizable sum of money, thus obligating the reporter to file something. The momentum builds as more reporters are sent in just to keep up with the competition. Everyone wants to sell papers, so everyone has to cover the same shit. And shit it often is.

Then the shit started all over again with a story that Pon and his UPI boss, Kim Willenson, ripped from the front page of the government's propaganda organ, *Lao Presse*: Souvanna had declared a state of emergency. Declining to call it martial law, they reported that General Ouane Rathikoun, the commander in chief of the Royal Lao Army, was ordered to "take all necessary measures for general security throughout the territory of the kingdom until order is re-established."

This was one of those ethical dilemmas Carl and Doolittle had discussed. The government said it, so it must be news, but that didn't make it true. Picking up on one of my favorite criticisms of journalism, the lack of perspective, I explained in one of my scrapbooks of news clippings the power the military had always had in Laos:

> The military has controlled the country at least since 1962. All power is in the hands of the MR [military region] commanders.

> The civilian government is charged with the task of maintaining the facade of neutrality and of providing minimal

services to the community. They clean Vientiane's sewers, for instance. But USAID takes care of the refugees. CIA provides for Vang Pao and his troops. The U.S. Embassy pays for the army, which is controlled by the generals anyway.

The civilian government has damned little power to do anything. They do manage foreign service appointments, but they do not collect taxes. They take care of water, postal, and electrical affairs.

Consequently the state of emergency giving control of the country to the army is only a formality, not a new change.

Having just sent soothing letters back to the States, this pissed me off, and I vented in my journal:

Despite this played-up report by Pon and Kim Willenson, Vientiane is very calm. There are no soldiers in the streets and no extra security precautions have been taken. It appears this is more for the benefit of the Americans. The ARVN invasion does not warrant this.

Then, just like that, two things happened to unsettle my view of the world: The Royal Lao Government expelled Fred Branfman, a journalist and antiwar activist, and Tammy told me he was getting ready to bug out.

Branfman gave every Official American he met a bad case of heartburn. He had been in country since 1967 and spoke Lao fluently; he had come to Laos to work off his draft board commitment, and he went native immediately, renting space in a village outside Vientiane. And he had discovered the refugees. What he learned, and what he refused to stop talking about, was how the refugees were fleeing American bombing more than the ground fighting or the communists.

The Official Americans knew that.[6] They just hated having anyone talk about it, and Fred could talk of nothing else, and he was not shy.

What happened to Branfman was what full-time journalists as well as freelance writers feared most. Getting kicked out of a country meant losing income. And it put a bull's eye on your back when you relocated to a new country. Because it scared the regulars, it scared me. I had already been booted out of one country.

Branfman got word on February 13, at the end of the first week of the actual ARVN attack in southern Laos, that he was being kicked out "at the convenience of the government," bureaucratic talk for "We're doing it, and we don't have to tell you why."

I'd met Fred several times and sat around the Constellation's low cocktail tables listening to his stories about hill tribe refugees. Tracking down refugee camps all over the Vientiane Plain, southwest of Long Cheng, Sam Thong and the Plain of Jars, and the mountains of Sam Neua, where the Meo had fought the Pathet Lao and North Vietnamese going back to the 1950s, he made no secret that he was collecting refugee stories and even crude line drawings of life under the bombing and planned to write a book about them.[7]

I wrote a terse note about his expulsion in my journal:

It is assumed that the RLG [Royal Lao Government]

---

6 I saw a U.S. Information Service report about refugees from the Plain of Jars dated July 10, 1970. It cited the U.S. Embassy's political section as concluding that "bombing is clearly the most compelling reason for moving." The statistics it cited were staggering: Of 268 refugees from 96 villages, 97% witnessed the bombing; 91% said the bombing made life difficult; 87% built shelters to escape the bombing; 75% had their homes damaged or destroyed by the bombing, and 63% could only eke out a subsistence living because of bombing.

7 The book, *Voices from the Plain of Jars: Life under an Air War,* was published in 1972.

believes he was supplying information to the NVNese &
Chinese from [Lao General] Thongphanh's briefings.... He
was giving info to CBS, but they refused to do anything
about his expulsion.

Four days later we learned more of the story behind
Branfman's ouster:

Irwin joined us. He was upset about a few things. While
he was at the People's Chinese Embassy for a cocktail
party, he learned about the Fred Branfman story. To wit,
Fred took copious notes on every conversation and meet-
ing he had. He gave some of these to NVNese & while in
Bangkok at the Atlanta Hotel, he showed them to Dr. Hen,
the proprietor. Dr. Hen turned out to be a CIA informant.
The Atlanta Hotel is a bad spot—trouble only.

It's possible that Branfman shared what he knew with the North
Vietnamese and Chinese, but it's unlikely that he had information
they did not. Besides, Fred told the same stories to everyone he met,
regardless of how long he had known them or what he might have
known about them. You could not shut him up when he got going
on the bombing and the refugees.

More likely, Branfman got the boot for his unending investi-
gation of the civilian toll of American bombing in northern Laos.
(A magazine profile of Fred years later reported that the American
Embassy had engineered his forced departure from Laos.)

A week after Branfman's departure and Souvanna's declara-
tion of emergency, Tammy Arbuckle threw me for a loop with his
worries. I had been trying to calm troubled waters in my letters
home, and here comes Buckle in something of a panic, reporting that the young Thai waiters and cooks at the Chinese Noodle

had decamped back to Thailand to avoid the Lao draft. I recorded Tammy's thoughts:

> Tammy and I talked a little. He considers the situation to be fairly serious. He is sending much of his material to Australia and [his wife] Soupy is packed and ready to head for Thailand at the first sign of an evacuation. I was surprised at this. I did not feel that there was anywhere near that much trouble. Now I don't know what to think. Tammy may be cautious because he has Soupy and [his daughter] Linda to look after.

Buckle's fears clearly had more to do with what the North Vietnamese were doing 70 miles northeast of Vientiane around Long Cheng than what the South Vietnamese were doing hundreds of miles south of the capital on the Ho Chi Minh Trail.

It was just one more lesson in foreign correspondence: Proximity dictates news.

Chapter 16
Tony Poe and the Meo
NOVEMBER 1970–MARCH 1971

The most we could hope for was to tie down a significant part of NVA elements that would otherwise go south and fight our troops in South Viet Nam.

Dick Johnson, 1970s CIA Unit Chief
at Long Cheng, September 1993

WHILE THE SAIGON press corps worried about Lam Son 719, the regulars at the Constellation focused more on Long Cheng, the secret center of the American war in northern Laos.

The "secret war" in Laos was outed the year before I arrived. American officials had kept a lid on it for more than a decade. But by 1969, the war had gotten so big, involved so many people, and cost so much that it was impossible to keep under wraps any longer. That year, Senator Stuart Symington of Missouri conducted closed-door hearings about the CIA's war. The record of the hearings revealed for the first time the full extent of American bombing in Laos, despite heavy deletions of the transcript by the Nixon White House, the State Department, and the CIA. And Senator J. William Fulbright of Arkansas, one of the earliest critics of the war in Viet Nam whom LBJ loved to taunt as Senator Halfbright, revealed that the CIA was operating a full-blown war in Laos.

Secrecy, by its nature, creates myths and legends. Three reporters, including Vientiane regular Coiffait, became legends in February 1970 when they walked away from a USAID dog-and-pony show at the refugee logistics center at Sam Thong and followed a newly graded dirt road into Long Cheng. They punctured the veil of secrecy, but their stories provided at best a snapshot taken over two hours. They reported finding a paved, all-weather runway "complete with landing lights" in the center of a tiny valley. Aircraft of all types and sizes—some with Air America or Royal Lao Air Force markings but others with no markings at all—landed or took off at the rate of one a minute. Windowless buildings studded with air conditioners bristled with antennas. The trio estimated that 40,000 people lived in Long Cheng, making it the second-largest city in Laos.

The U.S. Embassy charged each reporter $450 for the flight from Long Cheng back to Vientiane but in the process made them heroes.

The secrecy created other legends: Meo General Vang Pao, leader of the CIA's secret army; Edgar "Pop" Buell, a former Indiana farmer who ran the refugee operations that allowed VP's tribesmen to leave their villages and fight for the CIA; and perhaps the most fabled of all, Tony Poe, the crazy-heroic, invincible CIA spy and guerrilla leader.[8]

Everybody in Laos seemed to know all this but me. I had a lot of catching up to do.

Early in my metamorphosis from lost college student to whatever I was becoming, I started writing "stories," as I labeled them in the margins of my journal. They were summaries—100, 200, even 300 words long—of what I had learned about a subject that

8 American secrecy was so pervasive and so effective that the real architect of the CIA intervention, a lanky balding, and bespeckled CIA operative named Bill Lair, was not identified until the early 2000s, more than 35 years after U.S. involvement in Laos ended.

caught my eye. For instance, I wrote about the visit of the National Student Association guys to Hanoi by copying the stilted news style I read in the newspapers. I composed my thoughts about the anti-American violence in South Viet Nam, which might have affected me, and about a visit to Vientiane by one of the hard-core supporters of the war, Rep. G. V. "Sonny" Montgomery of Mississippi, who affected me not at all. I also described the 11 kinds of license plates issued in Laos, a country that could not have contained 25,000 vehicles. Soon enough, I discovered how awful these stories were; writing at night produced a warm euphoria of accomplishment that turned to ice in the light of day. Besides, writing a story is not the same as selling it.

Just after settling in Laos in mid-November, when I was hearing the war stories for the first time, I decided to write my own, well-documented version of the Meo, Vang Pao, Pop Buell, and Tony Poe. I quickly concluded that this material was scarce and scattered. That explained why I heard a bit here, a piece there. This realization at least gave me a focus as I scrounged up books, reports, and news clippings and asked questions during bull sessions at the Constellation.

I don't know if I had expressed it, but I had surely internalized that the Meo comprised a primitive society. They spoke a language different from Thai-Lao and Vietnamese and had no written language, no books, no histories. They preferred to live on the mountaintops, away from other hill tribes and the lowland ethnic Lao. They practiced slash-and-burn farming, cutting down and burning all the trees in small plots and planting the same crops year after year until the nutrients in the soil were depleted; then they moved on to another plot and repeated the process. They did not use paper money; they bartered for goods or traded in silver. Meo women dressed in baggy black tops and loose trousers with colorful embroidered flaps of cloth front and back around their waists. Their rolled silver necklaces and bracelets served as both ornament and family piggy bank.

And everyone in Laos just *knew* they were fierce fighters.

But where did the Meo come from? How did they decide to fight for the Americans? Were all Meo on the U.S. side? Was Vang Pao some kind of Meo prince? Touby Lyfoung, a rotund, 60-ish Meo who lived around the corner from the Constellation, had served in the National Assembly and in several cabinet positions and described himself as "king of the Meo." For that matter, why wasn't Touby leading the Meo troops? How many fighters were there? Hundreds? Thousands? Tens of thousands? Were all these refugees we kept hearing about Meo, or did they belong to other hill tribes, like the Yao and the Lu, the Khmu and Mien?

My questions catalogued my ignorance.

So the second week after my resettlement in Vientiane, I knocked on the door of Doolittle's writing aerie on the second floor of the Lido Hotel. Where would he suggest I start? He handed me Hugh Toye's book, *Laos: Battleground or Buffer State?* I thought the title asked a really good question and dug in.

Three days later, Ed Kelly loaned me two reports by the U.S. Embassy's resident scholar, 'Win' McKiethen. He described them as "propaganda," but one, *Life under the P.L. in the Xieng Khouangville Area,* struck me as potentially useful. I knew Xieng Khouang was the province northeast of Vientiane where much of the Meo fighting took place; I figured I could find nuggets even amid the propaganda.

The same day, I started reading Arthur Dommen's new book, *Conflict in Laos: The Politics of Neutralization.* It had not been formally published, but someone had gotten hold of a copy and loaned it to me.

On November 23, Ronk gave me the mother lode of Meo mythology, a biography of Pop Buell called *Mister Pop,* written by Don Schanche, a globe-trotting magazine writer.

Devouring hardly describes what I did with these materials. I read Dommen in two days, Schanche in a day and a half. That included taking extensive notes. I wasn't a reporter, but I knew how to do college research.

A couple of days later, I noted in my journal that I got more books from Doolittle: *"Some Congressional hearings and a field study on Laos."* Two days on, I picked up from Ronk a book about the broader U.S. war in Indochina (*At War with Asia*) by the outspoken leftist scholar Noam Chomsky, and I started reading the 1955 Human Relations Area Files *Handbook on Laos,* which I got from Doolittle.

In early December, Carl dropped off his copy of Senator Ted Kennedy's 1969 hearings on refugees in Southeast Asia. By this time, Gary Porter, a true scholar working on his Ph.D. at Cornell University, arrived and invited me to some of his interviews and shared his notes on others.

So in three weeks, I laid the foundation of my understanding of Lao history, the role of the Meo, and the convoluted Cold War politics that shaped this pretty little country that I was coming to love. I learned right off the inexactitude of almost everything I read. Sources frequently disagreed on dates and numbers.

For instance, I read that the Meo came to Laos from southern China 200 years earlier; another source said it was 150 years ago, or 75 to 100 years ago. They settled in villages of 6 to 10 houses or 20 to 25—take your pick. Their slash-and-burn farming forced them to move every 5 to ten 10—or 1 to 3 years. They grew opium as a medium for trade, or because the Chinese forced them to, or the French forced them to.

On one thing, the sources agreed: The Meo were quarrelsome. One of their interclan quarrels caused a split with tragic consequences for all Meo. In a nutshell, Touby Lyfoung's father married the sister of Faydang; the woman died, and a Hatfield-McCoy kind of feud ensued. Whatever one side did, the other did the opposite.

Touby's line sided with the French colonists; Faydang fought the French at every opportunity. After World War II, Faydang sided with the Lao Issara, the anti-French independence movement that evolved into the communist Pathet Lao. Touby stayed with the French and later became a cabinet minister in the independent Royal Lao Government.

Along the way, the governor of the area north and east of the royal capital of Luang Prabang, Chao Saykham, met a promising young Meo named Vang Pao. Saykham made sure that VP got some education in the French school system, and the boy joined the French colonial army, fighting in the last losing battle of Dien Bien Phu near the Lao border with Viet Nam. Vang Pao rose through the ranks of the Royal Lao Army and in late 1959 came to the notice of American military advisors and the CIA.[9]

Vang Pao would soon meet Buell, and the two would be inextricably linked for the next decade and a half. I read that Buell's wife died an untimely death, and he signed up as a volunteer with the pacifist International Voluntary Service, the same group Ronk joined in Viet Nam. Buell found himself in northeast Laos in June 1960 advising farmers on how to increase crop yields.

Two months after Buell's arrival, however, an unknown Lao army captain named Kong Le led a coup in disgust over the left-right-neutralist infighting and foreign intervention (American as well as North Vietnamese) in the affairs of Laos.

I marveled over the comic opera nature of Lao history. If I had read it in a novel, I would have considered it far-fetched.

In reality, the two-year civil war that followed Kong Le's coup inspired both the Eisenhower and Kennedy administrations to recruit thousands of Meo fighters to keep an eye on the North

---

9 Decades later, a key participant in the CIA's initial contact would recall Vang Pao asking him if the United States would abandon the Meo as the French had in 1954; the United States did.

Vietnamese; the first CIA case officers entered Laos in January 1961. One of them was named Tony Poe.

Poe was the shadowy king of American spies in Laos, the most famous man no one had ever met. We didn't even know if Poe was his real name. Some insisted it was; others said it was a nom de guerre.

He had helped rescue the Dalai Lama from the Chinese communists, or so the stories went, and he led intelligence-gathering forays into China at a time that getting caught meant torture and certain death.

In Laos he helped set up the CIA base at Long Cheng in 1962 and organized Meo commando raids behind Pathet Lao–North Vietnamese lines. Poe was ruthless to the point of savagery. I had heard that he paid bounties for the ears his tribesmen cut off their enemies; decades later his contemporaries confirmed the stories.

He was either the bravest man alive, or the craziest. Some said both. He was battle hardened and bore the scars, including two fingers missing from his right hand.

Those missing fingers inspired a dark, almost paranoid, joke that reporters loved to repeat. "What's this?" the joke teller would ask, raising his right hand with the two middle fingers bent over. "It's Tony Poe ordering four beers." Wild laughter invariably ensued. It was that kind of war, and Poe was that kind of legend.

In writing about the Meo, I became aware of the importance of geography in Laos. In the minds of the Lao elite and the U.S. Embassy, Vientiane was the center of the universe. Everything that occurred in recent Lao history was based on that assumption.

If you used a protractor to draw an arc on a map of Laos, with Vientiane as the base, all the military action in the north took place in a segment between 12:30 and 1:30. Three hundred miles from Vientiane at roughly 1:30 on the clock lay Hanoi, the capital of North Viet Nam. Had I, and perhaps other Americans, realized the importance of that proximity, we might have understood better the motivations of the North Vietnamese in Laos and the importance of the Plain of Jars.

Two hundred miles from Vientiane in the arc from one o'clock to 1:30 lay Sam Neua Province and its capital, Sam Neua, headquarters of the Pathet Lao and the homeland of most Meo living in Laos at the time. A little more than 100 miles from Vientiane as the crow flies toward one o'clock lay the Plain of Jars, more frequently called the PdJ after its French name, Plaine des Jarres. Closer still to Vientiane, 80 miles away in that same narrow arc, were Long Cheng, the CIA base, and Sam Thong, its refugee center.

All of the fighting in Laos from 1960 on took place along the 120-mile corridor running from the mountains around Long Cheng and Sam Thong northeast to Sam Neua, with Hanoi looming in the background.

Within months of the Kong Le coup, the Lao government forces and Vang Pao were driven off the Plain of Jars southward to the mountaintop of Padong. While the CIA replaced Meo flintlocks with modern automatic rifles, Pop Buell parachuted in and arranged for airdrops of rice to feed the troops and their families. An ill-fated alliance began.

The deepening war didn't just threaten the Meo army, it disrupted the entire fabric of Meo society. Of course, I started my study of the Meo not understanding that, and I'm not sure many Official Americans ever got it.

The Meo fight for one reason, I learned: To protect their families and their villages. In that postcoup era, the Pathet Lao and North Vietnamese threatened Meo villages throughout Sam Neua Province. When the Americans offered the Meo guns, ammunition, and other equipment to fight their enemies, they adopted the U.S. cause but insisted on staying with their families. They would use the American materiel against the invaders, but they were not in the habit of going to the aid of other villages.

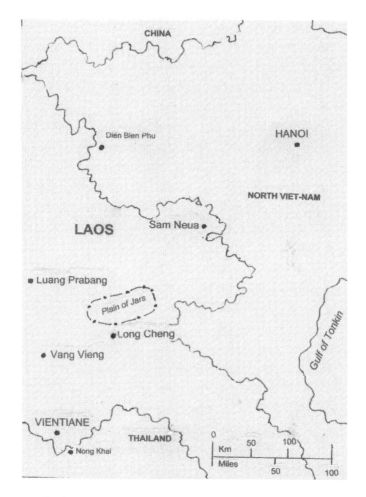

Buell's food supplies cut that link with the village. If someone made sure their families were fed, the Meo men could leave the villages to fight the enemy wherever they found him. This food-for-fighting link was the key to creating a mobile army, large and agile enough to strike beyond the range of a single village. It would keep the Meo on the move, retreating southwestward, advancing short-term, and then retreating again, until the Pathet Lao took control of the government of Laos in 1975.

Thirteen years before the end, in 1962, the great powers of the time agreed in Geneva that Laos would remain neutral in the Cold War contest between the super powers, with a coalition government including rightists, neutralists, and the communist Pathet Lao. The United States and North Viet Nam agreed to remove all their military forces.

This, I learned, was never more than a figment designed to keep the United States and Soviet Union from coming to blows over an insignificant, tiny landlocked jungle kingdom in Southeast Asia. By 1964, the fighting between communist and noncommunist forces resumed and settled into a back-and-forth pattern centered north and east of the Plain of Jars in Sam Neua Province. The Pathet Lao and their North Vietnamese allies attacked in the dry season (November to March) when they could truck in supplies over the dirt roads. The American–Meo army pushed back during the wet season using helicopters and airdrops to leapfrog over roads made impassable by rain and mud.

The United States started bombing Laos in 1964 as well, gradually escalating the number of sorties and targets as the PL-NVA advanced. By early 1970, as I prepared to spend a year studying in Viet Nam, U.S. B-52 bombers were dropping thousands of pounds of bombs a day to hold back the North Vietnamese around Long Cheng, and all the land, villages, and towns between Long Cheng and the North Viet Nam border were a free-fire zone.

The see-saw fighting, and even more so U.S. bombing, created refugees, fed and cared for by USAID under the direction of Pop Buell, by then retired from IVS. What started as a trickle of short-time refugees fleeing their villages during a battle became a flow and then a flood of homeless Meo and other hill tribes of the Lao-Theung as Americans forcibly evacuated villagers from huge areas to allow unrestricted bombing without the worry of civilian casualties. Carl had saved newspaper and magazine clippings in a hardcover scrapbook; I borrowed it and painstakingly constructed a day-by-day chronology of activities in Laos for the previous few years. Despite drawing up tables and making charts in pink-covered booklets purchased from Habeeb, I could never make sense of the numbers: The number of Meo. The number of other tribes fighting under Vang Pao. The number of killed and wounded. The number of part-time refugees and full-time resettled homeless. The number of human beings USAID fed and tried to provide a subsistence existence for to make up for or to enable the bombing. Nothing added up, and I suspected that was just how the Official Americans wanted it.

Finally, I simply accepted the conclusion of Senator Ted Kennedy's subcommittee on refugees on the disruption to life throughout the Lao battle zone: "Of an estimated population of 400,000 in 1960, at least 40-45 percent of the men have been killed and 25 percent of the women and children have fallen as casualties of war."

Meanwhile, Pop Buell, who had avoided the media for years, began speaking out in the late 1960s, at first merely answering questions, then lamenting what was happening to his beloved Meo.

In one clipping from May 1968, writer Robert Shaplen quoted Buell:

A few days ago I was with Vang Pao's officers when they rounded up 300 fresh Meo recruits. Thirty percent of the kids were 14 years old or less and about a dozen were only about 10 years old. Another 30 percent were 15 or 16. The rest were 35 or over. Where were the ones in between? I will tell you, they are all dead. Here were these little kids in their camouflage uniforms that were much too big for them, but they looked real neat, and when the King of Laos talked to them they were proud and cocky as could be.... They are too young and are not trained. In a few weeks 90 percent of them will be killed.

In early 1971, Buell told Gary Porter: "The Meo have been reduced by some 100,000 through war, hunger, massacres and disease."

As I continued to write my big story on the Meo, Buell told another reporter: "The Meo are terrifically worn down as fighters.... Their morale is shot, and they are slow to engage in battle. If you are going to have a guerrilla army, you to make your move fast and clear out fast. That is what the Meo used to do best; now they just don't do it."

My studies were turning me into a mini version of Ronk, Carl, and Doolittle: Cynical from an overload of irony.

Pop Buell wanted to help the Meo save their families and villages from outsiders—the Pathet Lao and North Vietnamese—only to see them destroy themselves in the cause of the American outsiders.

The United States was intent on saving the government of Laos from communism while disrupting the lives of one-quarter of its people, turning them into refugees in their own country.

And that press offensive inspired by the South Vietnamese invasion of southern Laos turned the spotlight instead on the disaster of the North Vietnamese occupation of northern Laos.

My new knowledge brought no understanding, however. None of what I learned was real. It was both academic and sanitary. I had not yet seen common people, fear in their eyes, fleeing their homes with only the goods they could carry on their backs. No soldier had died at my feet, not yet.

After all, I lived in Vientiane, the center of the universe, and the war never reached us.

Chapter 17
An Odd Kind of Normalcy
MARCH–MAY 1971

Time flies, but I don't know what I do.

Journal entry, 1971

THE OUT-OF-TOWN PRESS went back to where they had been; battles that we could not witness raged north and south; a numbing sameness overtook us.

I taught English for the Official Americans. I plugged away on my research for Antioch, spending a couple of hours a day raising dust in the archives of *Lao Presse* developing a detailed chronology of events in Laos from the end of World War II to the present.

I discovered kindred spirits in two farang teachers a few years older than I: Walt Haney, an American working for the Lao Ministry of Education, and a Frenchman named Georges Chebelier. We pooled our data and charts on the elite families of Laos—the na Champassaks, the Sananikones and Insisiengmais; the Abhays, Chounramanys, and Somsaniths; the Panyas, Sayasiths, and Louangkhots—and a half-dozen more. Topping the list, but not necessarily the most influential, were the royal and vice regal families of Luang Prabang. We charted how each clan married off their offspring to preserve the most money, influence, and power and to attract more.

My Indian merchant friend, Habeeb, offered me an unexpected deal on books: No charge on mysteries. I had bought and sold back most of the used mysteries in his ever-changing collection, taking a handful at a time and returning them a week later in exactly the same tattered condition. His margin on the buybacks wasn't much, and I was a great customer. Habeeb was making a Lao-sized fortune selling me notebooks, paper, Bic pens, aerograms and stamps, clipping books and glue, newspapers (the *Bangkok Post* and the *World* and the *International Herald Tribune*), and magazines (*Time* and *Newsweek*, the *Far East Economic Review* and *Playboy*). I took his deal as a touching gesture, knowing that he could afford to serve as my personal lending library.

I hunted down more academic books, monographs, and papers on Laos, buying what I could, borrowing the rest, but always taking detailed notes in my left-handed chicken scratching.

March, April, May passed. We were stalled in the early and hottest months of the rainy season, a misnomer since it also rains in the dry season in the tropics and the humidity rarely dips below 70 percent. Daytime temperatures hovered in the neighborhood of 35–36 degrees Celsius, which my body told me had to be the mid-90s and higher. The heat and humidity forced me to develop a strategy to control my perpetual diaper rash: Never run when you can walk, never walk when you can stand, never stand when you can sit, always walk on the shady side of the street, and take salt tablets.

Oppressed by the heat, I intentionally kept the map of my world small: My apartment; the Constellation; Haja and Habeeb; the Chinese cheese café for my late breakfast or early lunch; the Morning Market; USIS and the U.S. Embassy, as needed; the Chinese Noodle for dinner and late night conversation over tea and greasy doughnuts; and back to my apartment. I limited my photographic explorations, capturing scenes of daily life in Vientiane on Kodak TRI-X Pan black-and-white film, and making fewer and fewer visits to my favorite bench looking out on the shrinking Mekong.

And in the end, I still had way too much time on my hands, which I chipped away at in the Constellation bar or at the Chinese Noodle, writing letters back to the States. I wrote to my parents, my sisters, the occasional neighbor, guys from high school—one a full-fledged hippie living in a commune in central Wisconsin and another a budding Jesuit priest at Georgetown University in Washington, D.C. At Antioch, I wrote to Dan Grady and Paula Spier, and close friends Madi and Michael Adams, who looked after my stored possessions for me. And of course I wrote my friend, Liz, in Ohio.

My expulsion from Viet Nam intensified a habit I had picked up at Campion and kept up at Antioch of writing long letters. Letters in the pre-technology days before free long-distance phone calls, email, and social media kept a tenuous link to a more secure past.

Mail service between the States and Laos, however, proved to be both haphazard and expensive. In the United States, I could send a letter across town or across the country for six cents and expect that it would arrive the next day. Getting a letter from Vientiane delivered across the Pacific Ocean by "ground" service could take a month or more, so I always splurged on "air mail," a higher level of service that could deliver a missive in less than a week. But the cost was high: 125 kip, or 25 U.S. cents. And that was for a "flimsy," an air-thin piece of stationery that folded into its own envelope. I had to train my ham-fisted left hand to tread lightly so I wouldn't tear the paper.

Onto these flimsies I poured out my heart to Liz, ranted to my family, and penned long expositions on life in Laos to everyone.

Skippy Bacon, an intellectual friend from Campion studying at Georgetown, asked me to describe my life. I told him of my so-far unfulfilled desire to write:

The details of my life. I can only assure that I am not a nascent Hemingway. But to my day. Mornings are dedicated to early rising (7:00) and breakfast. Then about an hour of thumbing through my Lao dictionary. (I have no talent for languages, but Lao is enjoyable.) If I have something to write—an article, letter, or diary entry—I do it in the morning, taking a break to fetch mail.

*Until last week I was also teaching English for one hour in the late morning. Now that I have quit teaching, I usually walk down to USIS [United States Information Service] to see what news they have or talk to whomever I think of going to see. Sometime around noon, Don Ronk (*Washington Post), *Tammy Arbuckle (*Washington Star) *and I meet at the Constellation bar and compare notes, and so on.*

I go off to lunch and then somehow the afternoon melts away. I have been doing research in the Lao Presse *archives for a few months. I usually spend two hours or so scouring those old volumes.*

At 5:00 the press again assembles in the Constellation. More note comparing, discussion, haranguing (me for not writing), and Cameroon playing. Cameroon is a dice game played by two or more people, not unlike poker. But to dispel any illusion you may have, none of us drink. I prefer tea; Ronk, coffee; Arbuckle, fruit juice or tonic water; Carl Strock (AP), Pepsi and pot.

And the press corps here is quite small. Besides the above, there are only three more members, all non-American with families. Don, Tammy, and I place dice most evenings with me dropping out for dinner at 7:00. I walk or read till bedtime which comes early. I have neither the money nor the temperament for a rich nightlife.

We all try to keep informed of what's going on in the States, but the urgency of being part of the "mainstream of life" evaporates after a few months here. When we ask ourselves "Why go back?" the answer inevitably follows that there is no reason to. And so we stay.

I suspected my correspondents envisioned a different kind of life for me than I was living—waging a daily battle of survival, proving my courage—but so did I. I just didn't know what. And that was part of the problem. The heat and humidity, the lack of focus, the feeling of being out of place—I *should* have been in Viet Nam—produced a stultifying lethargy.

For once, my money situation was not dire. I had $600 tucked away. Teaching brought in $75 a month, and my rent was only $40. I was sitting pretty and bored out of my mind.

Ronk kept beating me up about not writing. Finally, probably just to shut him up, I agreed to write a sit rep—situation report—on Laos and send it to my hometown newspaper, the *Dubuque Telegraph-Herald*. Ronk loaned me his typewriter day to day, forcing me to keep working and show progress. I sweated bullets over it, writing and discarding 20 lead sentences. Ronk tore the first three pages apart, and I started over again. Finally, after weeks of work I decided to just let it go and spent $2.31—5 percent of my monthly rent—to mail 10 double-spaced pages along with 11 3-by-5 black-and-white photographs I had taken. Ten pages! It was a book. A Bible. An encyclopedia. Not surprising, the response came back in a month; the T-H decided to pass. I had my parents send it on to Grady at Antioch. At least it would show him I was doing *something*.

Ronk made me keep plugging.

What are you going to do, just sit here? he would ask.

Um.

You can't just sit here. You'll end up a junkie.

I'm working.

How many hours a day?

Well…

What are you going to do, just sit here the rest of your life?

So I hammered away on his borrowed typewriter at night, an exercise that never failed to produce a warm feeling of euphoria that did not survive the light of day. My evening masterpieces seemed cliché-ridden and boring the next morning.

Over time, I pulled together another 10-page tome on the military crisis in Laos, this one single-spaced.

In the south, the North Vietnamese—just months after being targeted in Lam Son 719—drove the last Lao off the Bolovens Plateau, west of the Ho Chi Minh Trail. The Official Americans pulled out of Pakse, farther to the west, but returned in a few days when they realized the North Vietnamese were not planning to get any closer to the Mekong. A Royal Lao Army effort to retake the Bolovens collapsed after two days, leaving the North Vietnamese more deeply entrenched and farther west into southern Laos than ever before.

My story produced another round of reject slips.

April melted into May, and I realized that under my original study plan, I should be packing up and heading back to Yellow Springs for the summer semester. Once again, I had a decision to make about staying in school. I was no more convinced of the value of a college degree compared with its cost than I had been when Dan Grady proposed his outrageous plan to send me to Viet Nam.

Complicating my decision was the chaos that had overtaken the Antioch campus. I couldn't be certain when it started because I relied for news on the weekly student newspapers mailed to me at irregular intervals, and I had been without a reliable address all through the fall until I decided to remain in Laos.

A small group of students had shut down the school in support of a strike by janitors. As a financial aid kid from a blue-collar home, I sympathized with the janitors, but I was leery of their student allies. I had seen them in action and considered them rich spoiled kids rebelling against their white-collar parents. I knew that when they got bored, they would simply move on to another cause, and the janitors would be left to mend their relations with the college after months without pay. (I turned out to be right, and the school entered a death spiral as parents refused to pay for the education their students were denied during the strike.)

I leaned toward sticking around in Laos for another year despite an undercurrent of discontent. What was I doing here? What was I supposed to be doing here? On campus, I thrived on creating independent studies, working one on one with my professors; here I found a bit too much independence, not enough focus. I didn't have Grady to whip me into shape. It did not help that the people I saw most frequently shared the same sense of unreality and disconnection from the world.

Despite the war going on up north and down south, in Vientiane nothing was happening. In fact, life seemed to be happening everywhere except where I was. The perfect example was a story in the *International Herald Tribune* in late March bearing the headline, "CIA Sponsors a 30,000-Man Force in Laos; It Finally Confirms 'Irregulars'." A Senate staff report blew the lid off the secret war in Laos. I felt cheated. I wasn't in Washington—or anywhere in the United States—where I should have been able to get a copy of the report. I was there in Laos and couldn't see the war. Someone else got "my" story, and I was on site where the story was taking place. I felt doubly cheated.

Worse yet, two investigators from the Senate Foreign Relations Committee spent two weeks in Laos in late April and early May, and I never knew it.

We were—at least I was—completely out of the loop.

But as the old saying goes, be careful what you wish for. You may get it. Things were about to happen, none of them good.

*The Hotel Constellation on Rue
Samsenthai in Vientiane. 1970.*

*At our usual table near the door in the Hotel
Constellation bar, left to right, the back of my head,
Don Ronk, Carl Strock (behind camera) and Jerry
Doolittle. 1971. Photo by Danielle Cavalarie.*

Tammy and Somboun "Soupy" Arbuckle on motorbike.
Women rode sidesaddle because of their ankle-
length sarongs known as pai-sins. May 1971.

Danielle Cavalarie in the Hotel
Constellation Bar. March 1971.

*The view looking toward the river from my balcony on
the fourth floor of 20 Rue Manthatourath. March 1971.*

*A lone soldier stands guard at the entrance to Pathet Lao
headquarters in Vientiane, directly across Lane Xang
Boulevard from the U.S. Embassy. February 1971.*

*A Lao Theung tribesman shows his flintlock to Brian
Mosser (with beard) of Grenada TV and John Swain of
AFP (shirtless). Shortly afterward, we crashed our Land
Rover on Route 13. March 1972. Photo by Don Ronk.*

Our Land Rover hangs over a steep ravine
where it landed after we blew a tire on Route
13. March 1972. Photo by Don Ronk.

Yao mother and child at the Vang Vieng airstrip.
My favorite picture of Laos. March 1972.

*I interview Jane Fonda on the tarmac of Wattay
Airport after she arrived from a two-week visit to North
Viet Nam. July 22, 1972. Photo by Don Ronk.*

Chapter 18
Our Unsettled Summer
JUNE–SEPTEMBER 1971

My bathroom leaked like a sieve. I couldn't even use the toilet the water was pouring in so heavily.

Journal entry, September 3, 1971

A T THE END of May, Carl got fired. I was devastated. If it had been Ronk or Arbuckle, I would have been pissed but not wounded. But this was Carl; this was personal.

Carl was the first guy I had met in Laos who took an interest in me. He didn't think I was stupid to want to come to Viet Nam to find out what the war was all about.

I identified with him. I could see myself growing into someone like him. He had lived in Viet Nam, spoke the language fluently, and had taken a Vietnamese wife.

He lacked Ronk's brooding gruffness. Though a skeptic, he lacked Doolittle's caustic cynicism. He had a warmth about him that the remote Buckle did not.

And now he was without a regular paycheck because Associated Press headquarters in New York felt he had improperly provided information to a Republican congressman, Rep. Pete McCloskey, during a fact-finding trip to Laos. I didn't get it. Every reporter I had met talked to visiting dignitaries and exchanged information. I

figured it might not have been the simple fact of sharing information but rather whom Carl was sharing it with. McCloskey, while
a Republican, had turned against the war. I was turning into a
real cynic.

Dick Pyle, the AP chief in Saigon and Carl's immediate boss,
promised to take up his cause. Meanwhile, one day passed, then
another. Carl kept filing stories for AP; no one asked for his telegraph card. Then, as so often happened in the state of mind known
as Laos, Carl's dismissal just faded into memory.

The episode probably caused a bigger impact among the small
Vientiane press corps than I recall. Little else was happening, and
more so than Fred Branfman's expulsion in February, this suggested
to me the fragility of a reporter's job. Fred was more of an activist
with a press card; Carl was a real reporter and relied on his position
to earn a living.

This was, in fact, his second brush with journalistic death in
two months. In late March, Max Coiffait and Danielle Cavalerie
heard from the Information Ministry that Carl was to be expelled
for something he had written about Prime Minister Souvanna
Phouma. Danielle was close to Bouaphet Sygnavong, the head of
the press section at the ministry and Souvanna's spokesman; she
had seen the undated letter of expulsion on Bouaphet's desk.

While it was never stated, the offending article was probably
his old antisecrecy piece, a version of which appeared in the *Far
East Economic Review* on January 30 under the headline, "No News
from Laos." Carl's point wasn't that there was nothing new happening here; he meant reporters weren't able to cover it. His lead put
it succinctly: "The Laotian government and the U.S. Embassy in
Vientiane seem determined to keep the war in Laos a secret." That
was nothing new and would not have merited a cranky call from
the U.S. press attaché.

What probably set the prime minister off was Carl's asser-
tion in the article that the Lao military region commanders and

the U.S. Embassy in Vientiane controlled transportation through-out the country more than Souvanna did. Carl wrote, "Odd man out is Premier Souvanna Phouma, whose personally signed travel orders for journalists are sometimes rejected by regional mili-tary commanders."

Even a neophyte like me understood that a prime minister (who also holds the Ministry of Defense portfolio in his govern-ment) is a politician in deep trouble when he can't get generals to obey his orders.

Again, one day bled into another with the threat hanging over Carl's head. He decided to go ahead with a planned weeklong trip to Luang Prabang. When he returned, things heated up. After a touch-and-go situation for two or three days, Souvanna called him in and castigated him for the article. After he finished his rant, the expulsion order simply disappeared.

Expulsion would have been devastating for Carl. Making a liv-ing in Southeast Asia by writing was possible for a single freelancer because the cost of living was so cheap, but even the AP stringer-ship didn't pay enough to support a wife and child. If Carl were expelled, he would lose his job and have to start over in another country without a steady income. I had had my plans destroyed by an expulsion, and I feared for Carl. In fact, I worried about all of them. They had become my friends, admired figures, and role models. I resented anyone who criticized or threatened them. I had my own opinions about their frailties, but I resented outside critics.

Carl dodged the bullet and that was that, except for the behav-ior of the Official Americans. Norm Barnes, the head of the U.S. Information Service in Laos, denied that the American Embassy had intervened with Souvanna to rescind the expulsion order. Later, however, U.S. Ambassador G. McMurtrie Godley told Carl that he had intervened personally. Even when they were doing a decent thing, the Americans couldn't help but lie about it and try to keep it secret. I didn't remember this kind of lesson from any of Dan Grady's political science classes.

Irwin Block felt the ax next, and this time it stuck. The *Bangkok Post* eliminated his job, claiming the paper was having money problems. I had noticed, however, that one of its Thai editors, Theh Chongkhadiki, was writing more and more frequently about Laos, mostly about hair-raising communist threats against Thailand. ("Reds," shorthand for communists, was one of the *Post*'s favorite headline words. In one week I clipped articles from the *Post* with these headlines: "Reds push west in Laos," "Reds build road to Mekong," and "Reds cut air link to Kompong Som." The stories involved three different flavors of Reds; in order, North Vietnamese, Chinese, and Cambodian.)

Whatever the reason, Irwin's job was gone, and he hustled to Bangkok to try to work a deal and salvage some kind of income.

Ronk was having a different kind of money problem. He was selling stories, but he wasn't receiving checks. I felt his pain. He and I relied on the mail for emotional as well as financial support more than most of the local reporters. We suspected someone was doing funny things with the mail because we just weren't getting any while the other guys were. Was it a coincidence that I shared a mailbox at the Constellation with Ronk? Paranoia was a friend I repeatedly encountered in Laos.

I had not heard from Antioch in months, and even my favorite correspondent, Liz, wasn't writing, or so it seemed. Ronk and I mentioned it to Maurice Cavalerie, the Constellation's owner and our biggest fixer, but the Lao postal service seemed impervious to his charm and influence.

Not hearing from Dan and Paula really bothered me. I was their baby, and I was feeling like the cradle had fallen hard, and no one was checking to see if I was still alive.

After a four-month hiatus, I heard at last from Paula. It was so unusual that I noted the event in my journal:

Paula Spier writes that crises look different when we are involved in them. She urges me to continue at Antioch, get the magic piece of paper, etc. I have written to Grady, explaining my reluctance to leave here [Laos] and asking for his advice.

I am still confused and have not made up my mind conclusively. I do not want to leave Laos, not until I have completed my study of the [elite Lao] families or until I have run aground for lack of information. I am equally reluctant to return to the U.S.

As I have noticed in foreign policy matters as well as daily life, rather than planning ahead we mere humans allow each day to follow another without specific purpose except to see the new day ahead. We eat and sleep, work and play, filling each day with inconsequential trivia.... I do it here in Laos; I will most certainly do it in the States.

I simply do not wish to leave what I have here for what I may have, or may not have, there. It is security in the familiar, fear of the future unknowns. Perhaps here I see myself fulfilling an exotic role which could only be replaced at my home with a commonplace role.

I sought advice about my next move wherever I could. Walt Haney, the education consultant and my fellow student of the Lao elites, offered himself as an example. When his two-year contract with the Royal Lao Government ended, he left to go to grad school. If I followed his cue, I should leave. My year abroad was up. Antioch beckoned.

Then I met with Professor George McT. Kahin during his short visit to Vientiane in June. Kahin had just retired as chairman of Cornell University's Southeast Asia Program, which I was eyeing as a place to land someday post-Laos. I had enjoyed my language studies at Cornell, and I saw him as an important contact to have in my pocket later on. We discussed my studies at length. I was particularly excited about some work I was doing on corruption in the Lao governments at the time—there was a terrible scandal unfolding involving cheap Thai cigarettes that were undercutting the government-subsidized Lao brand. Kahin advised me to stay on, to forget about the corruption and focus on the Lao elite genealogies. I was incensed that he did not share my outrage over the corruption; my growing cynicism apparently left room for some innocent idealism. That would change.

At this point, my older sister, Bonnie, a frequent correspondent and confidante, wrote to tell me she had met a man and planned to marry at the end of the summer of 1972. "I would like to be there for that," I noted in my journal. It gave me a reasonable deadline to shoot for: Summer of 1972.

If I followed that timeline, I wouldn't have to think about Antioch again for almost a year. With that tiny nudge, I reached my decision to drop out of Antioch, while leaving the door open to my eventual return.

Laos had that effect, I noticed. You decide one thing, then do the exact opposite and find nothing unusual about it.

My 21st birthday passed in late June without notice, and I realized that without Antioch behind me, I was well and truly on my own. Maybe I had been too hasty in my decision making, I thought. By July Fourth, I convinced myself I had made the right decision, for the time being.

Our moods, never buoyant, turned sour as we learned of events elsewhere that would affect the war in Laos.

In Cambodia, just south of Laos, a right-wing general named Lon Nol overthrew the government of Prince Norodom Sihanouk, a crafty old monarch intent on keeping his country out of the Vietnamese civil war. Meanwhile in the United States, the *New*

York Times and the *Washington Post* published parts of a secret Department of Defense history of the Viet Nam War that became known as the "Pentagon Papers." Those two events blew away any interest the American public might have had in our secret little war in Laos. I recorded no visits by outside journalists. We were on our own, and we were depressed.

The Official Americans probably loved having the attention pointed elsewhere—although I don't know that for a fact—but it didn't stop the secrecy or the lying. One pathetic incident that started on July Fourth illustrated what happened to us every day.

I had long since started reading the CIA's Foreign Broadcast Information Service translations of North Vietnamese and Pathet Lao radio broadcasts. On July 4, the PL reported that three mobile regiments of Vang Pao's "special forces" and some Thai forces, with the support of U.S. aircraft, had mounted "nibbling" attacks south of the Plain of Jars. Several days later, Lao Army General Thongphanh Knocksy repeatedly insisted at his daily briefing that the offensive against the plain was strictly "an American affair." Two days later, U.S. Embassy press attaché Andy Guzowski denounced the allegations that Americans were conducting the campaign against the Plain of Jars. In fact, he said, the Royal Lao Government "categorically denies" these allegations. At first, no Lao spokesman would comment, then the government disavowed Guzowski's statement. History showed that General Knocksy was correct; we had assumed that all along, but had no way of confirming it, stuck as we were in Vientiane.

I didn't trust the North Vietnamese and PL propaganda, but with the Lao government and the American Embassy contradicting one another, I found it easy to distrust everyone. The guys' cynicism was rubbing off on me.

As the summer months wore on, the monsoon rains intensified, falling harder and for longer periods each day. The monsoon winds from India started blowing as usual in March and, by April, were producing daily downpours. The rain increased each month, lashing down in sheets for an hour or two at a time before giving way to a hot sun that turned the humid air into a sauna. By August, the Mekong, which had revealed its sandy bed just months earlier, was flowing over its banks in places near Wattay Airport.

Ba Tan, the Vietnamese bartender at the Constellation, showed me photos of the water rising around her home as the river sneaked into the northern backside of Vientiane. By the middle of the month, I noted in a letter that the river had risen 26¼ feet from its dry season low point, and the benches where I used to sit and watch the sun set over the Mekong were half under water.

I was safe in my new apartment on the third floor of Rue Manthatourath, but Carl was not so lucky. (This had to be his summer in hell.) On the 21ˢᵗ, he moved to the second floor of his house, and he and a neighbor started building a dike around their houses. Too late. The next day, the ground floor tile was invisible under six inches of muddy water.

The long narrow dragon boats accustomed to hauling passengers and goods across the Mekong to Thailand taxied residents down the flooded streets of Vientiane. *Lao Presse*, which usually devoted the first page of its mimeographed news sheet to some government announcement or other, started reporting the water levels upriver at Luang Prabang and Ban Houei Sai; we watched the numbers inch upward and wondered where all that extra water would flow when it reached Vientiane.

A week after seeking shelter on the second floor of his home, Carl asked me if I would help him move some things over to a hotel. This would mean getting—God, I dreaded the thought—into the water. Not just any water, either. The muddy crud surging through Vientiane had started in the Tibetan plateau and flowed through southern China and back and forth across northern Laos to get here, picking up silt, animal droppings, human excrement, and all kinds of other nastiness along the way. In eastern Iowa, we spoke of the Muddy Mississippi, but the Mekong in flood made the Father of Waters look pristine.

Worse than the muck and germs, however, was my fear of drowning. I drank water from small glasses and showered so I wouldn't have to sit in a tub with several inches of water. I hated water. I hated the thought of water, but Carl needed help, and I wanted to help him. (Only decades later would I wonder why he had not asked Ronk. Doolittle had his own problems, and Arbuckle hated getting his feet wet, but I was chosen, not Ronk. I believe that is known as being the low man on the totem pole.) I rationalized that it wouldn't be so bad. I could walk in that crud; I wasn't going to fall into it.

Not wanting to ruin my leather sandals, I made a quick visit to Habeeb's to buy a pair of rubber flip-flops, the kind that every Asian in Vientiane wore. Carl carried me on the back of his motorbike to the edge of the flood about a block from his house. We took off our pants and shirts and waded into the water in just our underwear and flip-flops. I can't imagine what Carl's neighbors thought of the two skinny white farangs with their farmer tans high-stepping through water that reached our ribs. (We had to high-step to keep from losing our flip-flops and to keep from tripping and falling into the muck.) As we carried suitcases and boxes perched on our heads, I suspect the shorter Lao, Thai, and Vietnamese of the neighborhood were just a little jealous of our height, although as foreigners, in their minds, we probably should have been able to hire a boat and coolies to do the job. They didn't know that we were not Official Americans; we lived on tight budgets without government perks.

The job done, I raced back to my apartment and scrubbed my body below the neck over and over again, and doubled washed the pants and shirt I had put on over my wet underwear. I toyed with throwing the flip-flops away, but they were brand new and I was on a budget. I settled for a thorough scrubbing and vowed not to wear them except in an emergency. When it came time to pack a year later, I considered them tainted still and left them behind.

Another week passed, and the water stopped rising but didn't recede. *Lao Presse* reported the flooding might last another month. Tammy returned from a trip out of country, and we toured the edges of the flood on his motorbike. Vientiane had become an island.

> *Luang Prabang road is in bad shape*, I wrote in my journal. *Just loose gravel in some places. Farther on towards Wattay, however, it was in good shape. Hard to explain. The water was flowing across the road well before Continental [the Continental Air Services terminal at Wattay Airport] so we turned around, Buckle getting his feet wet doing it [a big no-no since Tammy hated getting his feet wet], and headed back to his house. Detoured to Fa Ngum Street. Noticed the water had again covered the floor of the Chinese pavilion. Buckle changed his shoes and I put on my sandals....*

> *This time out we went to Chinaimo [the headquarters for the Vientiane Military Region south of town near the Thadeua river crossing]. Water stopped us about 200 meters from it. The river was rolling across the road where just that morning Buckle said it had been high and dry. The road here, too, was in bad shape. Posts were placed on either side of the road so drivers could see where it went. The left hand lane... was crumbling. About two feet of it had disappeared completely.*

A huge storm blew in on September 3, making the curtains in my apartment fly parallel with the ceiling; sheets of rain doused the floor six feet inside each window. Thunder pounded through the night. The lights went out, and by the flashes of lightning alone, I hauled all my furniture—desk, tables, chairs, armoire, and even the bed—to the center of the room.

My bathroom leaked like a sieve. I couldn't even use the toilet the water was pouring in so heavily.... As I looked out my balcony door at the houses next door, I could only remember the movies I had seen of Florida typhoons.

If I hadn't been on the third floor, I might have been worried by all the water. With nothing more to be done, I went back to bed and slept well, if somewhat damply.

It was the most severe flood since 1966 and most likely had nothing to do with the U.S. Air Force effort to change the weather as a tactic of war. It was merely another sign of our summer of discontent.

By the end of September, Irwin Block was gone for good. I applied to replace him as a stringer for *Time* magazine, but its Southeast Asian correspondent chose Max Coiffait instead. Given my lack of experience—I hadn't sold a piece yet—I can't say I blamed them, although I was far more likely to provide them with the kind of colorful background material the editors in New York relied on to write their timeless pieces.

Mike Morrow visited Vientiane again but found that the American Embassy had blackballed him, probably because he had outed Tony Poe as the key CIA operative in America's secret war in Laos. In any case, no Official American would talk to him, and he soon left.

Buckle got word that he had been declared persona non grata in Thailand. Given that Soupy, his wife, was Thai, and that we all traveled to and from Laos via Bangkok, this was a serious blow.

Grady wrote, letting me know that he would remain in touch despite my non-student status. And he told me that the *Dayton Journal Herald* was willing to consider any political pieces I sent.

In other circumstances, that might have been great news. Given the summer we had had, with firings and layoffs, expulsions and lost checks, journalism didn't seem all that promising.

It was just one shitty episode after another, but it could have been worse. We could have been Lao.

Chapter 19
Mad Street Feeler
NOVEMBER 1971

I am shy of making acquaintance with strangers.

W. Somerset Maugham, *The Gentleman in the Parlour*

I CAN STILL SEE the Mad Street Feeler.

A dark-skinned man, he roamed the streets of Vientiane naked. It was said that he had been a sorcerer, an honorable occupation, and could charge top dollar for his magic—as much as two chickens and a bottle of "lao-lao" whisky. Over time, his magic gave out, and the patients stopped coming. He gave up clothing and stopped bathing; his uncovered skin darkened with filth, the kind that never washes off. He was not blind, at least that anyone could tell, but his eyes did not seem to take in the world. So he rabbit hopped along, feeling the streets for pebbles and sticks just the right size and shape to shove up his rectum.

I frequently observed the Mad Street Feeler from my perch at the Chinese Noodle, but I slowly realized that he represented a problem for me: Despite living in the capital of Laos, I knew no Lao personally.

About 132,000 people lived in Vientiane, according to official estimates, but no one really knew. Although the country had been independent almost 20 years, the Royal Lao Government still had not conducted a formal census. And in terms of Vientiane, I found it hard to tell where the "city" stopped and the countryside started. Outside the business center with its three- and four-story hotels and apartment buildings, rice paddies, open fields, and wooden houses with corrugated tin roofs existed side by side with one- and two-story masonry buildings.

Among Vientiane's uncounted residents, the Lao couldn't even find a place at the bottom of the social, economic, and political totem pole. It was as though they didn't exist—at least in my Lao world.

Atop the totem pole, of course, sat the 1,000 or so Official Americans and their dependents. They ran the war, and in Vientiane the war was everything. The men wore solid gold bracelets on their wrists and lived with their wives and children in their own American-style suburb, complete with ranch homes and an Olympic-size swimming pool, at a walled, guarded compound about four miles from the center of town, a place known by its road marker, KM 6. They had their own doctors and an American supermarket in the USAID compound in downtown Vientiane. I rarely saw an Official American in Haja or Habeeb's or standing in line at the cinemas around the corner from the Chinese Noodle. They seemed to visit the enormous Morning Market a stone's throw from the U.S. Embassy only to pick up quaint souvenirs at the end of their tours in this hazardous duty posting. In fact, if they didn't want to, they never had to see a Lao outside work.

Second on the power list were the North Vietnamese. They ran the other side of the war. Their official physical presence was limited to their embassy, but they intruded on every discussion or plan for the future: What will we do when the North Vietnamese march down Lane Xang Boulevard? Or more likely, how will we get out before the North Vietnamese start lobbing shells into the city?

In fact, thousands of Vietnamese lived in Vientiane. At the end of World War II, more Vietnamese (12,400) lived in the city than did Lao, most likely because the French used them to administer all three of their Indochinese colonies. That number shrank to around 9,000 by 1958, despite a flow of refugees from both the north and south after the partition of Viet Nam. If they no longer outnumbered the Lao, the Vietnamese still appeared to have the upper hand economically. One afternoon, I stood in the shade near the Royal Palace photographing the traffic. At least half of the couples and families passing me on motorbikes were Vietnamese. And Dennis Ross told me that upper-class South Vietnamese draft dodgers lived the life of ease in Vientiane.

Foreigners of all kinds, from the Thai to the French, served as merchants, tradesmen, and advisors, not just in downtown Vientiane and the other large towns but even in the villages. Thais from across the Mekong, distinguished from the local Lao only by their sense of superiority over their country bumpkin cousins, hauled goods, filled the markets, drove taxis, and pedaled the three-wheeled samlors. Chinese, Indian, and Vietnamese merchants ran the retail trade. My two favorite restaurants, the Chinese Noodle and the Chinese cheese sandwich shop, were run by Chinese or Vietnamese. Indians and Vietnamese sewed clothing in the tailor shops.

Ordinary lowland Lao played almost no role in the events consuming their country. And in their own capital, they were seldom seen except in the markets and in the small villages that made up Vientiane proper. The Lao just lived here.

Except for the French-educated elites in the military and the government bureaucracy, the ethnic Lao went unrecognized and unnoticed.

Of the few I met, none seemed to understand that or care. It was just another contradiction that made Laos more a state of mind than real.

I criticized the Official Americans for their remoteness from the Lao people, but I wasn't much better. I knew Souny, a typically short, smiling teenager dressed in the green uniform of the Lao government civil servant, who tutored me in the Lao language, but we didn't socialize, not even for a glass of tea. We sat side by side at the table in my room, he reciting from elementary school Lao books, I repeating his words, trying to match tone and inflection and rhythm. He was my teacher, that's all.

Sa Wan cleaned my apartment every day for almost two years, but I knew very little about her. She was pretty, short and stocky with straight black hair than hung to her waist. She admitted to being 20 and unmarried, which seemed odd in a nation where marriages took place young, but perhaps her experience reflected a scarcity of eligible men, most being off somewhere in the Royal Lao Army or the Pathet Lao. Toward the end of my time in Laos, she asked if she could borrow my portable transistor AM-FM radio while she did her chores. After that, I always knew where she was in the building from the sound of love songs beamed across the Mekong from Thailand, but I didn't know her.

The young women I taught at the Lao-American Association wanted to know all about life in the United States and dating habits, but LAA forbade teachers from fraternizing with the students. This was wise and protected me as one of very few male English teachers, but I never used the classes to learn about their lives and social habits.

Bouaphet Sygnavong, the foreign press liaison in the Ministry of Information, called me out on my indifference to the Lao when I went to get my press credentials renewed the first time. You never come to see us except when you want something, he said. I thought he was an asshole; I didn't recognize the invitation to visit him more often for what it was. Danielle Cavalerie was sweet on him, and that may have colored my opinion, since the more I saw of Danielle, the more I liked her. But Bouaphet was right.

I recognized I was no Fred Branfman or John Everingham. Branfman had rented space in a village headman's house just a few miles outside Vientiane from the first month he arrived. And Everingham, a brash, ballsy, obnoxious Australian my age, traipsed all over northern Laos and was eventually captured and held by the Pathet Lao for several days.

I admired their approach to life in a different country, but that wasn't me. Growing up in a small town with dozens and dozens of cousins, I had visited my aunts and uncles on their farms in Wisconsin and Illinois and I had used outhouses. Living without air conditioning and with cold water showers, even in a tropical climate, was roughing it enough for me. I liked running water, beds with mattresses, and (more or less) sanitary food, and I didn't like the stink of excrement, whether animal or human.

I also had the language problem. I didn't start studying Lao until the late spring of 1971 with Antioch paying the bill; as soon as I dropped out of school, the money for language lessons, cheap as they were, dried up. I had focused on learning Vietnamese before coming to Asia; now I found I couldn't speak either Vietnamese or Lao, and the language I limped along best in was my high school French. Merde.

Still, I could have used my opportunities to get to know the Lao better. So the Lao I knew best were the ones I encountered while watching Vientiane's street life. Dirty-faced young women, knockoffs of Sa Wan, who used shovels with handles longer than they were tall, cleaned black muck out of the open sewers that lined every street. Women just like them, but covered in white dust, worked beside the occasional man, shoveling gravel and rock, mixing mortar by hand, and hauling bricks up bamboo scaffolds at construction sites around the city. I passed plenty of bored soldiers and police standing watch over military buildings or wandering down streets, a pistol on their hip or rifle in their hand. Occasionally a military truck would barrel past the Constellation, hauling cheerless young conscripts slumped in their fresh green uniforms to who knows where.

Aside from the Constellation bar, our favorite observation post was the Chinese Noodle. Ronk seemed to have his own table. If his table was taken, he just didn't stay. His outdoor table sat close to the accordion metal gate that was pulled shut when the kitchen closed. There was a bit of wall, about as wide as the table, and after eating we tilted our backless stools and leaned against the wall. A knee-high planter separated the high-class Chinese banquet hall next door from our noodle kitchen, offering a little privacy from the Mercedes drivers parked out front swishing feather dusters across their spotless vehicles.

After Ronk introduced me to the noodle kitchen, I spent some time there every day. If no one was around, I would walk on by, exploring other parts of the "theater district" around the corner.

Many evenings I left the Constellation around 7:00, walked down to the Noodle, ate a large plate of noodles and beef, then went home to wash laundry, write letters, or read a paperback mystery acquired from Habeeb. Around 9:30 or 10:00, I would head back to the Noodle for conversation and people watching. Most often, I found Ronk or John Cornell or Phil or Dennis or some combination of ex-patriates. I would order a Thai iced tea with cream, lean back against the wall, and watch life pass by.

Sooner rather than later, the beggars came out.

Street kids seven, eight, or nine years old, living who knows where, arrived first in ragged shirts and shorts, grinning wide smiles and nattering, "Kip. Kip. Kip." If we gave them money, usually a five- or ten-kip note pulled crumpled from our pockets, we did it immediately. No foreplay, no hesitation. That way, if we did not plan to give—and our generosity had its limits—the street kids knew right away to move on. It was always the same group of kids, four boys and one girl. They ran in a pack, but unlike in Saigon, I had never seen or heard of them trying to steal. Ronk, who had started a house for shoeshine boys in Danang, South Viet Nam, knew them and kept them in line.

He also kept an informal census of the beggars. When he first arrived, he counted just three hard-core beggars. Within 20 months, he was keeping tabs on somewhere between 50 and 100 who haunted the shops and restaurants in the business and cinema districts.

There was the mother, prematurely aged, with a toddler gnawing at her varicose breast.

The young heavyset woman we called the "horse-face girl" because her face looked as if a horse had flattened it with a giant hoof, robbing her of both her looks and her wits.

And a young man—he should have been in the army, and perhaps had been—half his right foot gone, hobbling down a side street, stopping at shops to display his infirmity and collect ten kip (two cents).

Other beggars were disabled. A man without hands. One without legs. Another who wrapped his shriveled legs in old inner tubes. Two blind men led by a bored girl who appeared to be five or six.

During my time, they came and went.

I encountered one living in a tin-roofed cardboard house in an abandoned French cemetery behind the Morning Market. Eyes sunken, he looked like he had risen from one of the abandoned graves. He appeared suddenly and scared the bejeebers out of me. I shivered as I photographed his grinning face.

Others slept on doorsteps I passed regularly during my nocturnal rounds, but most simply disappeared when the noodle shops closed and reappeared when the sun rose.

Despite their poverty, Vientiane's beggars were better off than those I had seen elsewhere in Asia. The police seldom harassed them, and shopkeepers shooed them away like recalcitrant children. No one kicked or beat them. And Laotians were generous; no one needed to starve here.

But I learned that some would die of their impoverished conditions, especially the cai addicts. Cai was a by-product of manufacturing heroin. It was highly addictive and so ridiculously cheap that even poor Laotians could become addicts. A user told me the high quickly gave way to uncontrollable addiction and the glazed eyes, the distracted demeanor, and nodding head that addiction caused. Cai is the Lao word for chicken, and addicts resembled chickens roosting for the night.

Addicts were familiar faces among the parade of beggars.

Pan was one. A formerly muscular stevedore unloading the Thai boats along the banks of the Mekong, he got his name from the Lao word for 1,000 because it was said that he earned "pan kip" ($2) a day wiping dusty cars and begging. One hundred kip would buy a packet of twenty brown, gravel-sized nuggets of cai, enough to satisfy an experienced user for two to four hours. Pan's addiction apparently ran 24/7, and no one was surprised when he no longer showed up at the Noodle.

Souny, Sa Wan, Pan, the Horse-Face Girl and the Mad Street Feeler—these were the Lao I encountered. I knew they did not represent all the Laotians. I wanted to see the real Laos, and to do that, I would have to go witness the war.

Chapter 20

Playing Reporter

I think the secrecy part, we probably carried it further than it should have been.

Bill Lair, 1960s chief of CIA operations
in Laos, December 2001

BY THANKSGIVING OF 1971, I had lived in Laos for more than a year. I had dropped out of college and supported myself for a time by teaching English. I wanted to become a writer, but despite repeated attempts I had not sold a single piece.

I filled my days creating chronologies of events in a country few people had ever heard of and trying to identify relationship links for an elite group of half-educated families who ruled Laos.

Despite the legal availability of drugs—opium, heroin, cai, and marijuana, which sold 20 rolled joints with menthol filters in the Morning Market for about ten American cents—I was not addicted to anything beyond indolence.

I exhibited cruel indifference to those in the States who loved me, especially my parents, by repeatedly failing to reassure them of my health and well-being.

I took a hard look at the future in a letter to my high school friend Skip Bacon, and did not at all like what I saw:

I have been in Laos one year now. In Asia for 14 months. It does not seem that long, and then it seems an eternity. Apparently I shall be here for a good while longer. I can't see going back to the States. Nothing there. I withdrew from Antioch last July. I had, and still have, two quarters to finish, but that can be completed some other day. Money is a problem.

Until recently I was earning my living by teaching English. Now I am beginning to write for newspapers and by this time next month I will be sinking or swimming, or at least floating, on my writing ability. I am learning a great deal and have found that I do possess some writing talent. All I need to do is turn it into money.

I have pretty much given up the idea of becoming an Asia scholar.... The obvious question is what then? I don't know that either.

In mid-November, the government sparked a financial crisis when it devalued the kip by 20 percent. My dollars now bought 600 kip instead of 500, but my kip purchased less. I found the new 600-1 ratio impossible to calculate, so I stuck with the five-kip-equals-one-cent rule. It was close enough for the buying I did.

Unfortunately, however, I got caught holding 95,000 kip ($190), mainly because the Lao-American Association paid teachers in kip, not dollars. That translated into a $32 loss in the value of my money, almost half of one month's pay. Worse than that, merchants began holding back stock, and I couldn't find pipe tobacco, which was hard enough to find in normal times. I took to tamping loose cigarette tobacco into my pipe; the tobacco was plentiful and still cheap but tasted awful. I finally just switched to smoking cigarettes, Craven A's, British cigs made in Thailand. They reminded me of American Marlboros, which started my smoking habit in high school. I would have been happy to smoke local tobacco, but the Indian merchants stopped selling local cigarettes when the government froze the price at 58 kip per pack, nine and a half cents under the new conversion rate. Haja told me he was paying more for the cigarettes than he could sell them for, so he stopped.

U.S. Ambassador Godley tried to reassure Official Americans that this was for the best for the average Lao (although Americans made out quite well, getting 20 percent more kip for their dollar):

> All Americans must understand that the 20% change in the rate of exchange for kip into dollars does not mean a comparable change in the cost of living for the average Lao since he meets the bulk of his requirements from goods produced by the local economy, where one kip will always equal one kip.

I found that to be—as we said in Iowa—pure manure.

The average Lao, whether in Vientiane or in a village, produced almost no goods. They grew rice, maybe some vegetables, raised a few chickens, ducks, and the occasional pig. But if they wanted pots and pans, cups and bowls, shovels and hoes, seeds or clothing, they had to buy them, usually from Chinese or Vietnamese traders selling products imported from Thailand. As for "one kip will always equal one kip," I found it almost too stupid to refute. One kip at 500 to the dollar is worth more than a kip at 600 to the dollar.

It was just one more example of the Official Americans trying to rearrange reality to suit their desires.

Such nonsense, combined with my growing sense of inadequacy, almost drove me over the edge. Tammy Arbuckle, however, pulled me back from the brink and finally got me moving. He made me an offer I couldn't refuse: Accompany him to southern Laos to take a look at the war.

From a financial standpoint, I couldn't afford to do it. From a personal standpoint—Did I have the guts to face potential death in a war zone? That was the question that launched this whole Asian adventure—I couldn't afford *not* to do it.

Before we could go, I had to outfit myself. At the time, I was reading *Scoop,* Evelyn Waugh's hilarious fictional depiction of war correspondents, so I had an idea of the types of things I would need. I understood I could not show up in my normal dress—creased trousers, a short-sleeved sport shirt, and polished shoes. Waugh's hero, William Boot, took an inflatable boat with him into the outback. Given my fear of drowning, I figured I could save a bundle by avoiding the water.

Right off, Tammy told me to buy a pair of boots. With any luck, we would be out tramping around. Habeeb provided appropriately sized khaki canvas boots with rubber soles. Arbuckle approved of my purchase but ordered me to drill holes through the soles.

Why would I do that? I inquired, looking for a gotcha moment. I had just bought them.

Water drains out of them faster that way, he said

Everyone around the table in the Constellation nodded agreement at the sage advice.

Fortunately Habeeb found a way to drill the appropriate number and size of holes and did not seem fazed in the least by what I thought was a bizarre request.

I knew this trip would test my courage, but I never imagined the test would involve overcoming my greatest fear: Water.

My other purchase had to be a jacket. When I packed for a year of living in Saigon, which from all accounts was as hot as hell and twice as humid, I never guessed I would need a sweater, much less a coat. But here I was in Laos in November, with the temperature cooling to comfortable levels. Tammy and I hoped to get out onto the Bolovens Plateau, elevation 3,000-plus feet, where it would be cooler still, especially at night.

It is winter here, I wrote to my younger sister, Kathy. *Got down to 47 two nights ago. That means 47 inside and out, because of the houses here not having any heating equipment. Boy, do I get cold! I am temporarily reducing my shower schedule to once every three days. No one here really minds because they smell just as bad. You should try taking a shower with cold water when the temperature is about 55. You would be surprised how fast you can bathe. As for washing your hair, well, just grit your teeth and don't use much shampoo. It is a little hard to believe that in five months we will be stewing in 100 [degree] weather.*

I could find no jacket, coat, sweater, or poncho in the Morning Market, the all-purpose Lao superstore. I had admired the visiting TV correspondents in their beige safari suits, so I went to the Indian tailor a few doors down from Haja and Habeeb and had him fit me for a custom-made correspondent's jacket with breast pockets and button-down flaps, wide pockets at the hips, and slots for two pens on the right shoulder. The tailor mistakenly put the pen slots on the left shoulder, the way he did for real correspondents, all of whom were right-handed. I was left-handed and needed my pens to hand—from my right shoulder. He redid the khaki garment while I waited.

On December 2, Buckle and I hopped the Air America milk run to Pakse at the southernmost part of the country. Pakse was a little burg filled with wooden buildings and the occasional French colonial masonry leftover. Our hotel, the Hotel Municipal de Pakse, was of the latter variety. The rooms were clean and had private baths. The bar on the first floor doubled as a brothel. By the end of our 10-day stay, the girls greeted us as old friends, in a sisterly sort of way.

It felt good being out of Vientiane, even if I was with a baby-sitter. I was certain Ronk had never gotten to the south; he hated flying, and going overland down Route 13 along the Mekong was dangerous as well as tedious. The only other way was to boat across the Mekong to Thailand; grab the Nong Khai train to Bangkok; change trains at Nakhon Ratchasima far to the southwest; travel to the end of the line at Ubon; catch a bus for the 80-mile, half-day trip to the Mekong; recross the river by ferry; and take a cab from the river landing into Pakse. Even if Ronk made all the right travel connections, it was going to be a two-day trip one way. I didn't see that happening. I was finally one up on Ronk. I felt bigger somehow, more experienced, important.

Our plane ride covered the 300 miles between Vientiane and Pakse in about two hours. The flight reminded me that Larry Lifschultz, my American nemesis in Saigon, had demanded that he be able to fly into exile in Pakse rather than Bangkok. A year later, I felt comfortable that I would not be running into him, but otherwise I didn't know what to expect.

Pakse was the capital of Champassak Province and the headquarters for the Royal Lao Army's Military Region IV, which incorporated the six small, southernmost provinces of the country. The Mekong ran along the west side of town. To the east lay the Bolovens Plateau, a saucer of rolling hills and forests about 60 miles across at its widest point; beyond it lay the Ho Chi Minh Trail, the North Vietnamese supply route into South Viet Nam. South of Pakse, the Mekong dropped through the Khone Falls and poured into Cambodia.

Since the failure of Lam Son 719, South Viet Nam's attempt to shut down the trail, the North Vietnamese had aggressively pushed the Lao forces—no Meo down here—and the Thai "volunteers" farther and farther west toward the Mekong and away from the Ho Chi Minh Trail. Tammy and I wanted to learn what was happening in the Pakse area, and we hoped to be able to visit the "front."

Arbuckle shepherded me from one briefing to the next. I learned that my image of the Ho Chi Minh trail was imaginary. It resembled nothing like the bare path I walked single file in Antioch's Glen Helen forest.

It was actually a tangle of dirt and gravel roads largely hidden under layers of jungle canopy. The old French Route 96 ran north and south through the mountains bordering South Viet Nam. A second route was a north–south road through Ban Phon, a tiny village in the valley between the Bolovens Plateau and Route 96. The third lay farther west and south through Saravane and down old Route 23 onto the Bolovens and through burgs named Thateng and Ban Lao Ngam.

A Lao briefer claimed to know of 16 NVA battalions operating on the Bolovens, including those belonging to a fearsome unit known as the NVA 309th Regiment. Despite my father's World War II and post-war National Guard service, I was never too clear on how many men belonged to a company or a battalion or regiment and so on up the line. What I learned from our briefings was that no unit, regardless of size, was ever fully manned. The designations suggested a relative scale to summarize the size of battles; they weren't absolute numbers of soldiers.

Back in May, not long after ARVN's embarrassing retreat from Laos, the NVA had surged west and captured Saravane and the Bolovens Plateau, including Paksong at the plateau's heart. Prime Minister Souvanna Phouma ordered the army to recapture the towns, and it had retaken Saravane in late July and Paksong in mid-September. While the Royal Lao Army had chased the North Vietnamese off the Bolovens, it had not defeated them. Three weeks before we arrived in Military Region IV, the RLA launched a three-pronged attack to clear out a huge supply area around Thateng and drive the North Vietnamese away from the eastern edge of the Bolovens. That operation, dubbed Thao La, was still going on, and we wanted in.

The CIA did not want us anywhere near the action. I confided to my journal:

The Americans, especially Lt. Col. Don Wilson, the Army Attaché, were kind and generally helpful. Arbuckle was invaluable. CAS [Controlled American Source, the code name for CIA], the spooks, were not so friendly and tied us up... with the absurd charge that I was a "sensationalist." That without ever having even seen me or my writing.

Buckle was well-known for his anticommunist, pro-U.S. involvement sentiments. Anyone would pale in comparison, but I apparently paled to the point of being a yellow journalist without ever having published a single piece.

Each day we banged on the same doors, demanding, suggesting, begging that we be allowed to observe Operation Thao La. Each day, we were told a different story, about unsafe conditions, lack of transportation, and blah, blah, blah. We were told on the sly what was happening, and I did not want Buckle's association with me to prevent him from doing his job. Instead, it just seemed to piss him off. I was his protégé, and I was apparently going where he wanted to go.

While we engaged in our bloodless battle with the spooks, we used our time to look around and make side trips.

Tammy acquired a motorbike, and we putt-putted 25 miles down dusty Route 13, the closest thing to a national highway in Laos, to Champassak, the namesake of Champassak province and the na Champassak royal family. Boun Oum na Champassak, the patriarch of the family, had served as prime minister in the early 1960s and was the heart of the rightists in Lao politics. His brother, Boun Om—whom we witnessed taking a leak in public in a park named after his grandfather—represented the family's interests in the Vientiane cabinet as Minister of Religious Affairs. A nephew, Sisouk na Champassak, operated at Souvanna's right hand, variously serving as de facto minister of defense as well as minister of finance.

We found nothing in particular to recommend Champassak, aside from Boun Om's public micturition.

Opposite the town, on the west bank of the Mekong, we visited the 1,000-year-old ruins of Wat Phou, a stunning stone relic of a temple complex older than Angkor Wat in Cambodia, although not as extensive. I wrote to my parents:

> *While at Champassak, I also got up to the Wat Phou (literally, Mountain Temple) ruins. I liked it so much I almost stayed there. It is quiet and peaceful. It makes Vientiane seem like a huge city. I will never be able to return to civilization. Maybe I'll become a farmer.*

Becoming a farmer would have to wait. I had more to see in southern Laos, and we were allowed to visit Paksong and the PS (Papa Site) 49 airstrip, where nothing was going on. NVA probes against the town began a day or two after our visit.

My PS 49 experience exemplified the problems I (and others) had with Lao geography. Every piece of ground seemed to go by several names, and that didn't count the varieties of spellings as French, British, American, and other Western mapmakers tried to convert spoken Lao names to written Western spellings. (For instance, the Royal Laos Army briefer in Vientiane was variously identified as Thongphanh Knoksy, Thong Phanh Knokeh, Thong Phanh Knoskey, Thongphan Knocksy, Thongphanh Knosky, Thonephan Knoksy, and Thongpanh Knockey. It's pronounced tong-pahn nock-see.)

We found nothing at PS 49. It was just a tiny landing strip, used by the Japanese during WW II, about a kilometer east-northeast of Paksong. Someone I encountered, probably the Lao pilot who flew us there, referred to it as LS (Lima Site) 49, so that's what I called it in a letter home. Never mind that there is an LS 49 farther north at Lak Sao, a village east of Vientiane in Khammouane Province near the North Viet Nam border. A U.S. Air Force report about the fighting on the Bolovens Plateau identified the airstrip as LS 449, also known as Toong Set. But the index of lima sites shows LS 449 as Ban Nongkin, not to be confused with the nearby Nongkin Noy. On the detailed maps the U.S. military used, I found a Thongset three klicks east-northeast of Paksong.

In short, I did not know where I had been, but I did know where I wanted to go. And after four days of dithering, the U.S. country team, made up of the ambassador and every senior Official American in Laos, took up my case and finally gave permission.

There was another lesson learned: Be careful what you ask for. You just might get it.

Chapter 21
Death on the Ho Chi Minh Trail
December 1971

I do not bring back from a journey quite the same self that I took.

W. Somerset Maugham, *The Gentleman in the Parlour*

WE FLEW IN aboard a Royal Lao Air Force resupply helicopter, a lumbering Sikorsky CH-34 with a bulbous nose and the pilots tucked up so close to the rotor blades they would never need visit a barber again. The chopper bounced on landing—a sure sign of a novice at the controls—and churned up red dust over the trampled elephant grass. Brown-skinned soldiers waved us away, their arms crossing over their heads in the universal sign of "No. Go back."

Shit, I muttered. We're in the wrong place.

I looked at Buckle; he grimaced.

What have we gotten ourselves into? I wondered.

Operation Thao La was an all-Lao operation. That meant flying with pilots who probably didn't have a driver's license.

Up we went, only to plunge again moments later at a different landing zone that looked exactly like the one we had just unceremoniously departed. The pilot bounced the chopper to earth again, taking years off the life span of the landing gear and my heart.

Tammy and I jumped out, landing on both feet the way

soldiers are taught to do, and scurried out from under the whirl-ing blades and over to two parallel dirt paths divided by a strip of green. Welcome to Route 16.

At last, we had arrived on the legendary Ho Chi Minh Trail, 25 miles behind North Vietnamese lines, surrounded by 10-foot-tall elephant grass and who knows what else. I was scared shitless, my hemorrhoids sucked up around my throat. I was trying to act cool, like I had done this over and over again, but I wondered if that was right—maybe that was a sign that you had never done this before.

We tramped toward the command post, and I got my shoelaces tangled in the brush. Tammy told me to tie them into knots with the shortest loops possible. I didn't know.

At Groupe Mobile (GM) 33 headquarters, radio code name "Golden Panther," I saw a two-inch statue of the sitting Buddha atop a bamboo altar that was surrounded by rice and fruit offerings. A new U.S. M-16 rifle, looking hardly more real than its plastic toy imitation, leaned against the makeshift altar, and I noted the incon-gruity of religion and violence so intertwined. Two radios hanging over a pole made this the center of operations for four irregular Lao battalions. (The CIA owned all of the irregulars in Laos, paying, equipping, resupplying, and commanding them. Up north, they were Meo or other hill tribes and, more recently, Thai volunteers; in the south, they were most likely borrowed from other military regions, which Lao commanders resisted, or more likely they were Thai. I couldn't tell.)

Capt. Bounleut introduced himself as the groupe mobile's operations assistant and welcomed us. He spoke more than pass-able English and proclaimed himself a graduate of the U.S Army English language school in San Antonio, Texas. That explained his twangy accent and his umbrage that night when I asked about a latrine. He misinterpreted my question, "Where do you take a shit?" as "Something, something Texas shit."

Bounleut told how his GM had helicoptered into Ban Phon in

a valley on the northeast edge of the Bolovens Plateau three weeks earlier, on November 21. Ninety-two villagers lived there, just 45 hazardous miles from the South Viet Nam border and 100 miles as the crow flies to Danang and the South China Sea. They might as well have been living on a different planet for all these villagers knew about the outside world.

At the start of the Lao attack, North Vietnamese Army troops in the area scattered northeast and southeast of the town, deeper onto the Ho Chi Minh Trail. In the week that followed, GM 33 fought skirmishes with local Pathet Lao guerrillas and mixed Lao-Vietnamese units but had avoided any heavy action.

During that first week of Operation Thao La, the troops had found a .51 caliber heavy machine gun, an abandoned motor pool, some rice stores, and many well-dug enemy bunkers. They sent the machine gun back to Pakse, burned the rice, and mined the bunkers and parts of a new road the North Vietnamese were building. GM 33 then moved west along Route 16 with the mission of clearing out the areas north and south of the road.

Around their new command post in the middle of the North Vietnamese Thateng supply area, they found much better pickings: Nine Russian-built trucks; an American jeep; 250 gallons of fuel in 50-gallon drums; 32 tons of rice; more than 200 chickens, ducks, and pigs turned loose by the Vietnamese; 81 mm mortar and B-40 rocket rounds; 12 rucksacks; some heavy wire cutters for snipping through concertina wire; and an English compass. They destroyed what they could not send back to Pakse as trophies.

After Bounleut's briefing, we started hiking down Route 16, engulfed on either side by elephant grass and crossing from one rutted track to the other to avoid low-hanging branches. We could not see an inch beyond the first layer of grass, and my imagination placed NVA with their dark green boonie hats and AK-47s just an arm's length away.

There could be landmines planted in brown tracks of the road or booby traps known as Bouncing Betties in the green strip where veteran troops might choose to step. Behind the walls of green on either side of us, NVA or Pathet Lao ambushers could be lurking. Was this march an act of bravery? Did this count as courage?

Our guides, an eight-man patrol, showed no signs of distress or anxiety. Their weapons casually slung over their shoulders, the men strolled along, oblivious to the quiet around them. The patrol leader ambled along, occasionally grinning broadly to himself. Maybe they knew something we didn't, that this was just a set-up for the farang journalists. We could be in Thailand, miles from any danger greater than a traffic accident, for all we knew.

We came to a company outpost, and the CO, long-haired and dressed in blue jeans, disapproved of the size of our patrol. He collected six more men while teenage veterans toyed with their M-23 grenade launchers. All right, I thought. If it was a set-up, it was a very elaborate one. Perhaps we were facing some level of danger.

Properly escorted, we straggled another kilometer down Route 16 to a path—just a thin broken line on the map—that led to Ban Chakom Noi, the home of 19 Kha Nghe hill tribe families. Captain Bounleut pointed out where he had been ambushed on first coming to the village earlier in the week. We looked around, and I found a black arrow—thinner than a pencil, about a foot long with thin slices of aged bamboo as feathers—sticking in a tree stump. The soldiers laughed and said it must have been fired by a bad marksman. To me, it looked more like a booby trap that missed some lucky soldier. I dug the arrow out and showed it to Col. Bounthavy, the GM commander. He gave me a much-used crossbow as a souvenir and took pictures for the CIA of him and me and the crossbow. (And that, I thought, is how you get a CIA file.)

We eventually reached Chakom Noi, and I was happy to stop pounding my feet in my new boots. Sweat dripped off my nose and trickled down both sides of my crotch. I saw no young men in the village, but I suspected they had to be around. Young mothers, their sagging breasts bared, squatted in the center of the village.

Twok, the village chief, told about the Pathet Lao's last visit, only nine days earlier. The PL told the villagers to protect their rice and leave the village to escape the bombing.

But this is home, he said. His villagers had never been bombed before, and when one dies, well.... He let the idea hang. We all got the gist; these people were staying.

Twok said he knew the PL and Vietnamese were near as he pointed around the spots on the compass. Everyone smiled knowingly when we asked him who Ho Chi Minh was.

That night back at GM 33's command post, we dined on warm sticky rice rolled into balls and dipped into meat sauce made from C-rations. For a while, one officer commented, we only had rice, now we have lots of food. To prove it, Captain Bounleut produced some locally grown "muk eua." He translated it as pumpkin, but it tasted like squash. As I sipped sweet black coffee from a tin can, I marveled at his command of English. Despite months of study, I could not think of the Lao words for pumpkin or squash.

In the last dying light of the day, officers sent out small squads to set up ambushes. Bounleut and Major Bounchan, the GM's deputy commander, drew a checkerboard onto a cardboard box with a grease pencil and played a fast game by lantern light.

By seven o'clock, the jungle around us had lost all light. Tammy and I eased past sleeping figures and shallow foxholes to our poncho-covered grass beds. Our flashlights, dimmed with strips of toilet paper, lit the way. We wrapped ourselves in nylon parachutes and shivered the night away in the cold high plateau air.

Staccato rifle fire and the pop of hand grenades roused us around 5:00 a.m. as the first gray streaks of light appeared through the treetops. We were under attack! I made love to the ground, and GM commander Col. Bounthavy, code-named "Black Bear," which he resembled in more than one way, got on the radio demanding news.

Bounleut used the second radio to report a TIC (team in contact with the enemy) to the Air Operations Center in Pakse and requested air support. The threatening noises died long before a tiny single-engine aircraft began making lazy circles above us.

An American voice squawked over the green radio: "We just had a TIC down south, and you called us away for just a small ambush. We had a bunch of bad guys reported in the open down south there, and you call us away for an ambush. Use your head now and…" Angry over being called away from a heavier engagement to answer a false alarm, the American FAC (forward air controller) turned his little plane and buzzed back toward the south.

The camp commander pulled on his socks and ordered his aide to report the casualties from the ambush: One wounded. Not serious.

Get a medivac and get him out of here, the commander added.

We rose from our shallow foxholes and stomped around the camp, trying to restore circulation to stiff limbs and warm up. During breakfast—cold sticky rice with sauce made from C-rations—the commander of the 309th Irregular Battalion plowed into the command post in one of the captured Molotova trucks. It was one of his men who had been hit in the brief engagement.

Did the journalists want to visit the scene?

We did.

He ordered us to climb into the back of the six-wheeled heavy truck. This did not strike me as a good idea. I could only imagine bad things involving loud noises and flowing blood resulting from riding in a loud, open, unarmored truck down the Ho Chi Minh Trail.

The road from GM 33 headquarters to the 309th main camp was rough but adequate for bouncing along at 20 km per hour, with human cargo tossing from side to side among captured fuel drums and spare parts. Green-clad figures stepped out of the jungle to stare as the growling machine ground in and out of shell holes on the trail. Every one, I was certain, was a lucky North Vietnamese or Pathet Lao soldier about to bag a regimental commander and two farang journalists and liberate a precious gift of the Soviet people.

Was taking this trip courage? Foolishness? It was certainly unwise, and I felt more than a little stupid. But the battalion commander seemed to think it was all right; his grinning troops obviously thought nothing of it. Buckle didn't seem happy, I was glad to see. But were we—was I—demonstrating bravery by joyriding through jungle the NVA had occupied just days before? Are you being brave when you do something stupid just because others are doing it? Is that what happens in war? Soldiers face danger because others are? I debated in silence, warily eyeing what little I could see from the bouncing truck.

Ban Thounla, described as "the center of the Thateng supply area," consisted of seven houses overgrown with vines. Five other trucks and one recaptured U.S. Willys jeep sat on a slope the size of a football field that also served as a helicopter landing pad. Empty Spam and sardine cans and bunkers half-filled with loose dirt confirmed the recent presence of Lao government troops. Farther on in rolling rice fields, heaps of gray, smoldering rice lay under ruins of burned-out thatch huts. To the east near the tree line, Lao soldiers camouflaged with branches sat in ambush among the pepper plants. It was here that the grenade hit the wounded man now lying back in camp.

Here we learned the details of the engagement.

As the first rays of dawn crept over the forest, two Pathet Lao guerrillas stumbled into an ambush at the edge of a rice field. The government soldiers shot first, killing one Pathet Lao, but the second threw a grenade and ran. The grenade landed behind the victim, spattering him with shrapnel. His friends carried him on a bamboo litter back to battalion headquarters after dawn.

His companions stripped off his bloody uniform, leaving him in a pair of red-and-black swim trunks, the kind most Lao soldiers wear for bathing. A young medic wrapped gauze around his wounds. Members of the patrol that brought him in squatted around bowls of fish sauce, dipping balls of cold sticky rice. After their meal, they strolled back to their ambush in the woods.

The sun cartwheeled above the trees higher into the sky, and still no medivac arrived. Flies buzzed around the black clusters of dried blood; the medic swatted them viciously. Beads of sweat gathered on the wounded soldier's forehead, and he shivered under the soft tread of a black ant on his thigh. Throughout the afternoon, birds and animals in the forest around him kept silent in the muggy heat and in the presence of the soldiers.

We three—Buckle, the wounded soldier, and I—waited and waited for the chopper. At 2:30, more than eight hours after the ambush, the radio promised a helicopter would be there soon. An NVA attack on Paksong south of us was producing heavy casualties, and the choppers were evacuating the wounded there first.

At last, around four o'clock, after more insistent calls for medivac, a Lao CH-34 helicopter throbbed onto the dirt landing pad, tossing broken branches, leaves, and dust into the air. The wounded man closed his eyes and gritted his teeth.

Stretcher bearers, his companions, handed him gingerly into the helicopter, and a companion climbed in beside him. Buckle and I climbed in last, stepping over the wounded man on the floor, and plopped into the seat netting. More soldiers came running as the engine revved, carrying war booty that they tossed haphazardly into the cargo bay, jamming the chopper's starboard door open.

The pilot gunned the engine, filling the cargo bay with more dirt and leaves, and the chopper slowly lifted and started moving forward. We circled the field and set down again. The pilot didn't have enough power to clear the trees. We were sitting ducks for any Pathet Lao or North Vietnamese mortar. The evidence that they were around lay wounded at my feet. The longer we stayed on the ground, the more vulnerable we became.

Was this courage? Is that what it is, submitting your safety to the skills and efforts of another? It reminded me all too much of just plain stupidity, but there was nothing I could do. I had no other option.

Again the chopper lifted, lurched forward higher and higher and finally cleared the trees. We flew at treetop level to GM 33 headquarters to pick up more spoils of war. Running soldiers anxious to get off the landing zone lest an enemy with rockets be nearby hurled loads of captured wire cutters and rifles into the chopper, and a basket bashed the wounded man in the head. The pilot didn't linger and made it out of the landing zone on his first attempt, rising in slow circles to 5,000 feet.

Air that had been hot and muggy quickly turned cold, and I was glad to be wearing my correspondent's jacket. The seminaked wounded man at my feet shivered—whether from fear, cold or pain, I couldn't tell—and his companion clutched his stomach as the throbbing machine rose higher and higher. Tammy pulled his extra coat out of his duffel and placed it over the wounded man.

With the sun starting to set through the jammed cargo bay door, our machine flew slowly south for a half-hour to beleaguered Paksong, a Royal Lao Government town in the middle of the Bolovens Plateau. The Lao chopper jocks up front, seeming oblivious to the wounded man's condition, circled to watch three propeller-driven T-28s drop their bombs.

One after the other, the stubby aircraft rushed forward, rolled onto their sides and swooped to the earth, pulling away just before crashing, and dropping canisters of napalm that burst open and ignited a broad orange path along the green earth. As the second T-28 slammed its canister to the ground with a whump, the wounded soldier quivered, then relaxed and lay silent, his eyes half open. His companion tapped his cheek; no response. He lifted the man's eyelids; eyes stared blankly back. He kneaded the soldier's stomach; there was no shiver, no pain.

When the T-28s dropped their last bomb, the chopper turned toward Pakse, bobbing up and down through the dimly lit sky, following a brown track of road below. A convoy passed below; we circled and rattled on. Finally, the airstrip on the north side of the Xe Don River came into view and we dropped like an elevator without brakes. The chopper jolted hard onto the runway and sped toward the tarmac, its wheels squealing as we made a too-sharp turn. I envisioned myself dying after being tipped out of a helicopter as it raced along the ground.

We finally stopped far from any buildings or other aircraft, and Arbuckle and I climbed down. Buckle said it was the worst helicopter ride he had ever had, and he had played soldier many times before. I swore it would be my last.

The pilot and co-pilot, laughing at some private joke or their own escape from a humiliating ground accident, joined us at the cargo door. Told that the soldier had died, they grinned and shifted away; I had seen other Lao do this in embarrassing situations.

Buckle and I stared at one another and at the frightened Lao soldier still crouching over his dead companion. There were no medics, no ambulance to meet us, so maybe it was all for the best.

I was no stranger to death. I had met it before. I had visited my aged grandfather as he lay dying in the living room of my aunt's home. One of my co-op jobs at Antioch had taken me to Boston's Peter Bent Brigham Hospital, where I hauled dead patients, including one beautiful girl my age, to the cold morgue. It was no big deal, just a part of life. That's what I thought.

Not long after my trip to Pakse, I was invited to a wedding reception for Frank Albert, a U.S. Embassy official I liked. I made a stunning ass of myself, getting completely drunk on champagne and confronting U.S. Ambassador G. McMurtrie Godley, calling him a killer.

After I left Laos, Ronk, a witness to my behavior, got most of the details right in a story he wrote for the Bangkok Post.

David, one of those who went to Ban Houei Pamone in the turtle, got drunk the night he came back from another trip, to southern Laos, to attend a wedding reception for an embassy official in Vientiane. Very drunk.

For three hours he pulled on gin and tonics while the celebrants whirled about him clinking champagne glasses. And for three hours he told in at least one hundred ways about the Laotian soldier he watched die on the floorboards of the helicopter outside Pakse.

He talked about the blood. About the breathing. About the innards that kept creeping around the swath of bandages. About eyes that couldn't stay in focus but that he was sure kept trying to seek his.

And the boy died on the floorboards.

"Christ," David kept repeating through the din. "I've never seen a man die before."

And he kept asking celebrants if they had ever seen a man die. When each said he had, David would qualify his question with the shrewdness of a drunk and describe how the boy had died on the floorboards.

"Have you ever seen a man die like that?" he would ask.

David was not popular at the party. Mostly he bored people and mostly because he kept drunkenly repeating the same story and questions well beyond the point that these older, more experienced observers of war could empathize with his trauma, telling themselves, "That's the way it was for me, too, once.

He out-talked the sensitivity factor.

David was anti-war when he came to Laos; he was anti-war when he left Laos after a year, six months after he saw his first war casualty die, "almost in my lap," as he kept telling celebrants. He never spoke again about his helicopter ride to Pakse nor any other dying he saw, not because he had become inured to the dying, but because it had become part of his reality and the reality of Laos.

Then I understood my father's silent dark moods and occasional bouts of heavy drinking. For two years in World War II, he had witnessed deaths like the one I had just seen, but he had done it every day, day in and day out. He had been a medic, an ambulance driver, sergeant of a medical transportation platoon, and the medical liaison for his regiment. I realized I could never match his courage. I had tried, but I would have to learn to live with my own meager supply.

Chapter 22

Second Great Press Offensive, 1972

December 1971–January 1972

Seldom in world history has such a large and varied company meddled in the lives of so few.

Joel Martin Halpern, *Economy and Society of Laos,* 1964

I was ready for some boring normalcy after the trip south. Christmas was coming, and I had two invitations to dinner. Buckle handed off an assignment to me from the *New York Times* that promised a $100 payment. *New York Times*! One hundred bucks! Things were finally falling into place.

I wrote an ode to joy to my older sister, Bonnie:

Christmas seems to be upon us. I returned to Vientiane yesterday to find that Habeeb, my favorite Indian merchant, had completely changed his stock for the season. All manners of tinselly articles were draped over the door and ceiling, and, he informed me, half of the stock had been sold already. Good old Habeeb doesn't miss a trick.

We don't have a Christmas tree trimming party here, but Tammy Arbuckle of the Washington Star *tells me that Soupy, his Thai wife, is preparing a little get-together for the gang, i.e., Don Ronk and me. It should be fun.*

Soupy is typically Thai-Lao and can't stand to see an empty glass or a rested mouth. I went up to their apartment a few weeks ago to collect a duffel bag for my trip and ended up staying for dinner and three large glasses of gin—straight without ice, of course. When I finally managed to stagger out, I had completely forgotten why I had stopped in.

Then I embarrassed myself at Frank Albert's wedding. That was all my fault. I couldn't turn back the clock. I was prepared—after a few days to sober up—for any ribbing coming my way.

The North Vietnamese spared me that humiliation, however. They roared over the Plain of Jars and headed straight for Vang Pao's headquarters at Long Cheng while I was still hung over. The Official Americans had a full-blown crisis on their hands two months earlier than usual.

In the south, Saravane and Thateng fell to the North Vietnamese. The Royal Lao Army irregulars abandoned Saravane while Tammy and I were in the neighborhood trying to get out onto the Bolovens. A lot of Official Americans and Lao knew about it and failed to mention it to us. I stopped beating myself up over my behavior; there was worse behavior going on everywhere.

In Vientiane, I almost felt sorry for the Embassy's Polish-American briefer, Andy Guzowski. For three days in a row he had nothing but horrible news to report. Artillery bases on the ridge lines separating the NVA and Long Cheng's mixed bag of defenders—Panther, King Kong, Sting Ray, and Cobra—fell one after another. NVA antiaircraft fire prevented propeller-driven planes from flying anywhere nearby and took down three U.S. F-4 fighter-bombers and two T-28s in one day, the heaviest loss of aircraft since the 1967 offensive against Long Cheng.

Four days before Christmas, Guzowski reported that the

northwest anchor of the defensive line around Long Cheng had collapsed. The North Vietnamese were tightening their grip.

From my recent excursion, I had a small sense of what it might be like up north, but in Vientiane, the holiday spirit held sway even though most of the inhabitants did not celebrate Christmas.

I looked into my crystal ball and predicted the future of Laos:

1972 will be a year of decision, not the decisive year, but rather the year that paves the way for the ending. Continued government losses in MRs I, II & IV should be expected. LP [Luang Prabang] will again be attacked, but again not taken. In MR II, the J [Plain of Jars] and Long Cheng will be completely lost forever. The Meo may fight back one more time, but I have serious doubts about it. Farther south in MR IV, the entire Bolovens will go; Pakse will again be threatened. Arbuckle feels that 1973 will be the decisive year. I am inclined to go along with that.[10]

There was no briefing on Christmas Day, although the fighting raged. Ronk and I waged our own battle with good cheer and our friends' generosity, first at a turkey dinner with Jerry and Gretchen Doolittle and their five boys and then at Soupy and Tammy's.

I shared the sordid details with my parents:

Don and I, being the only bachelors in the press corps, were invited up to Tammy Arbuckle's house for snacks and drinks. I should have known better than to eat so much before Tammy's, and in fact I did know better but the temptation was too much for me, because we had another full course meal there. First, cheese and potato-onion

---

10 Buckle and I were correct. The Official Americans permitted the Royal Lao Government to sign a ceasefire agreement with the Pathet Lao in February 1973. The agreement gave the PL a significant voice in the government, leading to the communists' complete takeover in December 1975.

soup. (I was ready to throw up by this time, but tactfully didn't.) Then Soupy, Tammy's wife, brought in the "snacks." Snacks, my foot. The tray was as big as your silver turkey tray. On it was piled a huge mound of duck, chicken, steak and liver. Naturally, we had to eat some of each. And not just a little. Two helpings of each meat, plus the fried potatoes.

We also had three kinds of punch (which really packed a wallop). The punches were color-coded. Red had about 50% gin in it. Orange, 75%, and the green stuff was, or must have been, gin spiked with peppermint schnapps. Side dishes included popcorn, home-roasted nuts, cookies of many kinds and other things that I ate but have happily forgotten.

By the time we staggered out of there (after a toast to Soupy with straight gin,) I felt dead. It must have been 1:30 or 2 o'clock, so I went to bed and slept like a stuffed toad, which is what I felt like.

The next day I didn't eat anything. Tammy had Don and me back for leftovers, which we barely managed to dent, let alone finish. And that was Christmas.... I was really happy to go back to eating plain old noodles.

Several days after Christmas, we got word that the North Vietnamese had recaptured Paksong in the heart of the Bolovens Plateau. The NVA reversed in a matter of weeks all of the Royal Lao Government gains in the south over the previous six months, in large part because the Royal Lao Army had to send troops north to save Long Cheng.

As my first full year in Laos ended, I let my excitement turn morbid in a letter to an old high school friend:

Things are hopping over here. My decision to remain in Laos was a good one.

North Vietnamese and Pathet Lao troops have stormed out of the north overrunning the Plain of Jars, 103 miles northeast of here, and threatening to do the same in Long Cheng, the CIA headquarters in Laos. All of this two months earlier than usual. It looks as though the war in northern Laos is in its final stages. When Long Cheng falls, the Meo army will disintegrate, disband and head for the hills. This has been the goal of the Vietnamese ever since the army was organized in 1960 under the CIA.

The fighting in southern Laos, which I visited for two weeks early this month, continues, but the game there is also just about over.

1972 will see many changes and 1973 should see the Pathet Lao back in the government, probably in a very strong, but not dominant, position.

My feelings about this sudden turn of events are mixed. The present government could use a good shaking up. The Pathet Lao deserve a place in the government, but I have no idea how it will affect the villagers.

I had mixed emotions about a lot of things, especially my ability to make a living by writing or reporting or whatever it was I was trying to do.

Carl told me that his boss at AP, Dick Pyle, had offered him a job on contract in Phnom Penh, Cambodia, where the war was very hot, and reporters had freer rein to do their job. If he took it, he said, AP would pick me up as its stringer in Laos.

At the same time, three reject slips arrived one after another.

As 1972 started, I mailed off my economics year in review piece to the *New York Times*, already cashing the $100 check in my mind. Job opportunities popped up and burst like bubbles.

"*I was told about an hour ago that I may be offered a job as director of the Lao-American Association in Luang Prabang, the royal capital, in a few days. It pays $7,000.00 plus a year. I may [be] ridiculous enough to take it,*" I wrote to my friend Liz.

Seven thousand dollars a year was a fortune in Laos, even if it required working for Official America. It seemed unlikely, however, that the U.S. Embassy would hire a long-haired (in its view) free spirit from radical Antioch College who did not have a college degree and who hung out with the nagging press. Oh, and one who called the ambassador a killer to his face.

Someone started an English-language news sheet called the *Vientiane News* and was looking for an editor. I didn't get that job either.

In a deep funk, I wrote to two Antioch friends, who were studying abroad in France:

It is to an unexpected fit of depression that you owe this letter.... One of those traumatic and infrequent periods where major decisions are taken.

I am referring, of course, to the receipt of six rejection slips in a two-day period.... I have been invited to continue sending material to these people but their definitions of what they want are out of this world: "Insights that only a person living in a country can offer." That came after explaining why articles about Asian beggars, two "cai" (heroin) addicts, and the effects of the recent 20% devaluation [don't meet this criterion]. I am not sure they know what they want, but I am sure they will let me know IF they see it... ten years from now or so.

The rejections put me off writing for two days. I am just getting around to beginning again. I have articles pending with the Far Eastern Economic Review *and the* New York Times. *NANA, a news feature service, also has one of my pieces. For the sake of my bloody sanity, I hope someone picks up an article soon.*

Once again, the North Vietnamese saved my ashes from the fire. On New Year's Eve, their artillery shells struck Long Cheng valley. The Great Press Offensive of 1972 landed almost as soon as those shells.

This time I was ready. I would provide no free briefings, no ego-driven demonstration of how much more I knew about Laos than they did (or cared to know). I had learned my lesson, and I would be selling my knowledge dearly: Minimum fee, a meal at the restaurant of my choosing. I loved the Chinese Noodle, but I was getting tired of lo mein.

On January 8, Drew Pearson of ABC News hired me as a guide-consultant for $40 a day plus any meals I ate with him. Short-term, I didn't care if I ever sold an article. Consulting and guiding was easy compared with sweating blood over a typewriter. And there was no danger involved—the outside press corps couldn't get to the fighting any more than we could.

Word came on the 10th that the NVA had occupied Sam Thong, the huge USAID refugee center one mountain range from Long Cheng. I had taken to reading the Foreign Broadcast Information Service daily bulletins at USIS. The Pathet Lao radio claimed on the 12th that its forces had captured Long Cheng; Andy Guzowski gleefully noted that Vang Pao and his troops, while under heavy attack, still held the CIA base. This time he turned out to be correct.

After a week of not being able to see any action, Pearson and his crew flew back to Saigon, leaving me $200 richer and Long Cheng still besieged.

I wrote my parents an awkward letter that I intended to be reassuring:

No bad news this letter. But some good. I just completed five days of work for ABC News which brought in $200....

The war seems to be quieting down now after two weeks of very serious fighting up north and down south. There is undoubtedly more to come. I shall be watching it from the sidelines.

The addition to my cash flow would enable me to remain in Laos through March. I had been down pretty low before the press offensive, but as Ronk said, just when you hit bottom, something brings in money.

The cash infusion cheered me but did not keep me from writing to the editor of the *Bangkok Post* asking for Irwin Block's old job. I offered Arbuckle and Ronk as references; Jack Foisie of the *Los Angeles Times* hand-delivered the letter. I hoped those three names would carry some heft, which I clearly lacked, not having any clippings to send along.

If I had waited a few days, I could have included a published piece. Opening the January 22 issue of the *Far East Economic Review*, I found a piece by David Haase under a three-column wide headline that read, "Long Cheng: From Bastion to Forward Base." It was my first paid article—I was a writer!

I wrote my parents with the good news and, as usual, probably caused more heartburn than joy.

There is really quite a bit to write about in Laos, but for one reason or another, the big newspapers and the television networks never seem to make it here. The year looks as if it might be the decisive year in Indochina. Fighting will undoubtedly continue for years to come, but the

North Vietnamese and pro-Communist Pathet Lao and Khmer Rouge are gaining the upper hand. If they continue their offensive, as expected, they may have control of 75% of Laos by June. That would be a clear signal for the Royal Lao Government and the U.S. to begin negotiating.

It is an especially good time to be here. History in the making, and so on....

There is also the possibility of just continuing to write for a living. I like writing even though I find it quite difficult now. It really knocks the shit out of me, but when I finally finish a piece I feel absolutely great. And in writing, I am my own boss; at least now I am....

I am just undecided about what to do. I don't want to return to the States until I have some firm plans about what to do there. If I wander back, I know I will only return to Asia and do nothing. So...

By September, things should be sorting themselves out.

Given my new bona fide status as a published reporter, I paid even closer attention to the war between the Official Americans and the press. At the end of January, I wrote a long update on the latest battle. I thought it illuminated both sides, but neither in a good light:

We are in the midst of a very interesting controversy: Has the U.S. Embassy "opened up" its activities in Laos, or is secrecy still the byword? The question was opened two weeks ago on January 19 when the U.S. allowed 14 journalists... accompanied by [CIA Station Chief] Hugh Tovar to go to Long Cheng. Each person was required to pay a portion of the cost, which came to $252.06 per person.

Three ground rules prevailed: (1) No pictures of Americans; (2) no American names could be used; and (3) no direct mention of the CIA involvement at Long Cheng was permitted. The third ground rule was opposed by some locals, but most gave way in the end.

Originally the plan was to take only ten people up. Ton That Ky, the U.S. Embassy's favorite journalist here because of his unwavering support of the U.S. position, was personally invited at the last minute (3:30 p.m.) by press attaché Andrew Guzowski to attend the 4:00 p.m. (1/18) backgrounder. Don Ronk of the Washington Post *and Max Coiffait were not invited at all; nor were VOA or G. Nickerson [freelancer for ABC News].*

(The Japanese were left out completely as was a 3-man German TV crew; they both got a free trip up to LC a few days later provided by Minister of Defense Sisouk na Champassak.)

Ronk and Coiffait shouted their protests to Guzowski and then to Norm Barnes, director of USIS, who "found" seats for all. Ronk refused the invitation on principle and was supported by the Post.

Now special permission is required to go to Ban Son [LS 272], which was once the showcase of U.S. involvement in Laos. Nam Yu is also closed.

Space-available on US planes is also out. Chartering is in.

A second trip to LC is planned for Wednesday, February 2. The press will choose its people, not USIS. The U.S. is also offering, or hinting at least, that other places may be visited on Wednesday. Bouam Long is the most likely. The trip is charter and will, of course, cost whoever goes on it.

The charter basis effectively cuts down travel possibility because freelancers don't have the money and even the richest companies are not anxious to pay a few hundred dollars for every story they receive.

As Max Coiffait would say, "Plus ça change, plus c'est la même chose." The more things changed, the more they stayed the same.

Chapter 23
Déjà Vu All Over Again
FEBRUARY 1972

Long Cheng became our Dien Bien Phu.

Dick Johnson, 1970s CIA unit chief at Long Cheng
September 1993

FEBRUARY REWOUND THE tape and replayed January.
The North Vietnamese Army kept its death grip on Long
Cheng despite intense American B-52 bombing and an influx of
Royal Lao Army irregulars from other military regions and Thai
"volunteers" to back up Vang Pao's diminishing forces. I sent off
more freelance articles and got back reject slips to add to my growing collection. A new contingent of out-of-town newsmen arrived
for the second U.S. Embassy dog-and-pony show at Long Cheng.
And the Official Americans played new games that did nothing to boost their credibility or reduce the press corps' skepticism
and contempt.

Writing to Liz, I vacillated over a career in journalism.

*Am I thinking of being a war correspondent? I have
thought about it but have decided against it. I am a coward and don't want to get shot at (or up). Your worries are
groundless. I take very good care of myself.*

A few days later, I reported to my sister Bonnie: *"A few more rejection slips have come in. I think I will start a collection. (I don't seem to have any other choice.)"*
I wrote two and a half pages about the NVA offensive that I called "On the Move in Laos." I filled three and a half pages on "Long Cheng," a pretty mean feat since I had never been there.
In another story, I tried to demonstrate the impact of the war on the Laotian people. I added up the casualties—killed, wounded and missing in action—and divided them by the official population of Laos to determine a casualty rate. I then multiplied the U.S. population by that rate and found staggering numbers: In just four months, the U.S. would have suffered 99,200 men killed in combat, 290,400 wounded in action, and 32,000 captured or missing, if it suffered casualties at the same rate as the Lao.

The majority of government casualties are recorded not in large battles, I wrote, but in small encounters.

Clashes involving no more than 20 men kill and wound several soldiers daily. Few roads or trails are safe from ambushers who claim a victim or two before scurrying off.

Each day mines and booby traps blow away lives and limbs. And because few Laotian units keep maps of the minefields they lay, government as well as Pathet Lao and North Vietnamese troops repeatedly fall into their own traps.

During an average day recently, the Laotian Ministry of Defense reported that eight government troops were killed, 26 wounded and two were missing in nine clashes, eleven shellings and one mine incident. The tally at the end of the week was 46 killed, 140 wounded and two missing.

Years later, a historian quoted Hugh Tovar saying that a comparison of casualty rates and population figures would reveal "a proportionate… loss of life in the war in Laos vastly greater than that which the United States has suffered in the Indochina war." Tovar did not cite his source, but I was willing to bet that my story was the inspiration. With Laos and the CIA, however, you never knew.

On the first of the month, I heard back from *Bangkok Post* editor Bob Boys about my offer to replace Irwin Block: Thanks, but no thanks. The *New York Times* sent a check for $50 instead of the $100 I had counted on. And I wrote to friends studying in France, *"Some idiot beat me to the Vientiane News job by a few days. Such is life."*

That evening, a bit of good news arrived in the form of Bob Werner of ABC News; I had attended the correspondents' background briefing for the second Long Cheng trip and briefed Bob. He hired me for $40 a day.

As usual, laying out the ground rules for the trip had not gone smoothly. *"Andy [Guzowski] wanted the rules themselves to be put 'off the record',"* I told my journal. *"Carl and Tammy refused, and Andy let the matter drop. The rules, however, are probably to be considered on deep background."*

Background, deep background, off the record. They were part of the game reporters and government sources played throughout Indochina.

In the government and military, information is tightly held, although many, many people may know it. Certain officials are designated as spokesmen, and theoretically only they are authorized to speak with the press. Anyone else having contact with reporters risked unpleasant consequences if their actions become known. Over the years, a system of confidentiality ratings evolved that allowed reporters and sources to negotiate the transparency of their discussions.

The three levels, from most transparent to least transparent, were background, deep background, and off the record. On background, a reporter could describe the source but not use his name. For example, a reporter might attribute news of a skirmish to "an American embassy official." Deep background allowed the reporter to use the same information but limited his description of the source to something like "an official in the know." Off the record meant the source could not be identified in any way, and the information could only be used to guide further reporting.

It's all very silly, but the system persists because it allows reporters as well as sources to avoid responsibility for their actions.

U.S. Embassy spokesman Andy Guzowski laid down two rules for the second Long Cheng trip:

(1) U.S. personnel supporting and advising irregular units may not be filmed, photographed or otherwise identified by name or function.

(2) When in operational zones, newsmen must observe normal military security rules as determined by the local Lao commanders.

Andy wanted the rules themselves to be put "off the record." That essentially would have removed the Official Americans from any involvement in the trip, as least as far as the public would know. In short, the embassy did not want reporters to disclose that the rules even existed, while the reporters wanted to be able to cite the rules to explain why the descriptions of what they saw were so vague.

Carl and Tammy refused, and Andy let the matter drop.

This source-reporter rulemaking reached a level of absurdity on February 6 when Ronk, Tammy, and I learned that Vang Pao had launched another assault on the Plain of Jars, hoping to disrupt the flow of supplies to North Vietnamese troops and distract them from their campaign against Long Cheng. The embassy embargoed the story, meaning we could not report it until Guzowski released the information. An embargo is like postdating a check: The giver promises to pay but at a time he determines; the receiver accepts it, knowing that he cannot use it until the giver says.

Official Americans used embargoes throughout the Indochina war, especially in Viet Nam. Used sparingly and with a specific, short lead time, an embargo could give reporters notice of a story and time to gather resources to cover it. Too often, however, officials plastered an embargo on a story to wear down its news value. There is nothing staler than news that happened last week.

Guzowski's embargo of the Plain of Jars campaign was an example of the latter. There were no security reasons for it; once Vang Pao attacked, the North Vietnamese knew about it. I was told the embargo was intended to avoid embarrassing Richard Nixon, who was planning the first presidential visit to communist China later in the month. Everyone knew about it but the American people.

Eight days later, the embargo still held. We argued with Andy, who was a decent man in a horrible situation.

Don't you think the North Vietnamese know what's going on by now? we demanded.

Guzowski did the only thing he could: He took a deep breath, sighed, and declared: The embargo holds.

I noticed that the Official Americans were unusually jumpy; I attributed it to Tet, the days-long Vietnamese New Year celebration that was about to start. They probably feared a repeat of the massive 1968 Tet offensive throughout South Viet Nam, which despite its failure caused the American public to rethink its support for the war and contributed to Nixon's election as president.

"*Tet begins tomorrow,*" I noted in my journal. "*U.S. officials are still expecting a big push. This is more than possible but I rather feel that they will wait until everyone's guard is down, say late in Nixon's China trip.*"

In mid-February, 11 days into the embargo, Andy and I had words, as I recorded in my journal:

> *Guzowski appears to be covering up something. He said yesterday that radio silence was still being kept. He also said that all but one element was poised to strike and that action would certainly come in the evening (last evening). I asked him how he knew this if radio silence was being kept, and he said that "command officers" had been in and out a few times in low-flying helicopters since they began their long march.*
>
> *Max reported today that he knew of 17 Thai battalions at Long Cheng. Apparently they have replaced the regular Lao troops who are on this [Plain of Jars] offensive. Buckle and Ronk are getting restless, especially T.A.; Max Coiffait (AFP) is asking all the right questions.*
>
> *A Thai reporter from the* Bangkok Post *is snooping around the Wattay bars and has written about the offensive.*

The embargo expired the following night, just shy of two weeks of life. I added more insights to my journal:

> *I later learned that when [USIS Director] Norm Barnes phoned [Lao Defense Minister] Sisouk to ask if T.A. and I could go up to the PdJ, Sisouk blew up about us even knowing about it. Barnes very prudently did not ask the question. (USIS apparently was considering sending T.A. and myself—as a pool reporter—to the PdJ).*
>
> *The military embargo was lifted but USIS then wanted to impose a political embargo so that [Prime Minister Souvanna Phouma] would not be embarrassed by an*

offensive while Nixon is in China. No one was willing to go with it though.

As February ended, I wrote my last entry about Vang Pao's guerrilla campaign against the Plain of Jars. *"[It] is turning out to be something of a farce. [Arbuckle] returning from there on Friday told me last evening that the friendly troops are NOT moving around, nor have they crossed Route 4, as [ARMA Col. Bob] Mahan and Guzowski were saying. They are instead sitting in fixed positions."*

I made a little money off the offensive, but not as much as I had hoped. Werner only needed me for a day and a half, $60 worth of time. My continuing connection with ABC paid a dividend in credibility with Official Americans. They could not ignore me as easily as they had in the past, and they had apparently gotten over the notion that I was a sensationalist. Witness that they had considered sending me to the PdJ as a pool reporter.

The offensive also gave me another opportunity to try: Radio.

With Vang Pao's offensive finally out in the open, my career advisers at the Constellation told me I should try to write some 30-second radio scripts and offer them to ABC News. I wrote the first draft, got shot down, and wrote another. Ronk and Tom Jagninski, a new freelancer in town, rewrote them and I rehearsed them for timing in front of the guys. This was kindergarten show-and-tell at its worst. Lower your voice. Speak slower. Talk faster. At the rate I was going, the war would be over before I got the story and delivery right.

When the guys thought I had done the best I could, I asked Ba Tan, the Constellation bartender, to dial a phone line to Saigon for me. This whole effort was on spec, and I was paying for the call. I saw the meter running and hoped against hope for a quick, strong phone connection.

I summarized the experience in a note to Bonnie:

I did three radio news spots for ABC News last night, but our telephone line to Saigon was cut off. By the time we got it back, they had already transmitted their material to New York. It was a test run anyway so not much damage done. Those 30-second blurbs—This is Dave Haase, ABC News, Vientiane, Laos—are not as easy as they sound. I can't think of anything that can be said in 30 seconds that means anything.

I added a note in my journal as well.

[ABC News Saigon bureau chief] Kevin Delaney said they were too late and [he] would have only used one in any case. He said they were too documentary, need more attribution, want "time" phrases, but had good content. He is going to query New York about establishing a relationship.

The whole experience—my complete ignorance, the friendly unrelenting public criticism, my reliance on others to do my work, the awkward rehearsals in front of my buddies, the expensive and unsuccessful battle with the telephone and Kevin's informative rejection—left me feeling like a phony and pissed. Then I met Gloria Emerson of the *New York Times* and went ballistic.

I had crossed paths with Gloria in Saigon. She answered the phone at the *Times* bureau when I called to tell them I was being kicked out of the country and could not accept their job offer. She interrogated me for a moment and promised to get back with me. She never called back, and I got kicked out. I understood the two events were unconnected, but I still felt jilted.

In Vientiane, she tried to pick my brain for free, but she had missed that boat. I charged for my knowledge, and she wasn't paying. Then she insulted my colleagues and me, calling the local press corps "the worst except for Ethiopia's." I didn't know a thing about

Ethiopia or its resident press corps, but I found her comparison to be insufferably arrogant. It inflated her ego for having been to Ethiopia while it diminished our skills.

I thought of all kinds of excuses for how we reported the war in a climate of total secrecy and without the coddling from the U.S. military that the Saigon press corps, herself included, got. But I was still offended and tried to write a scathing report of my experience with one of the war's truly ballsy correspondents:

> *Gloria Emerson and her lackey, Nancy, arrived in Vientiane yesterday. I met them this morning at the Lane Xang Hotel. She is a very haughty, annoying person.... [She said] the best man here is Ton That Ky. She adores French food and, in my opinion, is looking for a social elite to replace the French. She is, of course, among that number, but very few others, I doubt, are up to Gloria's par.*

Her evaluation of Ky was pure B.S., but my feelings toward Gloria and Ky simply proved I could be arrogant and annoying, too.

Thanks to the U.S. Embassy's embargo of the biggest story of the month and nothing else to write about, I fell back into academic mode. I had found a genealogy of the Luang Prabang vice regal family, starting with its founder, Chao Maha Oupahat Oun Keo. It was 73 pages long—in Lao. I got out my Lao-English dictionary and started plowing through it, recording the details of one illustrious royal Lao after another. By the end of the month I was able to report to my parents that I had distilled the history to a list of names, dates, and relationships that filled both sides of nineteen legal pages.

> *I translated the important sections and then organized the family's genealogy, or family tree. It is a large family*

spanning six generations with over 400 members. My head
was swimming a few times with all the intermarriage. But
that is finished now and I have put it away.

Then I heard from my Antioch mentor, Dan Grady, who proposed yet another crazy scheme: I should return to the States and
attend graduate school on a fellowship. Hah. I almost laughed at
the thought. I had three years of college behind me, and one of
those years had not been evaluated or graded. Of course I should go
to grad school!

I laughed, but I didn't dismiss the thought. This was Grady.
He never suggested the impossible, and he never let a student run
alone. Besides, I was always up for a Grady challenge. It got me
thinking that maybe it was time to leave Laos.

I was not the only one wondering if the party was coming to
an end. Ronk, who hadn't traveled outside Vientiane except for the
rare R&R excursion to Bangkok, talked more and more often about
how boring Laos had become. Arbuckle, with an eye on his future,
was angling for a position with the *Star* in Washington. Carl was
having trouble with his wife and was looking for a way out.

This might be the time, I thought, but I still had one or two
misadventures to endure.

Chapter 24
Down Dangerous Roads
MARCH 1972

There never was any danger, only inconvenience and a sudden change of plans.

Letter home, October 6, 1970

NOTHING IS AS exhilarating—or as scary—as racing down a dirt road in Laos with no other traffic on it. Exhilarating because you can speed as fast as you want and not run into anyone, and scary because when there is no one to run into, there's a reason, and it's never good. When you see no trucks or buses ahead of or behind you, a smart person wonders where everyone has gone. What do they know that you don't? Why are you here alone? What if something happens and no one comes to help? Road travel tightens the sphincter muscles.

Route 13, the closest thing Laos had to a national road, ran from Luang Prabang in the far north down to Vientiane, and from there south along the Mekong to Pakse and into Cambodia. The Lao blacktopped a few short stretches but relied primarily on the native rusty red rock and soil known as laterite to create a hard surface. The only way out of Vientiane was Route 13 and its diet of dust—that was part of the road experience.

The longer I stayed in Laos, the more I longed to venture out of Vientiane. This was especially true after my trip south. I didn't count my foolhardy ride on a few miles of the Ho Chi Minh Trail as a test of road travel in Laos. During the second press offensive, Bruce Dunning and a CBS TV crew flew to Vang Vieng looking for a story about refugees. I went along.

East of Vang Vieng, North Vietnamese troops held Sam Thong, the huge USAID refugee center linked to Long Cheng, and threatened the backup base at Ban Son. Old men, women, and children fled out of the mountains toward Route 13 to escape the fighting and the bombing. As yet another fallback, USAID beefed up its refugee operations at Vang Vieng, 67 miles up Route 13 from Vientiane.

Bernie Chessin, a refugee advisor for USAID, met us at the dusty Vang Vieng airstrip and told us what to expect over a quick cup of American coffee. Bernie, the four of us American newsmen, and a Lao USIS photographer named Sisouphanh Vongnorath climbed into two jeeps and drove south about four miles to where thousands of refugees camped under canvas tents.

Still armed with Ronk's camera, I shot photo after photo documenting the living conditions. Boys and young men stood silently under a hot sun waiting to collect the day's allotment of rice. A shirtless Lao USAID worker measured rice in his hands, scooping it from a large tub into a dented metal wash pan. A barefoot hill tribe girl, maybe four years old, carried a naked infant in a sling across her back.

Yao women in black pajamas and turbans with colorful embroidered sashes and belts chatted with one another; an old hill tribe man wearing a thin black-and-white plaid turban carried bundles of bamboo and firewood balanced on a pole over his right shoulder. A woman dressed in black bent over jars of food while strips of some sort of dead animal hung over a bamboo rack, and light blankets and thin towels dried on clotheslines nearby.

Life went on.

Back in Vang Vieng, we ate tuna salad on white bread, a lunch only the Americans could provide, given the fragility of mayonnaise in tropical heat. Then we ventured north nine miles to Ban Na Dao. We had the road to ourselves. No trucks, buses, or pickup taxis passed us in either direction. None of my companions seemed to notice or care. Was I more observant or just less jaded?

We found Ban Na Dao all but abandoned. The one-story wooden houses, little more than shacks with corrugated tin roofs, sat empty, locked or nailed tight. One dark-haired woman in a traditional ankle-length wrap-around skirt waited at the side of the road with a three-year old child. Around her lay her belongings— three burlap bundles, a plastic handbag, rolled sleeping mats, a metal basin, and a bamboo cage holding two white chickens. She ignored us, and we left her waiting. I assumed she knew more about the taxi service than I did, but I wondered if indeed she would be rescued.

Farther north beyond the village, rocky karsts dotted with green shot straight up 1,000 feet or more.

Bruce and his CBS film crew flew out of Vang Vieng before dusk on an Air America helicopter. Sisouphanh and I stayed overnight at the USAID guesthouse. The next day we shot more film of soldiers and planes at the airstrip.

A signpost pointed the way to Mama Lulu's in Vientiane (57 km by air) and 283 miles in the opposite direction, Hanoi. A line of boy soldiers, sweating in baggy green uniforms with rifles thrown over their shoulders, kicked dust as they trudged single file on the side of the road. Nearby, another young soldier wearing a baseball cap sat alone on a cut-off barrel, his head hung down, looking lost and friendless in his own world. A pickup truck-taxi rolled past with man-sized bundles and a wheeled cart piled on top.

A dozen or more Yao men and women loitered at the side of the dirt runway. I captured a close-up photo of a mother in a black turban with a toddler riding on her back. The woman squinted in the bright sunlight, and the child wore a red cap with black tassels and a string of beads under his chin. Of the more than 1,800 frames of film I shot in Laos, I liked this one the best and printed a copy for my friend, Liz. I called it *Madonna and Child*.

Just before leaving Vang Vieng, I ran into Defense Minister Sisouk na Champassak and six Lao generals who flew in for a brief visit. As I watched, they decided to send in four battalions of Royal Lao Army troops to defend Vang Vieng and ordered the refugees to stay nearby. This would keep the homeless off the Vientiane Plain where their presence would only cause concern among the resident villagers, and it might—but probably wouldn't—inspire the new troops to fight harder if it came to that. At least, that was their reasoning.

My two-day excursion whetted my appetite for travel, and in mid-March I set out from Vientiane by road to test the American Embassy's new openness policy with the media.

John Swain, a lean, long-haired Frenchman sent as a temporary replacement for Max Coiffait, planned to drive Max's Land Rover to the Royal Lao Army headquarters at Muong Kasy, about 134 miles up Route 13 from Vientiane. I joined him.

I recorded the highlights of the trip in my journal:

We left at 8:45 and returned the same day at 7:05. We had two very close calls with Lao buses on the road. Route 13 is primarily a gravel-laterite road. We had ideal conditions, however, since it had rained a day or two before we left. The road was dry enough not to be slippery and wet enough not to generate clouds of dust, although there was plenty of dust. There are countless bridges... with steel frames and plank bottoms. One had two large holes burned in one track where the underlay was showing as well as the water below.

Phone Hong [45 miles north of Vientiane], where the road

turns off to the Nam Ngum Dam, is a large Lao village of perhaps 3,000 people. A few concrete houses indicate where the district chief and the rich merchants, mostly Chinese, live. The rest of the villagers live in bamboo houses elevated 2–4 feet off the ground....

Vang Vieng is returning to normal. Many of the shops that were closed when I last visited the town are now open. One Indian merchant said that he had evacuated himself and his wares to Vientiane. Three weeks [later], he moved back in. The 9,000 refugees who were crowded together south of the town have been resettled to the north. They are making new homes and only the plastic roofing on their still unfinished homes and their daily requisition of rice from USAID distinguish them from the old timers. Many people have also returned to the villages north of Vang Vieng although about one-third are still vacant.

At one outpost between Vang Vieng and Muong Kasy, a drunk soldier told us we could go no further. A companion, however, opened the gate and we drove on after giving them cigarettes. This was the only instance where we were stopped. Otherwise our white faces allowed us to pass without question.

The FAR [Forces Armee Royale] H.Q. near Kasy was as far north as we got. There we met a 12-year-old soldier [and] an American—probably CIA or U.S. Air Force—with a .38 special slung on his left hip who was being briefed. The [Lao] commander sat in a lounge chair in a T-shirt with his boots off. He answered Swank's questions about the military situation in French. He said that the PL [Pathet Lao] wouldn't attack again because it was too late in the year (dry season). Also said the government was making progress.

Two tanks—U.S., of course—were parked behind the H.Q. knoll. Their crews slept or played cards. Soldiers were stripping a white building that looked as if it had suffered minor fire damage. The area originally had about 30 houses, 10 of which were burned completely to the ground. Garbage of all kinds littered the ground, including spent artillery casings, detonators, etc.

The trip didn't produce news but was a grand adventure, the kind where danger lurks but never shows its face. We were ready for more, and we weren't sure how long the Official Americans would allow reporters to travel the countryside. Four days later, we decided to drive to Ban Son, USAID's replacement for Sam Thong as the major refugee center in northern Laos.

As before, Swain took the wheel. Ronk rode shotgun, and I sat in back. A balding, bearded British producer for Granada TV News, whom I knew only as Brian, joined me in back.

We planned to take Route 13 north through Vang Vieng and Muong Kasy to the junction with Route 7 at Sala Phou Khoun. Route 7 runs east to the heart of the Plain of Jars, but we weren't going anywhere near there. Somewhere east of the Nam Ming River, we expected to find an unnumbered road off Route 7 shooting southeast where we would pick up the track to Ban Son. It was all a little vague, but we were reporters and not just men afraid to ask for directions.

We need not have concerned ourselves about finding our way. Somewhere south of Vang Vieng, the left rear tire of the Land Rover blew out. I described what happened next in my journal:

Swain was doing about 70 plus kph [almost 45 mph], and we served left, straightened out for an instant, shot to the right (ass end flying left like nothing I've seen) and then left again and turned the car over on its right side.

Don had had his arm folded over the open window but pulled it in quickly. I flew to the roof and broke the light case with my head. Brian of Grenada TV scraped his arm as he flew across the back of the vehicle. Swain held the wheel and was unscathed.

We piled out, unshook ourselves, hailed a bus, and had it pull us out. The Land Rover came to rest one-quarter of the way over the side of a sharp 30-foot incline which ended in another sharper drop into a foot or more of marsh water.

Max's spare tire—the left rear was completely destroyed by the blow out and from being driven on—had a leak so John and I caught a truck intending to go to Ban Houei Pha Mome or Ban Son for air. We ended up in Vang Vieng. Bought a new inner tube for 1,000 kip [$2] which was bigger than the old one. Got a taxi to Phone Hong that first went north to the refugee village to pick up bananas. At least 50 kids skinny-dipped in the river while downstream women bathed and washed clothes.

About 1:30 (we blew at 10:30) [Swain and I] arrived in Ban Houei Pha Mome. They were bringing down the last of the victims of an ambush. We scooted down to [our] wreck site, changed tires, and went up to Pha Mome to look around.

We hung around Pha Mome listening and asking a few questions.... On the way home, a rock shot up on Ronk's side and shattered the door glass. We stopped and picked the thing to pieces.

Swain flew back to Vientiane faster than I would have preferred.

Some people never learned. I didn't. Dodging road-hogging buses, the blown tire, the rollover, the ambush, the shattered window, and Swain's driving did not deter me. The next day I was ready to go again.

But first I wrote a story. The *Far East Economic Review* published all but a few paragraphs in its April 15 edition under the headline "Taxi from Death."

Ban Houei Pa Mome: They ease the bloody soldier into the rear of the jeep, then wrestle a corpse onto the floor beside the first. Three dusty soldiers scramble off the road as the jeep roars past the uplifted checkpoint barrier. A 13-year-old, with pack and M-16 rifle at his feet, gazes after the disappearing jeep.

We had been warned in the lowlands, 83 miles to the south, of the risks involved in travelling through the mountain by road, even in midday. Now we believed. Wrinkled women chewing betel nut squat in the shade of big Isuzu buses. Inside the buses, younger women nurse quiet children while old men eye the road east.

A small taxi-truck wheels into the center of the road junction triangle. The driver jumps out, questions a group of men, and returns to his taxi. "Phone Hong! Phone Hong! Py Phone Hong! Going to Phone Hong!" he bellows. Six men approach the taxi, pay their fare and squeeze themselves into the truck. The driver shouts again, climbs into the cab, and drives off carrying news of the ambush down the road to Phone Hong on the Vientiane Plain.

A blue Peugeot suddenly careens west, down the Ban Son

road, and bounces to a stop at the checkpoint. A crowd of soldiers gathers, exchanging comments with the driver and peering through dusty windows. An unseen guard raises the checkpoint gate from his outpost 20 feet above the road and the car starts off up the road to Vang Vieng, a bare leg showing through the dust on the rear window.

Then the soldiers begin to talk.

Two supply trucks were returning from Ban Son, the American refugee center 18 miles northeast. Hiding in the tall bamboo growing right up to the road, the ambushers had opened fire with machine guns as the trucks rounded a bend 11 miles northeast of Ban Houei Pa Mome. Everyone was hit.

A village chief says 11 people were killed, 20 wounded. A taxi-driver from Vang Vieng disagrees: there were only 10 killed, but yes, 20 were wounded. All were soldiers going to Vientiane, the capital.

No, that isn't true, another man insists. He personally saw two young girls, their faces covered with blood, being taken to the hospital at Vang Vieng.

Who were the ambushers? Were they North Vietnamese?

No, not North Vietnamese.

Pathet Lao guerillas?

Yes, probably Pathet Lao.

Bandits?

Well, yes, maybe bandits.

In a bamboo hut overlooking the road junction, a grinning soldier points to the blood spots on the stocks of the victims' rifles.

Then, no longer grinning, he picks at the yellow dirt crammed into the muzzles when the ambushed soldiers fell.

Two and a half hours after the ambush, bus drivers roust passengers from the shade of trucks and wooden buildings.

People find their places on bright green seats in the buses and taxis and settle down for the last—and now dangerous—stretch of the journey to Ban Son.

One by one the gears rattle into low and the 15 vehicles jerk across the triangle and up the road.

The taxi driver from Vang Vieng watches the procession round the first curve and disappear in the dust.

Is the road safe now?

No, it isn't.

The Vang Vieng driver gets into his empty car and drives across the bridge, south toward Vientiane.

I was dumb enough to go looking for war again and still be surprised by what I found. I wondered if Dad had experienced that morbid curiosity or whether the blood eventually washed it away.

Chapter 25

Prelude to the Finale

FEBRUARY–APRIL 1972

If all goes well, we shall be gone by fall.

Journal entry, April 8, 1972

W<small>E ALL SENSED</small> it was the beginning of the end. The timing was uncertain, but soon. The outcome long determined: The Official Americans, Vang Pao and his Meo, Souvanna Phouma and the royalists would lose.

VP and the CIA were proving to be a one-trick pony. The NVA closed in on Long Cheng yet again; the Meo army—increasingly composed of hill tribe teenagers and older Thai "volunteers"— threatened the Plain of Jars and the North Vietnamese supply lines. This time, however, the troops mutinied. A new, unlikely source of information for me—a college-educated Meo who opposed Vang Pao's alliance with the Americans—whispered that two battalions of Thais had abandoned their posts and refused to fight.

None of us felt like staying around to watch the unequal seesaw of battle, but we suffered the same malaise: A tug of war between our awareness of the need to change and the Laos-induced lassitude. Road trips intensified the conflict. But we just couldn't make the decision to move on, even when a round of newcomers demonstrated how stagnant and isolated we had become.

Irwin Block proved the epitome of our communal dilemma. Since losing his gig with the *Bangkok Post*, he had left Vientiane and his girlfriend, Dao. He came back and left again. And returned yet one more time.

In February, Jerry Doolittle had finally taken his wife, Gretchen, and their five boys home to Connecticut. Max Coiffait had gone on vacation, leaving us temporarily with John Swain, the Land Rover racer. Swain said Max was due for reassignment any day.

We could all see that Carl would not last much longer. He and his wife simply did not get along; their cultures—his American and her Vietnamese—just did not mesh.

Buckle was traveling more, trying to gin up his value to the *Star*, still hoping for a position in Washington or as a traveling foreign correspondent. He even sneaked off to Washington at great expense in mid-March to plead his case in person.

The days melted into one another in the state of mind known as Laos, and Ronk complained daily of boredom. I understood what he meant, and I had not been in country nearly as long as he had. Despite his fear of flying, Ronk was working on a new dream, or scheme. He envisioned reprising John Steinbeck's *Travels with Charlie*, the author's grand tour of America with his dog. Instead of driving with a dog, Ronk thought to ride Greyhound buses for three or four months to reconnect with the States; then he figured he would return to Asia and give the Philippines a try.

Even Danielle Cavalerie was said to be counting the days until her 21st birthday, when she planned to escape to Paris. Danielle had joined our small press corps in recent months, serving as an assistant to Max. Indeed, Danielle played a far more influential role than I ever had. She could speak French and knew the locals; she could interpret and open doors. More important, she understood the Constellation's touchy telephone and could make it work whether it wanted to or not. She was a young businesswoman, a negotiator, and a fixer like her father, Maurice Cavalerie, the proprietor of the Hotel Constellation and half-owner of just about everything in Laos that a Westerner would ever need or desire, including the Heineken beer concession. When Westerners, including and perhaps especially reporters, needed anything from changing money to obtaining visas that did not officially exist, they spoke with Maurice. He was Monsieur Indispensable, and Danielle was maturing into his equally indispensable Belle Jeune Fille.

I admit I had a minor crush on her. No, I had a major hard-on for her.

I fell in love with every pretty girl I met in Southeast Asia. Vietnamese. Thai. Lao. Chinese. Hill tribe. French. It didn't matter. A bright, smiling face; a healthy bust; a well-formed calf (or ankle, whatever was showing), and I was hooked. Sometimes two, or even three, times a day.

My Ohio friend Liz had made clear before we parted that she was too young for anything serious, so everyone was fair game in my mind. I knew these infatuations were not serious. I could not speak any of their languages, Vietnamese, Thai, Lao, Chinese, or French.

I almost made an exception with a lovely westernized Lao-Vietnamese girl named Khamnoi. She was in one of my more advanced English classes at the Lao-American Association, but I felt it would be improper to make an approach while I was teaching her. In fact, I suspected that messing around with the students would cost me my job, so I waited until I left LAA. By then, however, she had taken up with a much older USAID employee, someone who had a job and might provide a comfortable future.

My infatuation with her, however, made me seek counsel from my nonreporter Western friends. (There was no way I was going to announce my interest in an Asian girl to those guys. I already took enough shit from them about my writing, my hair length, my sandals, my photography, and my general and specific lack of experience in just about everything they could think of.)

Walt Haney, who taught for the Lao government, was a different matter. He was a few years older and wiser and was discreet to boot. His advice was worth recording in my journal:

> After you've met a girl, you visit her family at the house and must spend many evenings in discussion with them. After an indefinite period, you will be invited to social gatherings with the family such as picnics, movies, and so on. After another period of unspecified duration, you may be able to just attend social functions with the same age group. In the evening visits after "three hours or so," the family just leaves and you are left alone to talk. And that is as far as Walt ever got.

That didn't discourage me from admiring the young lovelies.

And Danielle Cavalerie was lovely. Straight black hair tied in a ponytail that hung down the middle of her back. Her face a sweet welcoming combination of her French-Chinese-Vietnamese heritage. A soft voice with a lovely French accent. And she always wore dresses or skirts that showed off shapely calves.

I imagined we almost lived together, in a distant platonic way. After all, I saw her and spoke at least a few words with her every day. Despite some long talks, during which she expressed more and more frustration with what the Official Americans were doing to her adopted country, I never worked up the nerve to ask her out. I respected (feared) Maurice and kept my distance, just like I did for the fathers of any girl I ever dated or considered dating.

What really kept me at bay, however, was her mother, Rose, the Dragon Lady. In two years, she never smiled at me even once. I don't know that she smiled at anyone who hung out in her husband's hotel bar. Every time I spoke with Danielle for more than a few minutes, one of her younger brothers would magically appear from the family's living quarters behind the dining room and simply stand and watch; they never smiled at me either.

Danielle and me. Just one more ride on the roller coaster that was Laos.

Writing—as in writing enough to make a living—provided daily disappointments and long-term frustration. I vented in a letter to Liz:

> I am in one of those pissed off moods again. Sorry. Received two more reject slips today. Lost the NBC job the day after I wrote my last letter. The Bangkok Post refused my offer to write for them. Gloria Emerson of the New York Times came to Laos, tried to pick my brain and thoroughly enraged me, so I lost another consultant job there. And this evening three of the "old hands," namely the Washington Post, the Washington Star and the Toronto Globe, tore into my writing style and found it wanting... and wanting and wanting. The criticism was good, but I think I shall imbibe more frequently of smaller quantities so that I may avoid another such intoxicating experience.

In addition to trying to make a living on words, I was back chasing butterflies over Dan Grady's graduate school ploy: He proposed that I apply for a National Defense Foreign Language Fellowship at Ohio University. O.U., not to be confused with its football-crazy cousin Ohio State University, was in Athens, a tiny southern Ohio town like Yellow Springs. Grady knew people there, and we figured that since I had already received one NDFL fellowship for my Vietnamese studies at Cornell, I should be a shoo-in to study a different language (Indonesian) at a different school.

There were one or two minor differences from my Cornell experience. This was for a graduate program, and I had yet to graduate from Antioch. Also, unlike my desire to study Vietnamese, my enthusiasm for Indonesia, about which I knew absolutely nothing, never rose above halfhearted. Sure, I could do graduate school in the States, but it was never going to match my adventure in Laos.

Still, I managed to gin up enthusiasm in a letter to my sister Bonnie. Unfortunately, it also started an unfortunate chain of rumors and anticipation in our family.

Very new and possibly exciting: Dan Grady, my old advisor at Antioch, wrote me recently proposing that I apply for a graduate fellowship at Ohio University in Athens, Ohio. The full scholarship would require me to study Indonesian language, but would permit me to work intensively with John Cady, one of the best French Indochina historians. The only problem is finishing my B.A. Dan is working on that now.

I think I would enjoy going back to school for a while and a free M.A. is not to be scoffed at. The fellowship begins in September and would mean leaving here [this] summer. This wouldn't displease me. Don Ronk, one of my best friends here, is thinking of moving on, and Tammy Arbuckle, another very good friend, is angling for a position in Washington. If they leave, I would probably not stay here much longer.

Thus began an almost farcical chain of family correspondence—"He's finally coming home!" "That's not what he told me." "Yes, he is." "No, it all fell through."—and the most frustrating game of chasing butterflies since I was detained in Saigon. Once again, I filled out myriad applications and forms (although this time I at least had a typewriter, even if it did tend to break down at the most inconvenient times). I rounded up references—Grady, of course; Ronk; and my fellow Antiochian, Ed Kelly at the American Embassy—and endured one crushing blow after another. I started to dread checking my mailbox at the Constellation, fearing yet another change of fate delivered over thousands of miles by airmail and the overnight train from Bangkok.

I learned I did not qualify for the fellowship because I had not earned a bachelor's degree. In fact, I was not even in college, at least officially. Not to worry, Dan wrote; apply for a graduate assistantship, and we'll work on finishing your degree.

Mom and Dad got an announcement in the mail from Antioch saying that I would graduate with the Class of 1972 in June. This was intriguing but odd news. Antioch students go through a five-year program to graduate, and I had not even finished three years. Oh, well, I figured, never argue with the bureaucracy.

Oops, bureaucracy jumped the gun. I would not graduate. I would not be eligible until I evaluated the credits I earned while abroad and fixed up some phys ed and Level I physical science requirements.

Back and forth we went through the early spring.

Meanwhile, visitors from the outside world brought new insights and forced us regulars to question our lassitude.

Tom Jagninski, a Canadian freelancer who had worked for the *Toronto Globe* and then in radio, struck a chord with me. Taller, thinner, and at least 10 to 15 years older than I, Tom shared a sense of self-doubt that resonated. He had come to Laos to put himself in harm's way so that he could discover what kind of man he was. I thought he was a damned fool, despite the similarities between our doubts. He flew to Bouam Long, dozens of miles behind North Vietnamese lines and the last Meo outpost northeast of the Plain of Jars. For a week, he lived at LS 32, a 1,300-foot dirt landing strip on top of a 4,000-foot mountain surrounded by the Pathet Lao and NVA. His only company was a CIA case officer and a group of Meo soldiers led by Vang Pao's uncle. When he returned, he never told me whether he had passed his self-imposed test.

On the opposite end of the spectrum was Anne Darling Moehr,

a skinny, braless freelancer in her 30s who treated me like a kid brother. She specialized in dating Air American pilots to inveigle stories out of them. I was appalled by her journalistic tactics and feared the worst for her morals, but I enjoyed every moment I spent with her.

Joe Triester, a *New York Times* correspondent based in Saigon, and his wife, Barbara, made a long visit, at least by Vientiane standards. I shared my knowledge; they fed me. They also forced me to leave the confines of the Constellation. One day Barbara and I went in search of refugees. About twelve kilometers north on Route 13, we found 65 families camped along the road. Closer to Vientiane at the Chinese Association on Wattay Road, we discovered 45 Meo families living in one long house. I had never gone looking for refugees to interview before, despite Branfman's example and encouragement. I justified my lack of initiative by claiming I didn't have the money to pay for an interpreter. It was true, but I knew it was just an excuse.

Two academic visitors arrived and became long-time friends. George Davis was a robust Californian with a wavy mustache and the hint of an English accent he picked up studying for a Ph.D. at the London School of Economics. His wife, Penny, accompanied him and helped him research his dissertation: *External Intervention and the Mobilization of Ethnic Minorities in Laos, 1945–1973*. I shared all of my material with him and even some of my sources. The three of us spent hours talking about the specifics of the U.S. intervention in Indochina and aiming for broader lessons. One conclusion we shared was that no minority group ever did itself any good by allying with the U.S. government, which used its allies as long as it needed them and then left them to fend for themselves.

George and Penny also chimed in on the debate over whether I should stay in Laos longer or push harder to return to academia. They, along with three or four other academics who visited from Cornell, told me bluntly that the time had come to leave.

There was just one problem (in addition to all of the Antioch–Ohio University melodrama): Jobs were finally pouring in.

Westinghouse Broadcasting actually sent me a telegram asking if I wanted a radio job with them. Holy shit! I'd never met anyone from Westinghouse—this was totally out of the blue, and thus needed to be treated with the skepticism accorded every free lunch. I checked with Carl, who had had the job briefly some time before. He suggested I take it; I decided against it. Other stuff had come along.

Tammy Arbuckle had turned me on to Copley News Service, and its editors asked me to start submitting pieces regularly. The London *Financial Times* actually sent me a cable card so I could file material on deadline for them.

And one day I picked up the latest issue of the *Far East Economic Review* and found my Muong Kasy ambush story published inside. I had given up hope for that story.

Once again, I reported my prospects, and my dilemma, to my older sister, Bonnie:

Things are fair enough here....

Westinghouse Broadcasting Company offered me a job doing radio news for them. I turned it down. After doing the ambush piece, I decided I want to concentrate my sparse talents on writing for newspapers, not for radio. I have been recommended for two other jobs. One with the Financial Times *of London and the other with Copley News Service, a feature story outfit on the West Coast.... If all goes well, I will be swamped at the end of this month writing for them....*

If I don't get the fellowship, I stay here a while longer. I am getting tired of Laos though. I need a change. If I get the Copley and Times *jobs, and not the fellowship, I think I will start traveling much more. Thailand has a war that is fast heating up. Cambodia is good writing material. I may even try Viet Nam for very short periods of time. Perhaps Burma also.*

Then on Easter Sunday, we cremated Carl's baby daughter, Alexandra "Sandy" Strock. Writing in my journal that evening, I ignored the news that the North Vietnamese had launched a massive offensive throughout South Viet Nam and focused completely on my friend's tragedy:

Carl's baby daughter, Alexandra, was cremated this morning at 9:00. She died sometime Friday night of bronchial pneumonia at the age of three months.

Apparently she had the measles about two weeks ago, which unknown to us, damaged her heart. Later this developed into bronchial pneumonia which collapsed one of her lungs on Friday. Carl was with her when she died at O.B. Hospital.

We gathered at Carl's house around 8:30. The red-papered coffin lay on the floor at one end of the square room. Vases of flowers circled the coffin with two candles in front near the burning incense. About 20 people sat cross-legged on thatched mats.

Carl held Yola [his other daughter] until the time came to load the tiny coffin onto the truck. Biting back tears, Carl carried Sandy out [of] the house alone and placed [her] in back of the truck.

At the wat, a small pile of wood awaited the coffin, the white brick bier being too large for the coffin. Tears rolling freely down his face, Carl draped the coffin with black

cloth, placed flowers and incense on top of it, poured gas-
oline over it all. Truong clutched the cloth for a final sec-
ond before Carl led her away.

Fire gulped the bier when Carl lit it with his lighter, almost
taking him with it. The gas burned out but the wood caught
on. Clouds hung over the wat. The fire consumed all.

Chapter 26

A Real Reporter

APRIL—AUGUST 1972

I have been writing like a madman.

Letter to Tom Spicer, May 5, 1972

EVERYTHING CHANGED. TALK turned to action. Arbuckle flew to Saigon to cover the end of the North Vietnamese offensive and demonstrate his value to the *Washington Star*.

Carl left his wife and took their surviving daughter, Yola, with him.

Dick Pyle, the AP bureau chief in Saigon, wired that he wanted me to take Carl's old job as the AP stringer in Laos. $300 a month. Cable card to follow.

I was a real reporter at last, and all it took was the death of an infant. I felt like shit.

I decided that if I was going to profit from a friend's worst nightmare, I was going to do the job up right. I recognized I was still a novice. I knew just enough to know how much more I had to learn.

First, I had to learn how to write wire service stories—just the facts, ma'am—and how to put those stories into cable-ese, the foreign correspondent's shorthand that saved money at the telegraph office.

In my earliest days in Southeast Asia, I had sent a few telegrams. They were expensive. My initial plea for help to Dan Grady ran a mere 35 words but cost $6.13. I assumed that news organizations worked a deal with the telegraph companies for special rates, but even with a discount it would cost a bunch to dispatch a 100- or 200-word telegram. Do that every day, week in and week out, and you're talking money. So any steps to reduce the word count saved money. Enter cable-ese.

Cablese mixed pidgin English and Latin to eliminate unnecessary words without sacrificing clarity. I expected to pick it up quickly because I had studied Latin for years at Campion. I had translated Cicero's *Orations* and Caesar's *Commentaries*. Veni, vidi, scripsi. I came; I saw; I wrote.

Beyond the cable-ese, I had to master the craft of the wire service story, putting the most important information first, then filling in the detail. I combed through my scrapbooks and compiled a collection of clichés to guide me:

> *A published article can be, and often is, collected from many sources centered on one topic or theme under an eye-catching headline.*
>
> *Nonetheless, the lead paragraph must contain the foundations of the headline....*
>
> *For emphasis, the news of a story is introduced first, followed by 'reliable'... sources said (announced, revealed) here (there) today (yesterday [day of the week]) period, paragraph.*

Putting this formula into cable-ese, I started one of my first stories for AP this way:

*laotian troops saturday regained complete control of vital
skyline ridge overlooking former ccciiiaaa base of long
cheng eight miles northeast of vientiane informed sources
said monday para laotian forces charged onto charlie
whisky rpt charlie whisky etcharlie alpha rpt charlie alpha
pads on skyline ridge just after midnight on Saturday
morning sources said para*

Somewhere in the wide world of AP, a crusty old editor would translate that into something readable and slap on a tantalizing headline. It might end up something like this:

Laotian Troops Rout NVA, Save CIA Base

Royal Lao Government troops forced North Vietnamese regulars off a ridge overlooking a beleaguered CIA base in northern Laos over the weekend, well-informed sources told AP Monday.

Units composed of hill tribesmen and Thai volunteers under the command of Meo Gen. Vang Pao charged onto the last two helicopter landing pads, designated Charlie Whisky and Charlie Alpha, on Skyline Ridge that had been held for weeks by the North Vietnamese, the sources said.

Skyline Ridge looks down on the CIA headquarters at Long Cheng just 80 miles northeast of the Lao capital of Vientiane.

It was hardly my best work, and I would learn to cut repetitive material, but it was a start.

Identifying sources followed certain rules as well, but I had already struggled to understand the formula. I explained them in one of my rants to Liz:

> The briefing, dear Liz, is where we are told the Official Version of the war news. (We are the collective press corps, now standing at 7 men and one fairly pretty, but severely restricted, young lady.) Each morning shortly before noon, the American press attaché gives the press what is known as a "background" briefing. He runs through the military events reported in the previous 24 hours. His "news" is collected from the Royal Lao Army, ARMA (the U.S. Army attaché) and the CIA. We are allowed to print what he says but may not quote him. He is usually referred to as "informed sources" or "a government spokesman."
>
> On Monday [and] Friday afternoons, ARMA gives its own briefing covering the previous week or weekend, as the case may be. Here we are not allowed to indicate the briefer's occupation and nationality in the same clause. For instance, our briefer is always an Army colonel. We may use "military sources" or "American sources," but we may not say "American military sources." Got it?
>
> And Monday through Thursday, the Laotian military spokesman, General Thongphanh Knocksy, gives his briefing in French. There are no restrictions about naming him.

My new full-time job coincided with the early onset of the monsoons and a heat wave that pushed temperatures close to 100 degrees, day after miserable, muggy day for weeks. Local soothsayers predicted that flooding would be severe for the second year in a row. I complained to Bonnie:

> Hot season is progressing and rainy season opened officially today when the U.S. Army attaché's meteorologist

here declared it so. I missed his statement. I was out being blown all over town in a dust storm. Left a layer of grime all over my room. Tore down my maps for about the fourth or fifth time. Been about 100 every day for the past two weeks. It is pretty hot when I think about it. Pretty hot even when I don't think about it, too.

My third week as AP stringer I learned the power the job brought and a lesson in how a single line in a story could stir up a storm. As an afterthought to a short roundup of military news, I reported that the Lao National Assembly opened a new session and elected Chao Sopsaisana as vice president. I cabled the following bit of information that everyone in Vientiane knew to be fact:

chao sopsaisana retired from his post as vicepresident last year to become laotian ambassador to france but was recalled when french customs officials discovered aaa large quantity of heroin in his luggage.

In my journal that night, I noted that my report was causing "some stir" in Vientiane. Sopsaisana had come to the Constellation asking for me. I didn't recognize him, and he apparently didn't recognize me.

I also discovered how flexible my sense of ethics could be. After filing the first few stories at the telegraph office, I realized the teletype operators added each new telegram to the bottom of a stack. A 500 or 1,000-kip note—a small fortune in Laos—discreetly folded in with my copy could move my telegram to the top of the pile. A bottle of lao-lao rice whisky made the clerks smile every time I walked in the door, which was at least once or twice a day. When I sought reimbursement for these payments, which I accurately identified as bribes, I received a quick phone call from Saigon informing me that these expenses were more properly reported as "representation."

Despite the rush of adrenaline I got from the Chao Sopsaisana story, I quickly tired of the monotony of wire service work. It was time-consuming and boring at the same time. The news never varied: The Pathet Lao and North Vietnamese attacked and the Royal Lao forces retreated despite the rainy season, when the opposite should be happening. The battle lines shifted closer and closer toward the Mekong all up and down the country. One skirmish, roadside ambush, or overnight excursion after another produced new casualties.

Collecting the details, tracing the location of each new disaster on a map and trying to substantiate the official version just chewed up time. I raced from my apartment to the Constellation to the U.S. press office in the USIS building, then up to the embassy, back to my apartment to write my story and over to the Radiodiffusion Nationale Lao telegraph office to file it. In between I tried to speak with more than the usual official sources, interviewed people for my freelance work and wrote up notes on all the information I was gathering that did not become part of a story.

"*Am up earlier and to bed later,*" I wrote a Campion friend. "*Eat meals more irregularly at night, but am pretty much off noodles now. I write more, although much of it is just note taking, cross referencing, and so on, and not necessarily for publication.*"

"*I have been writing like a madman,*" I complained to Tom and Gretchen Spicer, friends from Antioch who were scratching out a living on a commune in Wisconsin. "They require a couple hundred words almost daily."

To others I wrote, "*My head is spinning from the wire service shit I have to churn out. Everything I write for them sounds exactly like the piece I did the day before. Ugh.*"

What's the adage? Be careful what you ask for; you just might get it.

I did finally get what I wanted. A full-time job as a correspondent for a real news organization. But I had no more than started the AP gig when I began to plan my departure from Laos.

Ohio University offered me a graduate assistantship and a free master's degree. All I could think was that when it rains, it pours.

I wrote George and Penny Davis, now back in London, asking if I might stay with them for a few days on my way back to the States.

I received word yesterday from Ohio University. I was accepted, but did not get the NDFL Fellowship I requested. Instead, they offered me a full Course Assistantship which includes a $2,600 stipend, full tuition in return for an 18-hour workweek. I was not enthused about the work (cleaning erasers or some shit like that) but have decided to accept anyway.

I reluctantly started to prepare to leave, all the while wondering if Antioch would screw me. I laughed at the irony of possibly showing up at Ohio University only to discover that I no longer qualified because I did not have an undergraduate degree.

So there I was in my new job already talking about who would replace me.

Don and I had dinner at Pizzeria last night. Talked of going home. If Ohio does not drop the fellowship, I am only 9 weeks away from departure. Don is planning to make a bid for the AP job when I leave. Tim Allman brought back word from Saigon that someone is badmouthing Don there. Don suspects Peter Osnos, his nominal chief. Since he wasn't invited to the cocktail party for the new USIS chief, he has been a bit paranoid. A good case can be

*made that the American Mission is ostracizing him. He is
despised by more than a few.*

Other reporters wrote stories just as skeptical and critical of the
Official Americans as Ronk but did not generate the antagonism
that he did. Ten days after the USIS party, I was invited to a cocktail party marking Ed and Kitty Kelly's return from a three-month
home leave; again, Ronk was not invited.

I noted in my journal that the Official Americans seemed to be
cozying up to me. I wondered if this was a major change in policy
toward the press; I couldn't recall the guys attending embassy cocktail parties in the past, although maybe they had and just didn't tell
me about them. I understood it was not personal; the Americans
were playing nice with AP, not me. (To my credit, I at least recognized that; I had met reporters who thought it was all about them.)
Nonetheless, I liked the attention, but felt that I was being disloyal
to my friend. I was becoming a news whore, sucking up to people
I didn't particularly like just so I could improve me chances of getting the story first. God, I wanted out of there.

I tried to explain my situation to Tom and Gretchen at
the commune:

> *The bright lights have undoubtedly changed me. Am cyni-
> cal and bitter. Am enjoying good food. Servants. Have
> become all that I intended not to back [at Campion]. (It is
> actually not as bad as all that, but change is inevitable.)*
>
> *I can still do hard work now and then. Wrote 27 stories in
> May and 16 so far this month. Also sent out a roll of film
> to AP. I really love it. Hate to even think of leaving.*

In mid-June we went through one of the occasional failures of
the international (or perhaps just the Lao) postal system. I finally
received one letter that had been mailed in May 1971; it had sat

more than a year just three blocks away at the Lane Xang Hotel, despite having the Constellation's correct address.

The mail situation also caused understandable panic back home over where I was and what I was planning to do. I displayed a considerable lack of understanding in a letter to my older sister:

> *According to Mother's latest letter, Dan [Grady] understands that either I have been busy or the mail isn't getting through. I have been busy and it appears that the mail isn't getting through. I see no—repeat no—cause for anxiety on anyone's part. I said I would probably be home in August and I probably will. If I don't make it then, I shall write and explain why.*

In a letter to my parents the next day, I demonstrated a callousness that embarrasses me still:

> *Received your worried letter of the 14th yesterday [June 20]. I am well and fine and overworked but enjoying it. This is my fifth letter home since May 25. Mail must be bad. You should be used to it by now. Can't see why you aren't.*

> *Still have not heard anything from Grady. Don't really care much though. Have just about convinced myself to stay on here another year. Really like the writing work I am doing.*

While my academic fate hung in the air, I acted as if I planned to leave Laos late in the summer. I counted the weeks and started packing close to 100 pounds of books, monographs, papers, and maps that I had collected. I hit up contacts for more books and documents (secret as well as public) and held long interviews. I photographed wats, stupas, and ordinary places I had passed dozens and even hundreds of times without noticing before. In short, I did all the things I could have been doing over the last 18 months or so.

On July 1, with no further word from Antioch or Ohio University, I told my Jesuit friend Skippy Bacon that I had started reconsidering my options.

> *I may stay here another year. Which would be nice since I am enjoying myself. In any case, the situation is very confused. I am waiting for Antioch to straighten things out. This may be a mistake in judgment on my part but when you are so far away from everything, I feel it is best to throw the thing right back where it started."*

The next day I confided to my journal some anxiety about going back to the States:

> *If I am actually leaving on Aug. 10, there are less than 6 weeks remaining. Hard to believe. No word yet from Antioch. It is difficult to write about returning to the States.... Frightening in that it may be a terrible bore."*

In mid-July, I catalogued the latest round of advice I was getting about whether to go or stay.

> *Letter from Grady advises me to stay in Laos if I am doing well, but warns that I will have to pick up the Antioch science credits sooner or later to get the Antioch B.A.*

> *Don advises me to leave; not to get caught up in the Asia quagmire which ruins ambition—believes the Ohio fellowship is still good and that I should forget about Antioch.*

> *Gene Bruns [a visiting academic from Cornell], after some thought and a 180 degree switch, advises me to go now, try to work out BA and MA concurrently—sees staying on*

here as a risky business, which could backfire if [future graduate position at] Cornell doesn't come through.

David Wyatt [a Cornell professor also visiting Vientiane] whom I expected to advise the same, thinks I should stay on till December, apply early to Ohio, Cornell and Michigan and get the Antioch degree during spring.

I am inclined to leave. Two years is enough. Perhaps too much. There may be greater opportunities ahead but I do not trust myself to take advantage of them when they come along.

It was déjà vu all over again, and I was back in 1969, facing money problems, questioning the value of a college degree, and looking for a quick fix out of my dilemma, the same kind of quick fix that sent me to Viet Nam and then on to Laos.

The days raced by. I dispatched story after story to AP, documenting one travail for the Lao government after another: Attacks continued against Long Cheng; Pathet Lao seized a rice barge as it headed up the Mekong to Luang Prabang; 17 bridges were destroyed on Route 13 between Vientiane and Savannakhet, threatening to cut off southern Laos; the Finance Ministry closed all banks for a day to sort out panic over its ban on selling dollars to the public, then the ministry slapped price controls on food in Vientiane; Lao police arrested the only Meo member of the National Assembly for opium possession amid a crackdown on traffickers; Vang Pao's latest offensive bogged down in the rain; Souvanna reshuffled his cabinet yet again; and flooding halted operations at the American refugee center at Ban Son.

One day I attended the public burning of 700 gallons of chemicals used to process heroin, an event put on just for the press, with almost laughable consequences when the wind shifted and Lao and American dignitaries scrambled to escape the fumes. I reported one plane crash after another up and down the length of the country and, like watching a tennis match, kept track of the umpteenth offer and counteroffer of peace talks between Souvanna Phouma and the Pathet Lao.

At the end of July, I experienced the high point of my journalistic career in Laos. Jane Fonda, the movie actress and antiwar activist, landed at Wattay Airport on the weekly flight from Hanoi. She had spent two weeks in North Viet Nam posing for propaganda photos and was on her way to Paris en route to the United States. I met her on the tarmac as she stepped off the Soviet Aeroflot aircraft and dogged her steps into the terminal during the flight layover. She wore a three-quarter-length sleeved Lao top and black peasant pajama bottoms and sandals. Even without makeup, she was Hollywood beautiful, her blonde hair blowing freely in the wind. While Ronk photographed us, I pestered her with question after question about her activities in the North, including a photo taken of her sitting at an antiaircraft gun. She politely refused to answer every question. She said she was holding an international press conference in Paris; I understood that no AP stringer in Laos was going to scoop that.

I didn't care. I had met someone famous, and I was going to write about it. My brief story probably served to alert AP that she had left the country and was bound for France. This is the text of my entire cable:

presse
associated tokyo
haase 01945 vientiane 22/7

jane fonda cma american actress et antiwar activist cma late saturday afternoon left hanoi et arrived vientianes wattay airport for thirty minute stopover on first leg of long trip back to united states via moscow et paris para miss fonda cma wearing black silk vietnamese trousers cma refused to comment on her trip to north vietnam saying she will hold press conference in paris para an outspoken opponent of vietnam war miss fonda has been accused of treason by american congessman for her activities in north vietnam during last two weeks endit

David L. Haase
carte de presse 274
hotel constellation

That turned out to be one of the last cables I ever wrote from Laos. I bought my airline ticket, started hauling small bundles of books wrapped in brown paper to the Poste, Telegraphes et Telephones du Laos, and wrote one last letter home:

I am leaving Laos just two weeks from today. I have decided to get out now for various reasons, which I can explain more fully at our leisure in the future. I am planning to attend Ohio University this fall if they have no objections. I will write Ohio later today to explain a few things and then let it go at that.

Friday, August 11, smack dab between my sisters' birthdays on the 7th and 15th, I looked around my room at 20 Rue Manthatourath the last time. The place looked naked without my maps and Lao propaganda posters on the walls.

Ronk and I had said our farewells earlier in the day. We would see one another again soon, we promised. Maybe. Sometime.

I hauled my bags down four flights of stairs and dragged them a half block up to Rue Setthathirath. A cab whipped across two lanes of traffic and stopped. The driver hefted my overweight bags into his rusted trunk. A novice might have wondered if the sheet metal would hold the weight; an old hand like myself figured it would, or it wouldn't. Baw pen yang. Que sera, sera. Whatever.

At Thadeua, I let the cabbie drag my suitcases the short distance to the ferry. The Mekong was high; the boat rode low in the roiling chocolate water. I was scared as always, but more jaded now. Whatever happened… well, it happened. We pushed off from shore, and the ferryman pointed the boat upriver. With luck, we would keep ahead of the current and land directly across the Mekong at the Nong Khai landing.

I did not look back.

I would do that over the next 40 years.

Chapter 27

Afterthoughts

January 2016

We did—Branfman, myself, et al.—grow up with the war and, sorry, but we don't know anything else. It bled us, now we'll bleed it.

Letter from Don Ronk, July 6, 1973

I WENT TO VIET Nam in September 1970, just three months after my 20th birthday.

I went not as a soldier, as so many of my male peers did, but as a student. I planned to continue my college education with a year abroad at a Buddhist university in Saigon while a Cold War–inspired civil war raged. It would be a somewhat unusual year abroad, but an educational experience nonetheless. That, at least, was the pretext.

In fact, my real motivations were less scholarly and far more self-centered.

I wanted to prove to my father—and perhaps more important, to myself—that I was not a coward, not afraid to face war just because I opposed this one.

And I wanted to demonstrate my presumed moral superiority over young men my own age who chose paths different from mine: Those who complied with the draft and went to war; those who fled to Canada or Sweden to avoid the draft; and those who stayed behind in the United States, cowering behind their student deferments. My moral righteousness suffered from a severe case of myopia as I played the Selective Service game from Southeast Asia and won a permanent reprieve from military service owing to my 4F physically unfit exemption.

After my return to the United States in mid-August 1972, I endured graduate school for six months before dropping out in sheer boredom. (A decade would pass before I finished the Antioch B.A.) I got a job in public television with the father of one friend and then a career at a daily newspaper through the father of another friend. I eventually wore down sweet Liz—I called her Elizabeth by then—married her and had two children.

I tried writing about my experiences, meager though they were, but the ever-present need to make a living and support a family let me postpone the project for many years.

Elizabeth contracted life-threatening cancer in 2015. When I asked her what she wanted for her birthday, she said she wanted me to write a book. This is that birthday gift.

I find I am not alone these days in my obsession with the experiences of my youth. Oral history interviews and memoirs by CIA operatives, Air America pilots, and humanitarian volunteers fill a niche in Amazon's collection of Viet Nam War histories. Some 300 aging former newspeople from that era make up a Google discussion group called the Old Vietnam Hacks, devoted to talking about the old days and monitoring the changes that have occurred since.

As I looked back, I found time a slippery creature. It plays games with the memory. Things that I swore were true—knew to be true because I lived them, wrote about them—turned out never to have happened. Other events occurred at different times and with different people than my memory assured me was the case. In writing my story, I have relied on my journals as much as I could.

Where I couldn't, I have recorded what I believe to be true. It's all I have.

So I went to Viet Nam, got kicked out, and fled to the relative safety of Laos. Here was a backwater of the Indochina War where the CIA waged a secret two-pronged war, not against the Lao but against the North Vietnamese. The Lao, who never shared the repressed ferocity of their Cambodian neighbors or the overt aggressiveness of the Vietnamese, were caught in the middle—never master, always victim—in their own country. It was "a tiny, land-locked jungle kingdom" where the United States dropped more bombs than it had in Europe and Japan throughout World War II.

Much of what I learned, I picked up in the air-conditioned comfort of the Hotel Constellation bar, far from the dying, and distant even from the lives of ordinary Laotians and Thais, Vietnamese, and Chinese among whom I lived for 22 months in my apartment in downtown Vientiane.

What did I learn?

I put myself in harm's way for no real reason, and that was a foolish thing to do. Rather than demonstrating my courage, it mocked the courage of the young men who wore uniforms for one side or the other and faced death, disease, or injury day after day after day.

And things I did dispelled any notion of superiority, moral or otherwise. At best, I was an ordinary person just trying to make it.

Yes, I experienced things that almost no one of my generation could match, but I left so many opportunities on the table to learn more, see more, travel more, do more, understand more. That is all on me.

If I had it to do over again, I would travel every chance I got, riding buses and motorbikes, staying overnight in villages, attempting to talk to ordinary people. I would force myself to speak, read, and write Lao. I would imitate the best journalists I heard of, learning to work the phones like George McArthur of the *Los Angeles*

Times or brazenly witnessing whatever there was to see like the king of the Asia freelancers, Tim Allman.

Most of all, I would have changed my behavior toward my parents, keeping in better touch and trying to alleviate their concerns. As a parent and grandparent, I understand belatedly how much they must have worried every day I was gone. They deserved better.

So there you have it.

I did what I did, I saw what I saw. And this is the story of how it all fell out for me between September 1970 and August 1972, when I was too innocent to know better but knew enough to take notes.

Acknowledgments

A writer no more drafts a memoir alone than an individual lives life alone. Many, many people helped me live through this time and others subsequently helped me to remember what that time was like. I am indebted to all.

Dan Grady, Paula Spier, Lance Woodruff, Carl Strock, Don Ronk, Jerry Doolittle, and Tammy Arbuckle saw me through this adventure in real time. Claude Bernard made the adventure possible with a timely, generous loan.

Carl Strock, Don Ronk, and Jerry Doolittle shared their libraries with me, and Ed Kelly, Edwin T. "Win" McKiethen, Walt Haney, and George Davis loaned me special editions as well.

The research and reference librarians at Antioch College, Cornell University, Ohio University, and the Library of Congress located numerous books, monographs, and articles that seldom saw the light of day.

The staff of *Lao Presse* tried to make me comfortable in unbearable heat and humidity and seemed to enjoy my daily vigils.

Habeeb—I regret knowing his name only from the sign above his door—loaned me mysteries and adventure novels for free, and in doing so may have established the first lending library in Laos.

Northern Virginia artist Karen Chin graciously made umpteen versions of the maps.

A corps of readers took on early versions of individual chapters or large chunks of the manuscript and provided insightful feedback. My most loyal readers included Elizabeth Turner Haase, Richard

Haase, Donna Verdier, Sylvia Smith, Frank Phillippi, Eric Legg, Jason Dick, and David Leavitt. Sylvia Smith gets extra credit for editing the manuscript while Donna Verdier did the tedious copy edit. The members of the Royal Writers Secret Society reviewed chapters during our monthly critiques and forced me over and over to remember the reader. They include Bill Grigg, Patrick Hyde, Tom Milani, Rick Pullen, Patricia Schultheis, and Stacy Woodson. Finally, Royal Writer Ken Lawrence endured long anguished lunches and demanded that I be true to my inner voice, just the advice I needed.

I thank them for every error they caught and every passage they marked as vague, overstated, or just plain unclear. They did their job well; any failures of memory or errors are entirely my own.

Where Did They Go?

ARBUCKLE, Linda — Emigrated to England, grew up, has a teenage son and lives outside London.

ARBUCKLE, Somboun "Soupy" — Emigrated to England with Tammy and Linda. She died of cancer in 1998.

ARBUCKLE, Tammy – Returned to Edinburgh, Scotland, and earned his master's degree in politics. He wrote on military and foreign policy matters until his retirement in 2003. He lives in Edinburgh.

BLOCK, Irwin – Left Asia and returned home to Canada. He lives in Montreal.

BRANFMAN, Fred – Founded the Indochina Resource Center in Washington, D.C., and never stopped his advocacy against the bombing and for its victims. He died in 2014 at the age of 72.

CAVALERIE, Danielle – Married a French diplomat and had two children. She lives in France.

CAVALERIE, Maurice — Emigrated to Brisbane, Australia, after the Pathet Lao takeover in 1975. He died in 2010 at the age of 86.

CHANTHARAJ, Pon – Fled Laos with his wife and six young daughters in 1975 the day before Pathet Lao authorities arrived at his home to arrest him. He traveled to Bangkok

and Paris before settling in Houston, Texas, where he lives
in retirement.

COIFFAIT, Max – I lost track of Max after leaving Laos.

CORNELL, John – Left Laos with his girlfriend, Christine
Segalini, about the time I did, and I lost track of them.

DAVIS, George E. – Finished his Ph.D., moved to California and
became a venture capitalist. I have since lost track of him
and his wife, Penny.

DOOLITTLE, Jerry – Returned to Connecticut and became a
writer, serving as a speechwriter for President Carter. His
first novel, *The Bombing Officer,* is about Laos; it was published in 1982. He is retired and lives in Connecticut.

GRADY, Dan – Left Antioch and was twice a senior U.S. Senate
aide, a fund-raising expert, and in 2016 owned a consult-
ing firm in Rockville, MD.

GUZOWSKI, Andy – I lost track of him after leaving Laos.

HANEY, Walt – Returned to the United States, completed a
Ph.D., and is a professor of education at Boston College.

HEROD, Bill – Worked with a number of aid organizations and
retired to Sen Monorom, Mondulkiri Province, Cambodia,
along the border with Viet Nam, where he writes an occasional blog called Mondulkiri Meditations.

JAGNINSKI, Tom – Returned to Canada and wrote a novel
based on his experiences at LS 36, Bouam Long, entitled
Zero Casualties.

KELLY, Ed – Returned to the United States to serve on the Laos
Desk at the State Department. In 2015, he was actively
retired and living in Shepherdstown, WV.

PHOUMA, Souvanna – Was replaced as prime minister by Lao
Communist Party Secretary Kaysone Phomvihane in

December 1975. He died in Vientiane in 1984 at the age of 82.

POE, Tony (Anthony A. Poshepny) – Left Laos to run a guerrilla training camp in Thailand before I arrived in Southeast Asia. He retired from the CIA in 1975, returned to California in the 1990s, and died in 2003.

RONK, Don – Was expelled from Laos for his coverage of Prime Minister Souvanna Phouma in 1973; he was allowed to return briefly but left voluntarily before the communist takeover in 1975. He kicked around Southeast Asia, writing, editing, and working with refugees in Hong Kong and the Philippines. He died in Southeast Asia in 2001.

SPIER, Paula – Finished her career helping young Antiochians follow their dreams abroad. She died in 2011 of Parkinson's disease. Antioch named an Education Abroad scholarship after her in 2012.

STROCK, Carl — Never kicked the journalism bug or his sense of justice. He still writes occasionally from his home in upstate New York.

TURNER HAASE, Elizabeth "Liz" — Earned her Ph.D. in clinical psychology and practices in Washington, D.C., and Northern Virginia. She also married me, and we have two children and two grandchildren.

WOODRUFF, Lance – Remained in Thailand and continues to practice photojournalism from Bangkok.

Glossary and Acronyms

AFP – Agence France Presse: A French-language news service

AFSC — American Friends Service Committee: A Quaker peace group

Air America — U.S. airline controlled by CIA

AP — Associated Press: A U.S. news service

ARVN – Army of the Republic of Viet Nam: The South Vietnamese army

baht — Thai currency valued at 20B to the U.S. dollar in the 1970s

ban — Lao word for village, as in Ban Na

CAS — Controlled American Source: Code name for CIA

CCAS — Committee of Concerned Asian Scholars: An anti-war group of college graduate students and young university faculty members

CIA — Central Intelligence Agency: Primary U.S. spy agency abroad

CN — Chinese Noodle: A restaurant on a side street near the Anou Hotel where Ronk and other ex-pats hung out at night; formally known as Cuong Ky

CS — Cheese sandwich: A restaurant on Rue Samsenthai

down the street from the Constellation; formally called
Boua Kham

DMZ — Demilitarized Zone: Boundary between North Viet
Nam and South Viet Nam running roughly along the
17th parallel

DNS — Dispatch News Service: An alternative news service relying on freelancers and focusing on the war in Viet Nam

Dry Season — In Laos, November to March

FAR — Forces Armee Royale, Royal Lao Army

GM — Groupe Mobile: Three battalions and one
105-mm howitzer

Hmong – The name Meo adopted for themselves after the war

IVS — International Voluntary Service: A private nonprofit organization that placed volunteers in development programs
in Laos, Viet Nam and a half-dozen other underdeveloped countries

kip — Laotian currency; 500 kip = US $1 until devaluation to 600
to the dollar in late 1971

km — Kilometer: 1,000 meters, or about 3/5 of a mile

Lam Son 719 – South Vietnamese invasion of Ho Chi Minh Trail
in early 1971

Lane Xang — Name of the old Kingdom of Vientiane; also the
largest boulevard in Vientiane, and the most expensive hotel

Long Cheng – CIA headquarters in northern Laos from about
1962; AKA LS 20 Alternate or LS 98

LS — Lima Site: Aircraft landing site, often just a dirt air strip,
used by Air America and other aircraft leased to work with
the CIA and USAID

Luang Prabang — Royal capital of Laos and home of Lao royal family; north of Vientiane on the Mekong River

Meo – Hill tribe living at highest mountain levels recruited by CIA to fight Pathet Lao and North Vietnamese; now known as Hmong

monsoon — Seasonal wind that blows heavy rains to Laos April through September

Muong — Lao word for town, as in Muong Kasi

MR – Military Region: The Royal Lao Government divided the country into five military regions with most fighting confined to MR II in the north and MR IV in the south

Nam — Lao word for river or water, as in Nam Tha or sa nam hon (hot tea)

NVA — North Vietnamese Army

PL — Pathet Lao (Land of the Lao): Communist opposition in Laos, supported by the North Vietnamese government. Formally called Neo Lao Hak Sat, Lao Patriotic Front

Rainy Season — April through September

Reuters – A British news service

RLA — Royal Lao Army

RLG — Royal Lao Government

Sam Thong — USAID refugee headquarters in northern Laos, several miles southwest of Long Cheng

SVN — South Viet Nam

Tet — Vietnamese new year celebration lasting several days

UPI — United Press International: A U.S. news service

USAID — U.S. Agency for International Development: In Laos,

it served as a front for and provided logistical services to CIA operations

USIS — U.S. Information Service: An agency of the U.S. State Department, it distributed news and information from the U.S. government abroad

Vang Pao – General in the Royal Lao Army, commander of MR II and leader of the anti-communist Meo army suppled and controlled by the CIA; known as VP

VCS — Viet Nam Christian Service: A volunteer service organization

Vientiane — Administrative capital of Laos, located on the Mekong River on the Thai-Lao border; south of the royal capital at Luang Prabang

VP – Meo General Vang Pao

Wattay – Vientiane's international airport just west of the city; a key air link to Hanoi, North Viet Nam

Pronunciations

Nothing distracts me like encountering foreign names and words. They slow me down as I puzzle over an unfamiliar mixture of vowels and consonants, slow my comprehension, and detract from my enjoyment of the story. My eye wants to move forward, but my brain says, "Slow down. Let's figure this out."

The English spelling of Lao sounds comes to us by way of French pronunciations. Thus we are actually transliterating two languages at once. This has resulted in numerous spellings of the same sounds. For instance, I note in the text the eight variations I found for spelling General Thongphanh Knocksy's name, none of which accurately capture the Lao pronunciation, including the one above.

Two rules on Lao transliterations might help: There is no F sound associated with the letter combination "ph." Thus, the Lao word for spirit, phi, is pronounced pee, not fee or fie. In addition, the Lao language does not contain the sound formed by the letter duo "th," as in this or that. When you see "th," pronounce it like a plain hard "t." Thus, Thailand is pronounced Tie-land.

For those interested in understanding the pronunciation of Lao names and vocabulary (as well as an assortment of French, Hindi, Thai, and Vietnamese), I have listed the most frequently used non-English names, words, and phrases below, followed by the phonetic pronunciation.

Also bear in mind that this is a memoir. I have used the spellings I encountered in Laos. Many have changed in the intervening years; for instance, Vientiane—pronounced vee-en-chun—is now often seen as Viang Chan, which in fact is much closer to the Lao, at least to my Midwestern ear.

In addition, and this may spark controversy or hurt feelings, I continued to use the word Meo to refer to the hill tribe that for years comprised the bulk of the anti-Communist forces fighting in Laos for the CIA. Since the end of the war, this ethnic group has preferred to call itself Hmong, claiming rightly that Meo comes from the Chinese word for "slave."

This is a book about events I lived through more than 40 years ago. "Meo" never carried a derogatory connotation for me, and none of the Meo I met ever referred to themselves by any other term. I mean no offense in using the term here.

The language of origin is noted in parentheses using this code:

F – French
H – Hindi
L – Lao
M – Meo
T – Thai
V – Vietnamese

Ayutthaya (T) – ah-yoot-ah-yah

baci (L) – bah-see

Ban Houei Pha Mome (L) – bahn hoo-ee pa mome

Ban Houei Sai (L) – bahn hoo-ee sigh

Bolovens (L) – bo-low-vens

Boua Kham (L) – boo-ah kahm

Bouaphet Sygnavong (L) – boo-ah-pet sign-yah-vong

Bounkhong (L) – boon-kong

cai (L) – kie

Champassak (L) – cham-pah-sock

Chao Saykham (L) – chow sy-kahm

Chao Sopsaisana (L) – chow sop-sy-sahn-na

Cuong Ky (V) – coo-ong key

Dien Bien Phu (V) – dee-en bee-en foo

Diep Quang Hong (V) – dee-ep kwahng hong

Major General Etam Singvongsa (L) – a-tahm sing-vong-sah

farang (L) – fah-rahng

Faydang (M) – fie-dahng

Habeeb (H) – Just like it looks

Haja (H) – Ha-zha

Huynh Huu-Luan (V) – hine who loo-ahn

Khoun Boulom (L) – koon boo-lome

Lane Xang (L) – lahn sahng

Lao (L) – lah-oh

La Paix (F) – la pay

Le Cong Chat (V) – lay kong chat

Luang Prabang (L) – loo-ong pra-bahng

Manthatourath (L) – mahn-tah-too-raht

Meo (M) – may-oh

Muong Kasi (L) – Moo-ong kah-see

My Lai (V) – me lie

Nam Phou (L) – nahm poo

Nguyen Van Thieu (V) – win van tee-oo

General Duong Van "Big" Minh (V) – doo-ong van min

Nong Khai (T) – nong kie

nuoc mam (V) – nook mahm

Om Tong (V) – oam tong

Pakse (L) – pahk-say

Pang Kham – pahng kahm

Pathet Lao (L) – pah-tate lah-oh

General Phoumi Nosavan (L) – poo-me no-sah-vahn

Plaine des Jarres (F) – plane day zhar

Pon Chantharaj (L) – pone chan-tar-eye

Pongvichit (L) – pong-vee-chit

Rue (F) – roo (street)

sa bai di (L) – sah buy dee

Samsenthai (L) – saam-sen-tie

sa nam hon (L) – sah nahm hawn

Savang Vatthana (L) – sah-vahng vah-tah-nah

Setthathirath (L) – set-tah-tee-raht

Siddhartha (H) – sid-ar-tah

Sisouk na Champassak (L) – see-sook nah cham-pah-sock

Sisouphanh Vongnorath (L) – see-soo-pahn vong-nor-aht

Soth Petrasy (L) – soat peh-trah-see

Souk Vongsak (L) – sook vong-sahk

Souphanouvong (L) – soo-pahn-oo-vong

Souvanna Phouma (L) – soo-vah-na poo-ma

Tan Son Nhut (V) – tahn sun nee-yut

Thadeua (L) – tah-do-ah

Theh Chongkhadiki (T) – tay chong-kah-dee-kee

That Dam (L) – taht dahm

That Luang (L) – taht loo-ong

Thich Minh Chau (V) – tick min chow

Thich Nhat Hahn (V) – tick nee-yaht hahn

Dr. Ton That Thien (V) – tone taht tee-en

Tran Thien Khiem (V) – tran tee-en key-em

Touby Lyfoung (M) – too-bee lee-foong

tuk-tuk (T) – took-took

Van Hanh (V) – vahn hine

Vang Pao (M) – vahng pow

Vang Vieng (L) – vahng vee-eng

Vientiane (L) – vee-en-chun

Wah Lampo (T) – wah lahm-poe

Wat Ing Peng (L) – waht ing peng

Wat Ong Teu (L) – waht ong too

Wat Mixai (L) – waht me-sie

Wattay (L) – waht-tie

Xat Lao (L) – saht lah-oh

Xieng Khouang (L) – see-eng kwahng

Selected Sources

Adams, Nina S., and Alfred W. McCoy (eds.). *Laos: War and Revolution*. New York: Harper and Row, 1970.
  The first look at post-World War II Lao history and U.S. involvement by a young generation of skeptical historians and investigators.

Ahern, Thomas L., Jr. *Undercover Armies: CIA and Surrogate Warfare in Laos, 1961–1973*. Washington, DC: Center for the Study of Intelligence, 2006. Available at *http://nsarchive.gwu.edu/NSAEBB/NSAEBB284/6-UNDERCOVER_ARMIES.pdf*.
  Quasi-official CIA history of secret operations over more than a decade, with a focus on northern Laos. Filled with detail, this declassified secret study blanks out most footnotes, operative names (even where widely identified elsewhere), operation code names, and even entire pages. Released February 19, 2009.

Anthony, Victor B., and Richard R. Sexton. *The United States Air Force in Southeast Asia: The War in Northern Laos, 1954-1973*. Washington, DC: Center for Air Force History, 1993.
  Quasi-official history of U.S. bombing and secret operations in northern Laos.

Barney, G. Linwood. "The Meo of Xieng Khouang Province, Laos." Pages 271–294 in *Southeast Asian Tribes, Minorities*

and Nations, edited by Peter Kunstadter. Princeton, N.J.:
Princeton University Press, 1967.

Barney explains Hmong social organization, customs, mores, folk-
lore, local history, and some politics.

Blaufarb, Douglas S. *Organizing and Managing Unconventional
War in Laos.* Santa Monica, CA: RAND, January 1972.
Released August 5, 1997. Available at *https://www.rand.org/
content/dam/rand/pubs/reports/2006/R919.pdf.*

Insightful insider's story of how the CIA waged secret
war in Laos.

Castle, Timothy N. *At War in the Shadow of Vietnam: U.S. Military
Aid to the Royal Lao Government, 1955-1975.* New York:
Columbia University Press, 1993.

Superb overall history of U.S. operations in northern
Laos with comprehensive list of source documents.

Conboy, Kenneth, with James Morrison. *Shadow War: The CIA'S
Secret War in Laos.* Boulder, CO: Paladin Press, 1995.

Conboy documents the growth of the CIA operation
in Laos from a small, flexible, seat-of-the-pants operation
relying on guerrilla operations to a massive bureaucracy
devoted to intensive bombing and set-piece battles by large
units. He records the destruction of the Hmong.

Davis, George Ellsworth. *External Intervention and the
Mobilization of Ethnic Minorities in Laos (1945–1973).*
(Ph.D. dissertation, University of London School of
Economics, 1973).

In 1980, I noted it was the most recent account of
the Hmong as warriors, concentrating on U.S. efforts
to recruit them to fight the North Vietnamese and
Pathet Lao.

Dommen, Arthur J. *Conflict in Laos: The Politics of Neutralization.* New York: Praeger, 1971.
This, along with Hugh Toye (see below), provided the basis of understanding Laos for every newbie.

Halpern, Joel, and Kunstadter, Peter. "Laos: Introduction." Pages 233–258 in *Southeast Asian Tribes, Minorities and Nations,* edited by Peter Kunstadter. Princeton, N.J.: Princeton University Press, 1967.
Historical background on Laos puts the Hmong in context. Contains a good bibliography and table of tribal population estimates. Considered the standard work on Laotian tribes at the time.

Hickey, Gerald C., ed. *Area Handbook on Laos.* HRAF-23. Chicago: University of Chicago for the Human Relations Area Files, 1955.
Basic statistical information about Laos.

Leary, W. M. United States Special Operations in Laos, August 1969–June 1973. Available at *http://www.utdallas.edu/library/specialcollections/hac/cataam/notebooks/.*
Leary's notebooks on the history of Air America document special operations that relied heavily on air transport and support.

Manich, M. L. *History of Laos.* Bangkok: Chalermnit, 1971. Available at http://www.reninc.org/bookshelf/history_of_laos_manich.pdf.
History of Laos from the perspective of a non-Westerner.

Marcus, Russell. *English-Lao, Lao-English Dictionary.* Rutland, VT: Charles E. Tuttle Co., 1970.

More of a glossary than a dictionary, but it was, and is, the only thing like it.

Robbins, Christopher. *The Ravens: The Men Who Flew America's Secret War in Laos.* New York: Crown, 1987.
One of the first books to pierce the secrecy of U.S. Air Force involvement in bombing Laos.

Schanche, Don A. *Mister Pop.* New York: David McKay Co., Inc., 1970.
Adventures of an Indiana farmer, Edgar "Pop" Buell, among the Hmong in the 1960s, working on behalf of the CIA. A blend of fact, speculation, and legend.

Stevenson, Charles A. *The End of Nowhere: American Policy Toward Laos Since 1954.* Boston: Beacon Press, 1972.
By a U.S. Senate staff aide, it includes continual references to Hmong as an instrument of U.S. policy.

Stuart-Fox, Martin. *A History of Laos.* Cambridge: Cambridge University Press, 1997.
Laos from its earliest recorded history through the first two decades of Communist administration, written by an Australian journalist who covered Laos early in his career, married the eldest daughter of Maurice Cavalerie, and continues to write about Laos.

Toye, Hugh. *Laos: Buffer State or Battleground.* London: Oxford University Press, 1968.
An overview of the situation as it stood in the late 1960s, by the former British military attaché in Vientiane.

U.S. Congress. House of Representatives. Committee on Government Operations. *Economy and Efficiency of U.S. Aid Programs in Laos and Cambodia.* Hearing Before a Subcommittee of the Committee on Government

Operations, July 12, 1971. Washington, DC: US Government Printing Office, 1971.

This and the other congressional hearings and reports that follow put a time and date stamp on U.S. activities in Laos that were kept from the American public and resulted in limits on those secret activities.

U.S. Congress. Senate. Committee on Foreign Relations. *AID Activities in Laos.* Hearing of the Subcommittee on U.S. Security Agreement and Commitments Abroad, April 13, 1972 (sanitized July 30, 1972).

————. *Laos: April 1971.* Staff report prepared for the use of the Subcommittee on U.S. Security Agreements and Commitments Abroad, 92d Cong., 1st sess., 1971.

————. *Thailand, Laos, and Cambodia: January 1972.* Staff report. May 8, 1972.

————. *U.S. Agreements and Commitments Abroad,* Part 2, *Kingdom of Laos.* Hearings of October 20-22, 28, 1969 before the Subcommittee on U.S. Security Agreements and Commitments Abroad.

U.S. Congress. Senate. Committee on the Judiciary. *Problems of War Victims in Indochina,* Part II: *Cambodia and Laos.* Hearings of the Subcommittee on Refugees and Escapees, May 9, 1972

————. *Refugee and Civilian War Casualty Problems in Indochina.* Staff report, 91st Cong., 2d sess., September 28, 1970.

————. *Refugee and Civilian War Casualty Problems in Laos and Cambodia.* Hearings before the Subcommittee on Refugees and Escapees, May 7, 1970.

————. *War-Related Civilian Problems in Indochina,* Part II: *Laos and Cambodia.* Hearings of the Subcommittee on Refugees and Escapees, April 21–22, 1971.

Warner, Roger. *Shooting at the Moon*. South Royalton, VT: Steerforth Press, 1996.

    With a fiction writer's deftness and ear for a good story, Warner documents the glory years to the destruction of the Hmong as an anti-Communist fighting force.

Whitaker, Donald P., Helen A. Barth, Sylvan M. Berman, Judith M. Heimann, John E. MacDonald, Kenneth W. Martindale, and Rinn-Sup Shinn. *Area Handbook for Laos*. Washington, DC: American University Foreign Area Studies, 1972. Available at https://babel.hathitrust.org/cgi/pt?id=uva.x001642414;view=1up;seq=1.

    Updated version of the overview of Laos.